YELP & GOBBLE, INC.

How Restoring the Wild Turkey Spurred on a Game Call Innovation Boom

By Brent Rogers

Foreword by Jim Casada

Artwork by Sherry Brown

YELP & GOBBLE, INC.

© 2024 Brent Rogers

All rights reserved.

For inquiries, please contact:

Brent Rogers
17489 Blackhawk Road
Ottumwa, IA 52501

Email: Therogersroost@outlook.com

No part of this publication may be reproduced, stored in a retrieval system, or transmitted, in any form or by any means, electronic, mechanical, photocopying, recording or otherwise, without the written permission of the author.

ISBN: 979-8-9896459-0-9

Printed in the United States of America

DEDICATION

For my late father, Danny Rogers,
and my mother, Rosanne Rogers,
whose love and encouragement
have been my greatest asset.

And to the visionaries who restored
the wild turkey to our land.
May future generations be as committed
to leaving things better
than they found them.

TABLE OF CONTENTS

FOREWORD 7

PREFACE – THE SURVIVOR 13

ACKNOWLEDGMENTS 17

INTRODUCTION – ANSWERING THE CALL 19

CHAPTER 1 – KNIGHT & HALE 29

CHAPTER 2 – PRIMOS® HUNTING 73

CHAPTER 3 – QUAKER BOY® 127

CHAPTER 4 – MIKE BATTEY: THE CALL DR. 169

CHAPTER 5 – ANTHONY FOSTER: THE MILLWORKER 201

SOURCES 222

APPENDIX – WILD TURKEY HISTORICAL TIMELINE 225

ABOUT THE AUTHOR 227

FOREWORD

The gifted wordsmith and sage of the South Santee River, Archibald Rutledge, also happened to be an old school turkey hunter who wrote widely and wonderfully well about America's big-game bird. In one of his memorable quotations associated with the sport of wild turkey hunting he stated: "Some men are mere hunters; others are turkey hunters." He was making the distinction, one that any dyed-in-the-wool aficionado of the grand quest knows all too well, suggesting that turkey hunters are a breed apart. As someone who belongs to the clan and long ago lost a corner of his soul to the wild gobbler, I can only nod in full understanding and deep appreciation of the manner in which Old Flintlock (as Rutledge was known to his family and hunting friends) described the marvelous malady that likely afflicts anyone about to read the pages to follow.

The late Larry Hearn, a fascinating fellow, owner of turkey call patents, and skilled turkey hunter whom I was privileged to know once laughingly said to me: "Medical specialists and law enforcement think they got problems with cocaine and other drugs; they don't realize that such things don't even compare to the plight of an highly addicted turkey hunter." Or, to present things in another fashion, take the title of a delightful though little-known book on the sport, Phil Phillips' *The Grand Obsession*. Turkey hunting can indeed become an obsession, one that is all encompassing to an almost unimaginable degree.

Archibald Rutledge realized as much, and his devotion to turkey hunting closely approximated fanaticism. Yet the quotation from him offered above does not quite capture the ultimate level in turkey infatuation. That comes with individuals such as the author of this book, Brent Rogers. He is, as old-timers in the Southern Appalachian region of my raising variously described pronounced degrees of compulsion, "eaten up with it." Possibly another example of applicable mountain talk comes from the words used to describe a distinctive character trait or defining aspect of an individual's personality—"bad to." Sometimes this was used as a term of opprobrium, such as "he was bad to drink," "she was bad to gossip," or "he was bad to chase women." But "bad to" has another gentler and more persuasive connotation that applies to a fascination or fixation with a hobby or pursuit. The finest example I know is an epitaph found on a simple tombstone marking a grave in a country cemetery. It reads: "He was bad to fish."

With that by way of background, it should be clear why I maintain that Brent Rogers is "bad" about most anything connected to the world of the wild turkey. Simply put, he is "bad to collect turkey stuff"--a man deeply devoted to the folklore, paraphernalia, collectibles, and wisdom of the wonderful world of the wild turkey.

That devotion first came to my attention when he bought some books from me on turkey hunting—both ones I had written and those by others. Then there followed the acquisition of calls and other tools of the trade, phone calls earnestly seeking information, and indications he had literary plans in the works. Rogers realized he had found something of a kindred soul, a fellow who was "bad to collect" turkey treasures of pretty much any kind. Indeed, so pronounced is my turkey affliction that a fellow sporting scribe who has published a bunch of books on the subject (including a highly useful guidebook and a trilogy of tales involving dealings with *Bad Birds*), Jim Spencer, once wrote of our shared passion in the Foreword to my *The Literature of Turkey Hunting*: "Neither of us, probably, would go to Hell to kill a turkey gobbler, but if one was gobbling hard enough down there we'd pilfer around the edges until we fell in."

The author of the book you have before you suffers from the same sort of compulsion. The first of the seven deadly sins of the *Bible* is lust. Its religious context refers to sexual matters, and former president Jimmy Carter created a whirlwind of controversy when he once acknowledged "lust in the heart." Rest assured what you have before you is a chronicle growing straight out of lust, but in this case there is no sin involved—just a man determined to share what he considers important milestones in the modern evolution of the sport, insight on notable figures involved in its advances, and information that shows dedication and determination to preserving these developments and the figures behind them for posterity. Although he has previously done some writing on various aspects of the sport in magazines and in a book for collectors co-authored with George Denka, this is Rogers' first full-scale venture into the sport's literary vineyards.

Generally speaking, he has chosen his subject matter wisely and done his research well. As someone who has reviewed books for various publications throughout his career as well as having written a bunch of them, let me assure you that there are always things to quibble about, criticisms to be offered, and doubts to be expressed regarding any book. As I've told the author in the fashion which long ago earned me richly deserved evaluation as a guy singularly lacking in diplomatic genes, I don't agree with everything found in these pages. I'm picky as an old maid school teacher when it comes to matters of style, punctuation, grammar, and the like, and I think it only fair to say that Brent never met a comma he wasn't inclined to use and that detailed lessons in diagramming sentences had left the standard upper elementary school curriculum before he came along. To 99 out of 100 readers that simply doesn't matter, and if this finds its way into print it will indicate that Brent has taken my goading in good stead. What readers want is hard information, well-researched material, and depths of insight that bring understanding. Those they get in these pages—in spades. Also on offer is a general time line, something students of the world of the wild turkey will find interesting, especially inasmuch as it closely parallels the dawning and unfolding of the golden era of restoration and hunting.

Also worthy of mention are the individuals and businesses Rogers has chosen to cover. Again, my choices might have been a bit different or wider ranging, but for the most part there's delight aplenty here awaiting the eyes of discerning readers. Over the years I've been privileged to know and in many cases hunt or share hunt camps with key individuals associated with the first three chapters—Harold Knight and David Hale, Will and Jimmy Primos (and "Cuz" Strickland back when he was videoing for them), and Dick and Chris Kirby of Quaker Boy along with their longtime public relations guy, Ernie Calandrelli. What warm, winsome memories these names evoke!

I think of a time in the Knight & Hale production facility in Cadiz when they met with the late Larry Hearn and me prior to several days of hunting in their home and stomping grounds Land Between the Lakes. Hearn, who was a raconteur fully capable of talking the ears off a Georgia mule, held Harold and David, along their entire staff, entranced as he demonstrated an adjustable, suction-type yelper he had patented. Or there was the time, during a truck ride connected with a deer and tundra swan hunt in eastern North Carolina, when Harold explained to me the basics of using a diaphragm and started me down the road to at least a marginal degree of proficiency with mouth calls. Of course my cherished friend and fellow writer, the late Wade Bourne, told their story, and told it with customary skill and wordsmithing, in *Harold Knight & David Hale's Ultimate Turkey Hunting*. But a full three decades have come and gone since that book's appearance in 1993, and the focus here is more on the evolution of a company and its place in the world of making calls than on the ins and outs of turkey hunting tactics and techniques.

Then there was another hunt with the Knight & Hale gang where we struck a turkey in late morning, after two fruitless days of hard hunting, thanks to a friendly game warden offering information on where he had heard one gobbling. Videographer Chuck Jones and I eased into the woods and in fairly short order had the loud-mouthed bird on the march. He came to within 25 yards, Chuck indicated that he had good footage and to go ahead and shoot. I did, ignominiously putting the full load of Number 6s squarely in an oak tree at a height at least 18 inches above the gobbler's outstretched neck. It was a classic case of failure to follow the timeless wisdom of getting "wood to wood"—the wooden-headed hunter (yours truly) watched from on high rather than getting his cheek down on the wood of the gunstock. The turkey, rather than suddenly remembering it had urgent business two counties away, gobbled and then went erect again. My second shot didn't miss and Knight & Hale had some excellent footage of a fool of a hunter and a lovelorn gobbler that was even more foolish and paid the ultimate price. They subsequently used the material to good avail.

Yet the most poignant memory from that hunt did not involve the unusual and decidedly lucky kill. Instead, it focused on the frivolity that ensued when we got back to Harold, the game warden, and two or three others awaiting our return. The warden looked deeply concerned while Harold broke into delighted laughter when he saw the gobbler slung over my shoulder. It turned out that when they heard my second shot a minute or more after the first one, Harold had quick wittedly said: "You never know about Jim. He's an old hillbilly and he probably just up and shot two turkeys." Since only one bird a day was allowed, that statement understandably had the good-natured warden deeply concerned.

In the case of Primos, my mind goes directly back to a time when Will and I were easing up to a green field on an afternoon hunt and debated whether or not to call. I wanted to run a few yelps on a wingbone while he argued that a silent sneak was better. There are valid points on both sides, as there are for about any other tactical situation you can posit in the sport, but there's no denying that on a comparative basis I was the rank novice and Primos the expert.

That was somewhere around 1990, and a great deal has transpired in my world and Will's since then. Most significantly though, through sheer savvy, shrewd business sense, and dogged determination, the Primos gang built a callmaking operation (along with production of other innovative gear) that became a model of success.

Will would be the first to tell you he didn't do it alone. Jimmy Primos is a gregarious, instantly likeable guy with a genuine knack for promotion, and in the early years individuals like Ronnie "Cuz" Strickland (read his *Truth* trilogy for more information) helped shape and mold what would become and continues to be a powerhouse brand. The Primos story falls squarely into the "American dream" or Horatio Alger path of success that citizens of this country have always admired.

As for the Quaker Boy gang, over time I have shared hunts with them in a lot of settings involving numerous scenarios—turkey hunting in New York, Missouri, Iowa, Texas, Virginia, and probably other locales that escape my inept memory; a grand deer hunt in Missouri; and even catching monster crappie at a little pond in Kentucky. Chris Kirby has witnessed me miss a turkey (something at which I'm an accomplished master) as well as kill some, and Ernie Calandrelli and I have had numerous laughter-filled adventures.

Among them were him poking fun at my feeble attempts at owl hooting after his stellar efforts imitating a barred owl produced naught but the sound of silence. Let the record state that gobblers responded from everywhere (no doubt truly shocked at such an intrusive and different noise!) at my owling. That drew Ernie's derision but also a wry acknowledgment that it had somehow worked. Another time he laughed at my chase after a wounded gobbler that ended up in a briar thicket with yours truly thoroughly scratched and shredded while the hapless gobbler was minus most of its tail feathers. I carried the bird back to where Ernie

FOREWORD

lay, literally rolling on the ground in laughter. He blithely ignored my protestations about his lack of assistance and proceeded to laugh some more at my expense.

Then there were occasions when we jointly almost managed to set a 200-year-old cabin afire while trying to deep fry a whole turkey, Italian cuisine he cooked for a whole camp of deer hunters that was indescribably delicious, a fine mess of fried crappie and all the fixings, along with much, much more. To be with Ernie was to have fun, and he had a real knack for promoting the Quaker Boy brand.

Those sorts of good times and good memories go beyond just a writer interacting with delightful guys. They give a glimpse of how the vision of Dick Kirby, combined with the sharp business sense of Chris Kirby and the gregariousness of Ernie Calandrelli, served as underpinning for what started out as a champion caller turning into a callmaker. From that emerged an ongoing evolution into the remarkable Quaker Boy tale of success on the hunting market trail.

All of these eventually thriving businesses began on a shoestring, a whistle and a prayer, and the vision of their founders. Coupled with that, and of transcendent importance, was an abiding love of turkey hunting. Will Primos was a hunter straight out of the old school—confident and competent in his woodsmanship, possessed of exceptional determination (something of great value not only in the turkey woods but in business), and someone who learned as he went while absorbing lessons of the hunt of the selling of calls like a thirsty sponge.

Dick Kirby was decidedly different, and should I be asked to select one characteristic of the man that stood out above all others, it would be his competitiveness. He had a deeply rooted thing, a sort of "mad on" if you will, about turkeys. Simply put, he was obsessed with calling in and killing gobblers. It was something he did with single-minded intensity, and I strongly suspect that hunter's hard edge had its equivalent application in business. I shared turkey camps with Dick on more than one occasion, and you can rest assured no one went at it harder or with greater dedication than he did. His was an ongoing, never ending hunter's war with his quarry. Some may find that distasteful, but in my eyes it was palpably real. Moreover, Dick was unapologetic about the level of his "armed conflict" with gobblers; almost ruthless you might say, and something of a similar mindset no doubt guided him as Quaker Boy grew and thrived. Also, and I would be remiss if I didn't note this, both his son Chris and his public relations director, Ernie Calandrelli, were perfect foils. They smoothed the sharp edges, knew how to garner meaningful publicity and public good will, and were in many ways the yin to Dick's yang.

On a personal level, I probably identify more readily with David Hale and especially Harold Knight than any of the figures covered in this book. Like me, they are sons of hills and hollows country, and I don't think they would take exception to being called hillbillies. Indeed, that description is likely one that both of them would, as is certainly the case with this writer, wear as a badge of honor. They were born to hunt and blessed by being able to link passion to profession.

In-depth looks at three of the longtime, major players in the turkey callmaking field form the heart of this book. Yet, as anyone who has taken the time to look into the details of commercial call production knows, the companies are just a part of the whole. Whether it is an employee with a keen ear and years of knowledge tuning box calls, a gifted craftsman figuring out new ways to invent whatever you would call turkey hunting's equivalent of a better mouse trap, or some innovator constantly taking his thinking to different realms while contemplating calls that are not only new and novel but that have the potential to be noteworthy, folks behind the scenes make a huge difference. Even if you are someone like me who has labored in the vineyards of the world of the wild turkey and the paraphernalia of the sport for much of his adult life, chances are excellent you don't know many guys of this ilk.

Anthony Foster, who is the subject of this book's final chapter, is a prime example. Until I read this manuscript, I had never heard of the man. My educated guess is that suits him just fine and that he is someone who is quite willing to work his wonders in obscurity. Mind you, not all of those wondrous talents who work the sort of wonders Foster has performed for decades fit that mold, and there are even those who hanker for renown with an unquenchable and often unseemly thirst. Such is clearly not the case with Foster, and for that reason alone coverage of the man and his career here is a signal achievement. I have no idea how Brent Rogers convinced the man to share the details of a career that heretofore had been cloaked in obscurity, but discerning readers will recognize we are better for him having done so.

Foster, in effect, serves as an exemplar for the unknown and under-appreciated fellows of the call making world. There are scores of them who have, in varying degrees, been a vital part of this whole scene. Quite simply, without these often nameless and always obscure men of rare talent, commercial call making as we know it today could not exist. They were a key if largely silent component—men who with a few notable exceptions had no interest in tooting their own horn, self-aggrandizement, or indeed anything except utilizing expertise in a way that has proven beneficial to legions of turkey hunters. Foster's story is one that might be repeated, at least to some degree, for dozens of others. Rogers' decision to include him in these pages was, quite simply, a fortuitous one.

This chronicling of what might be termed the unknown underside or background story for the emergence of modern call production is one that far surpasses the numbers of calls associated with the Turpin clan (they were really custom call makers) or even M. L. Lynch (the closest thing to an operation involved in mass production of calls in the pre-restoration era). It is a welcome and much-needed addition to the literature of the sport and its history, a volume that should find a place of some prominence on the shelves of any truly serious turkey man.

– Jim Casada

PREFACE – THE SURVIVOR

"I am the last of my race, my name ends with me."

This was the justified lament in a local newspaper when the extinction of the heath hen was officially recognized.[1] Once bountiful across New England, overhunting and habitat loss shouldered them out. A subspecies of the greater prairie chicken, it had been a dependable source of food for generations of Native Americans and the Pilgrims. By 1870, it was extinct on the mainland, and with the final few on Martha's Vineyard eliminated in 1933, its booming was eternally silenced. [2]

This was not something new but a troubling pattern. In 1852, the great auk, found along the coast of upper North America, was reduced to a memory, as was New England's Labrador duck by 1878. [3] In 1914, the last known passenger pigeon, with none to return its soft calls, took the final breath of an entire species. In 1918, the last colorful Carolina parakeets would follow that course to extinction. [4] More recently, it is feared that "The Lord God Bird," the Ivory-billed woodpecker of the southeast, is likely extinct due to the loss of old-growth forests.

Don't be alarmed; I am not here to harangue you with gloom and doom. However, it is important to establish that this book came close to never being written. The American wild turkey was on the same path to extinction; thankfully, it is a survivor. We are just a century removed from grim days when it looked like our proud, native bird was a goner. Early explorers, settlers, and naturalists, up to the early 1800s, enthusiastically reported large concentrations of wild turkeys. Naturalist William Bartram reported in the late 1770s, "The high forests ring with the noise… of these social sentinels, the watch-word being caught and repeated, from one to another, for hundreds of miles around; insomuch that the whole country, is for an hour or more, in a universal shout." [5] Even today one can only imagine a chain of gobbles for hundreds of miles.

How fortunes can change! In the 1830s, just half a century after Bartram penned those words, the now-renowned John James Audubon noted a decline in the number of wild turkeys. He wrote that they were "less plentiful in Georgia and the Carolinas" and were "becoming less numerous in every portion of the United States." [6] The wild turkey population plummeted from an estimated ten million when Europeans first set foot in North America to less than

200,000 by 1920. [7] The wild turkey, too, seemed to be on the brink of extinction. [8]

It was not a simple thing to save a species. It required sacrifice, effort, and an investment of time and resources from many. Those endeavors came in the passage and enforcement of laws, closed seasons, reduced bag limits, resolute landowners, and disciplined hunters. It required these different stakeholders to band together to form conservation organizations. Still, lessons had to be learned using new game management practices and utilizing new technologies before they got it right. Technology adapted from World War II included the development of cannon nets (then rocket nets) to fire over turkeys, allowing their safe and effective capture and transport. It also included radio telemetry, which was a critical tool for biologists to monitor the success of transferred turkeys.

As a united force, they overcame the myth of the game farm turkey, muted the poacher's gun, and championed better land management practices. [9] By the 1970s and 1980s, they established a new nationwide generation; those born after the 1980s won't likely recall a time without wild turkeys in their state.

It took five decades of law, learning, and effort to restore the population to one million turkeys by the 1970s, and by the year 2000, the population exceeded five million birds. [10] To put that in context, there are now eight individual states whose wild turkey populations each exceed the total number in existence just seventy years earlier. [11] Significantly, the conservation efforts on behalf of the wild turkey have also benefitted many other game and non-game species. It turns out that what is suitable for the wild turkey is good for its neighbors.

This post-restoration era has seen all fifty states, except Alaska, enjoy new revenues from the sale of turkey hunting licenses, tags, and stamps, funding more conservation work. The federal Pittman-Robertson Act uses money collected from hunting license sales and taxes on firearms and ammunition to restore, manage, and enhance wild birds and mammals and their habitat. Most who criticize hunters do so without realizing the wildlife and natural areas they enjoy are often tied directly to dollars coming from hunters. The National Shooting Sports Foundation reported in 2018 that "Hunter spending generates more than $185 million per day for the U.S. economy." In 2016, "Hunters spent over seven billion dollars on equipment alone." [12]. The wild turkey is a wildlife success story that was enabled by and through hunters. [13]

Out of that success story, the foundation was laid for the subject matter of this book. Despite a close call on the ability to have and hunt wild turkeys, we have been blessed with a privilege that requires our diligence to avoid past mistakes. Now, I must qualify the scope of this book.

I revere the American wild turkey (that should now be obvious!) and the American bison. Those two members of our North American fauna are symbolic of the spirit of freedom and wildness associated with the history of the United States. Given enough time, anyone who has engaged in a conversation with me knows that I can turn any discussion to wild turkeys.

PREFACE

So much of my passion revolves around the wild turkey that much of my leisure time is spent in pursuit of knowledge and collectibles associated with them.

The American wild turkey is worthy of praise. There are mutterings of well-meaning but misled farmers who see turkeys in their fields during the daytime eating bugs, weed seeds, and waste grain and blame them for crop damage. In reality, squirrels, nocturnal raccoons, and deer do most of that damage. [14] Understandably frustrated are urban dwellers living in close quarters with turkeys taking advantage of backyard feeders and the lack of predators. The truth is that the wild turkey is marvelous at eking out a living in a world where everything that breathes seems to want to eat it.

The wild turkey earns respect from those who take the time to study it. They are a pleasure to observe, with their sleekness of form, the stealth of their movements, and the shimmering robes of iridescent plumage they wear. It has proven its mettle and adaptability by living in swamps, rainforests, deserts, mountains, and just about any habitat found between the Pacific and Atlantic oceans that contains some trees and fresh water. Also, like *Homo sapiens,* they are omnivores and social creatures whose depths of spirit were captured firsthand by ethologist (a scientist who studies animal behaviors) Joe Hutto in his eye-opening book, *Illumination In The Flatwoods.* [15]. PBS *Nature* would later produce the documentary "My Life As A Turkey" based on Hutto's experiences over two years with his imprinted wild turkey brood. [16]

In greatest admiration of the turkey are those whom one might least expect: the hunter. I place myself in that class. There are slobs among us, those who exploit such wildlife or whose interest is confined to reveling in that basest part of the process, the kill. The honorable hunter loves the turkey's life more than its death. We live closer to it than others and come to know its vulnerabilities and its seemingly supernatural abilities. Its brain is a pitiful size compared to ours, yet it humbles us in ways only hunters fully comprehend. Its death gives us life, and our triumph comes with a twinge of regret. Those heartfelt feelings keep good hunters honest, and we are bettered by knowing the actual cost of the sustenance on our tables.

While this story will celebrate the origins and innovations of some production turkey call companies, the real story I will tell here is about people. *People* run businesses. *People* design, make, and produce turkey calls and other outdoor products. *People* purchase those products and hunt turkeys. Although I provide a fair amount of data and information that will help establish some historical records and serve as a guide for collectors, this is a human interest and business innovation story.

In the following pages, I will cover the journey of a few successful companies started by people who were uniquely placed in time to accomplish what they did. These individuals fit Malcolm Gladwell's definition of *Outliers* in his book of the same name. [17] Many enterprises to make turkey calls and products for the masses were launched, but few persevered and succeeded over decades.

In early 2023, I co-authored a book with George Denka, the *Turkey Call and Literature Collector's Guide*. [18]. It is a continuation of the late turkey call enthusiast Earl Mickel's books that provide short biographies on turkey callmakers and a perspective on the collectability and value of their calls. [19] This was George's fourth edition since being handed the reins by Mickel. I have become obsessed with collecting the tangible items of turkey hunting: books, magazines, calls, audio, video, clothing, stamps, art, and anything turkey hunting-related I can find. In George's book, my contribution was primarily on wild turkey literature; here, I delve more into the history of "factory" calls and products.

As much as I love the "stuff," such items will eventually lose meaning if the stories behind them aren't captured for posterity. We have mostly lost the generation that lived in the "lean years" when wild turkeys were scarce in this country. As the wild turkey flourished again, a new generation of turkey hunters rose to re-forge this great tradition. I consider that the greatest generation of turkey hunters, which we are now starting to lose. For those who will never get to meet them, their passion and personalities are preserved for us through their calls, recorded voices, and images. This book is an effort to capture for posterity their accomplishments and impact. They made kids like me dream and then were part of making my dreams come true.

– Brent Rogers
Ottumwa, IA 2024

ACKNOWLEDGMENTS

There are many without whose time and attention I could not have brought this book to print. Realizing it isn't possible to thank everyone who has provided encouragement, information, or support of some kind, I seek here to recognize the elite few. A brief note of gratitude follows for those individuals who provided essential elements that helped shape *Yelp & Gobble, Inc.* You have my enduring thanks for your part in celebrating this history through the art of storytelling so that it may be passed along and appreciated long after we are gone.

Anthony Foster, Bev Kirby, Chris Kirby, David Hale, Harold Knight, Jimmy Primos, Mike Battey, and Will Primos endured hundreds of questions from me over many hours and days as this was written. Any error is wholly mine, and I am forever grateful for your patience and kindness. Thank you for your contributions to my success in the woods!

Bill Jordan, Bob Wozniak, Brad Farris, Brad Johnston, Craig "Cornbread" Corbett, Eric Hughes, Ernie Calandrelli, Jeff D'Agostino, Jim Strelec, John Phillips, Keith Wahlig, Lorena Lipe, Mark Prudhomme, Marlin Watkins, Mary O'Reilly, Matt Stewart, Paul Butski, Preston Pittman, Rob Keck, Ron Jolly, Ronnie Smith, Shannon "Guv" Knight, and others I interviewed or received photos from are all a big part of this story; your contributions enriched this book.

Jessi Cole, Daniel Haas, Neill Haas, Toxey Haas, Ronnie "Cuz" Strickland, and the Mossy Oak team provided help, information, stories, quotes, and photos. You are a great part of the history linked to the wild turkey restoration.

Jim Casada is a writer whose shadow many such as I happily walk in. He is an authority on wild turkey history and bettered this book through constructive criticisms. Jim, I am grateful for your help and honored by your excellent Foreword to this book.

Sherry Brown is a gifted artist who provided the pen and ink sketches used throughout the book. Thank you Sherry for bringing life to this book's pages with elegant wild turkey artwork.

Tom "Doc" Weddle issued helpful guidance on book publishing. You are one of a kind and my turkey-hunting superhero!

Kevin Rhoades, thanks for your patience and guidance in bringing my text and photos to life through your formatting and help getting the book published on time and in full!

Alex Lee White, Brad Reid, Jason Worley, Korby Taylor, and Todd Johnson are fellow collectors who inspired, provided information, and helped with editing. You are fellow "keepers of the flame" for wild turkey history.

Al Smith, Chris McDonald, Danny Ellis, David James, Delano Kruzan, George Denka, Herb Mckee, Jim McGinnis, Joe Hutto, Larry Proffit, Ralph Permar, Ray Berryhill, Rick Powell, and Roger Parks are but a few examples of the people from whom I have learned and benefitted.

To my many wild turkey collector friends, while we spend a lot of each other's money, remember not to let your spouse sell your collectibles for what you said you bought them for!

For the last thirty years, my professional colleagues in the food R&D world have helped shape my research savvy and interest in innovation, which spilled over into this leisure pursuit.

A special thanks to my late father, Danny Rogers, my wife, Renee, my children, Cyrus and Hannah, my brothers Curt & Andy, and my mentors, Tom, Sam, and Austin, for all being my hunting partners. My best days have been spent with you in God's great outdoors.

INTRODUCTION: ANSWERING THE CALL

Necessity is the mother of invention, and the return of the wild turkey was a call to action for some. With wild turkeys being restored to former habitats and expanded into new ones, the 1970s and 1980s were heady times for enterprising turkey hunters. At first, their focus was to support their passion and put food on their table. They made their own calls, clothes, and accessories because they couldn't get or afford the few available local options. They then improved on what they used or found, selling to friends and local sporting goods stores. They learned how to use new industrial processes and materials to make game calls and accessories that could be marketed nationally through new channels. In the end, they not only put food on their table but that of many others through creating jobs and helping make hunters successful.

Their opportunity required timing and technology to ideally converge for what they would do. No one could have predicted this unique moment in time, as it hinged on what was a quick re-establishment of the nation's wild turkeys. Even companies that existed at the time and offered only a handful of turkey calls for a few decades prior failed to recognize and seize the growth opportunity. All I interviewed agreed that what they did then could not have happened outside of a small window that aligned newly huntable populations of the wild turkey, their passion, new technologies, and many other supporting factors.

Following the decimation of our wild turkey flocks to feed the stomachs of a growing non-native population and the consumption of natural resources that were the wild turkeys' home, it would have been hard for most to succeed with a turkey hunting business. M.L. Lynch, whose calls were first available in 1940, certainly did; his success was likely a barrier to others, given the period's regional and minimal turkey call market. [1] In addition, the wild turkey is native only to North America, so it has a more limited hunting community than other species distributed worldwide (waterfowl, deer, sheep, etc.).

Even with few turkeys, there were enough people captivated by this wily, native bird to keep it on the radar of sportsmen. I have identified over 150 sporting magazine articles from the late 1800s through 1940 (and I am sure there are many more) focusing on turkey hunting and turkey calls. Some may be articles written by inexperienced turkey hunters to turn a buck; a few are very good. In any case, no one was getting rich on wild turkeys in those decades. Author Jim Spencer captures it best in his book of enjoyable tales, *Bad Birds.* He writes, "I imagine the bleak days of the 1930s and 1940s..when turkeys were mostly imaginary, and a few old-timers continued to hunt them against all reason." [2]

During this time, hunters earned a reputation for their dogged persistence and secrecy. Hearing a turkey constituted a successful hunt; seeing one was unheard of, and putting one on the table made you a local legend. Turkey hunters today are sometimes considered eccentric within hunting circles, willing to pursue something whose ears and eyes are more fearsome than tooth and claw when wielded on the field of battle.

Following WWII, those returning from military service found the outdoors an enticing and practical leisure pursuit. Golf may be fun, but you can't eat a golf ball. There were improvements to facilities in our parklands and expansion and management of public hunting and fishing. Accessibility increased through the creation of an interstate highway system and affordable automobiles. There was a reason for sportsmen and women to acquire those unique tools and products. This all became relevant for turkey hunters because of the amazing restoration of their population.

If you are not a hunter, it may surprise you that hunting is big business. Billions of dollars each year are spent on such products and hunting. [3] Where there is oil, there are oil wells, and where there are hunters, there are Bass Pro Shops and Cabela's carrying thousands of products to cater to their needs. Visionary people were behind those products, and much of their success can be traced back to restoring the wild turkey to the American landscape.

"It seems like it was just yesterday," the iconic game call company founder Harold Knight said about his early days chasing turkeys and making tube turkey calls. All of us can relate to that sentiment, as the things we love are firmly etched into our minds and hearts such that the memories never fade. Most turkey hunters can recall a moment when their lives became forever intertwined with the wild turkey. It may have been hearing a gobbler on the roost, getting a gobble in response to their calling, or slinging their first turkey over their shoulder. In the quest to reproduce that experience, turkey hunters will leave no stone unturned in finding that call or product that provides an advantage.

Turkey hunters have a well-earned reputation for their eccentricity and zeal, and many of us make turkey hunting a lifestyle. We dedicate our time from March through May to turkey season, and when driving, we scour the landscape all year to spot turkeys. We are eager to tell our stories of the tribulations and triumphs of our hunts, and we gather at conventions to meet up with old friends and see what's new. Some of us even ascribe national treasure status to those special turkey calls that have gone to battle with us, or we go down the sordid road of becoming 'turkey call collectors,' which causes spouses to grimace and wallets to shrink!

In a sense, game calls such as turkey calls are a musical instrument. Their entire purpose is to produce sound within a narrow range of pitch and tone like an animal, which the target species will recognize. Often, the 'voice' reproduced by the instrument or call is that of the hunted species. It is more common when hunting predators to mimic the voices of the species they hunt to entice them to come to dinner. For many species, hunters must study their game

INTRODUCTION

species and understand the language they will replicate with the call to know what they are saying and to whom. Calls may trigger protective responses, challenge the "pecking order," convey emotions such as contentment, speak to physical activity such as feeding, or provide seasonal mating invitations.

Tracing the first hunting call used is a difficult exercise, but there is speculation that 12,000-year-old coot-bone whistles found in Israel might have been used to reproduce the voice of a bird of prey to "scare up" ducks to offer hunters a target to capture. [4] While hunting horns were used long ago, they served as a signal to other hunters or their dogs instead of issuing a call to their quarry. Early calling made to animals being hunted could have been through manipulating a hunter's voice (some gifted people are "natural voice" callers). Turkeys may have been amongst the first North American species to be hunted with game calls. There are Native American sites in which turkey wing bones have been found, which were believed to have been used to call turkeys by sucking through one end of the bone. That is still practiced by hunters today. Whether native Americans did it or not, early non-indigenous turkey hunters in North America employed objects to call turkeys. [5] Blowing across leaves to call was one such method, similar to using a modern-day tube call. [6]

Individual turkeys have unique "voices," so there is some forgiveness in the sound of turkey calls. In addition to sound, the cadence, volume, and frequency of calling the user employs can be crucial. The numerous styles of turkey calls are ever-growing, and the wild turkey's voice lends itself to being recreated well with air (forced air and suction) and friction (two items coming in contact to emit a sound). The wild turkeys' complex language may lend itself to a wider variety of calls than other game species. [5] David Hale said it well, "There is not that kind of differentiation in deer calls. You've only got one or two. Same way with geese. How many goose calls do you need? A goose is a goose. But a turkey ain't just a turkey. A turkey's got a vocabulary that's extremely complicated." [7]

Anyone who has heard turkeys gobble in a barnyard or a large, prefabricated building full of market turkeys has not experienced a real gobble, let alone the grace and beauty of a wild turkey. Though they share genetics, the domesticated turkey has lost the traits that put the 'wild' in wild turkey. Wild turkeys domesticated by Native Americans in what is now Mexico were transported to Europe in the early 1500s by Spanish Conquistadors. [8] Those domesticated turkeys were returned to this hemisphere when the first European settlers came. Sadly, those specimens are all that residents in most other countries know, and those Galliformes are but poor representatives of the wild turkey in voice, body, and spirit.

It has been commonly stated that if turkeys could smell, hunters could never kill one. Their eyesight is keen and hearing acute, and hunting a wild turkey takes persistence. Ironically, a wild turkey's greatest vulnerability is its eyes and ears. Generations of turkey hunters know that the birds' flocking instinct and breeding season behaviors can be used in hunting methods and tools. The sight or sound of what may be another turkey can often entice the otherwise cautious turkey into the hunter's shooting range. Hunters purchase turkey calls and turkey decoys because they work!

While vintage waterfowl calls and decoys can fetch sales prices well into five figures at auction, few turkey calls achieve such feats. [9] Truly rare calls, such as calls made by historically significant turkey hunters like Charles L. Jordan and Henry E. Davis, have fetched such sums. Danny Ellis of Charlotte, NC, has put together such calls into a historically significant collection. [10] One can hope that the innovations and craftsmanship in turkey calls will gain appeal internationally; remember that making turkey calls is a truly North American art and craft, given the wild turkey is native only to that continent. In addition to custom-made calls, some production turkey calls now interest aging collectors who used them for hunting in their youth. Who can say what will tickle the fancy of tomorrow's collector of antiquities?

The innovative people covered in this book started by making their turkey calls for personal use, then for a few others, leading to industrializing those processes and expanding beyond wild turkey calls to make other game calls and products. Regardless, their inclusion in this book suggests they all kept a strong identity with turkey hunting as part of their past and ongoing success. As Will Primos told me about such companies that made game calls, "We all started with turkey calls. We expanded to other calls but always kept our passion and fondness for turkeys first." The companies I cover "answered the call" (a phrase oft used by the National Wild Turkey Federation's former CEO Rob Keck) of the wild turkey hunter and will forever be industry icons within that realm. I am not ignorant of the many other excellent companies that were part of this journey, but I believe these few are representative of the many.

In this book I will focus on three companies originating from the restoration of the wild turkey. As the popularity of turkey hunting grew a few new turkey hunters would begin turkey call businesses in the 1970s. All developed turkey hunting products to be manufactured on a production (factory) line and sold under a nationally distributed brand. Some products were made 'in-house' and some by third-party manufacturers. Of course, the prototypes for these calls are hand-made, and hand-tuning or assembling the final product is sometimes required. The KNIGHT & HALE, PRIMOS®, and QUAKER BOY® stories are featured in this book. QUAKER BOY® is still family-owned after forty-six years, PRIMOS® continues to thrive under new ownership, and the the KNIGHT & HALE brand is under new ownership (though sadly does not seem to be making products).

While this book tells the story of the people who manufactured turkey calls through highly mechanized processes, not all turkey calls are made in bulk or in factories. Some of those factory calls might still be hand-assembled or hand-tuned. However, they differ from hand-made custom calls (often using mechanized tools) which are made one at a time and sold by private individuals. Both types of call production require innovation, but custom callmakers have more degrees of freedom. Some might qualify lesser quality custom calls as being more folk-art; suffice it to say that the quality of turkey calls can be highly variable regardless of their method of manufacture but is in direct correlation to the skill of the person or people behind it.

INTRODUCTION

Mass-producing calls requires innovations in materials and processes to get a product made consistently. Individuals like Henry Gibson, Tom Turpin, Neil Cost, and D.D. Adams helped pave the way for the production of turkey calls by leaps forward in the design and quality of turkey calls for those coming behind. In more recent years, Lamar Williams, Billy Buice, Ralph Permar, and Marlin Watkins are a few of many who exemplify excellence (to me) in contemporary custom callmaking. Consider custom calls like "small-batch" bourbon, distinguished products made by masters of their craft for fewer people willing to pay.

A production call for the sake of definition in this book must have been manufactured by the thousands at a time and been available nationwide through major retailers. These products must have been priced for the average "Jake" or "Jenny" hunter to afford to purchase them locally. Production doesn't (or shouldn't) mean it is cheaply made or not dependable, and that criteria may be subjective to an individual hunter. While a custom call's value, if cared for, can be expected to appreciate, it is wrong to assume the same cannot be true of some production calls. Some of the earlier factory-made calls have become scarce, thereby attracting the interest of collectors and the hunting community. The recent collectability of production turkey calls has astonished some vintage collectors.

I believe nostalgia is big medicine for collectability, and thousands of hunters who began using some of those calls in the last fifty years now have an affinity for them. A new generation of hunters also enjoys those "retro" items as they gain a passion for the sport and seek to connect to its roots. Obtaining an old-stock call that is still new in the package is a way for hunters to relive the memories they made or to exhibit their passion. Displaying such things in man caves, dens, hunting cabins, or living rooms is a way to surround themselves with what they love. The same goes for vintage camouflage clothing or some early turkey shotguns made; one will likely have to pay more for it now than the original sticker price!

All turkey calls are made for the love of turkey hunting and profit. Both are noble endeavors, in the author's opinion. While this book will go much deeper into one facet of callmaking, an excellent supplement is Howard Harlan's 1994 masterpiece *Turkey Calls: An Enduring American Folk Art.* Harlan's book is a must-read. It addresses the history of wild turkey callmaking, particularly the earliest known calls. [6] Earl Mickel's trilogy of books featuring callmakers, the first of which was also released in 1994 and is titled *Turkey Callmakers Past and Present,* offers a wonderful look at the personalities and products of a host of callmakers. [11]

There are other companies I don't cover in detail, which may seem like naïve omissions to some. An explanation is that this book provides a few strong examples of companies that rode the wave of the post-restoration era as wild turkeys once again populated this country. There are others. A few companies have been around even longer, selling turkey calls before those I chose to cover. P.S. Olt Co., Johnny Stewart, Herter's, and Faulk's are examples. Those historic brands are still around in some form, though they have always had few offerings for turkey calls. Likewise, Lohman has an active brand under Cabela's (no longer offering turkey calls), but starting with Bill Harper, who owned the company from 1979-1989, they had a full line of turkey calls and would put together a great ProStaff. I did not provide coverage of the company M.L. Lynch, the original production turkey call company, as Raymond M. Masciarella II has already done a superb job of that in his treatise on Lynch calls in his book *The Most Perfect.* [1]

Several once prominent game call companies that I did not cover are no longer in business. They merit a book or books of their own. Penn's Woods (Roger Latham, Frank Piper) and Ben Lee Calls (Ben Rodgers Lee) would have certainly been included had they still been solvent today. Lynch, Latham, Piper, and Lee have also been ably covered in Jim Casada's fantastic 2012 book *Remembering The Greats.* [12] The chapters that Casada did on those men, as well as Dick Kirby, first gave me the idea for this book. Jim suggested, as I echo, that timing was essential to their success. I decided to include Kirby's company, QUAKER BOY®, as the business continues under his family's ownership. Ashby sold years ago, and I regret not getting to talk to Ike Ashby about his company. Perfection, which Jim Clay and Tom Duvall owned, is another I intended to cover, along with M.A.D. Calls (founded by Mark A. Drury); H.S. Strut had a ProStaff I greatly admired. Tom Stuckey is one such person and he worked for Penn's Woods, Ben Lee Calls, and H.S. Strut; he alone would be able to fill a book with his experiences and stories. All such companies are a significant part of history and turkey hunting culture; alas, this one book has too little room for many who are deserving.

A host of smaller but notable companies made turkey calls. It was common for competition turkey callers to start making their own calls. Some of these would qualify by definition as

INTRODUCTION

production companies (versus custom callmakers), given they hired employees to make calls, hired out to third parties, etc. Regardless, they were part of that core group that rode the wave of wild turkey restoration and contributed to turkey hunting and callmaking heritage. Rob Keck pointed out that Perry County, PA was an area rich in competition callers, and as competitive callers sought to improve calls, many innovations and improvements to turkey calls originated there. I would argue that the three companies I covered are significant in being earlier than some, familiar to many, and bigger than most in scale and success. If anything, I apologize for the inability to include more in this book; my admiration has led to an extensive collection of calls from many companies and custom callmakers.

For the sake of the book's length and the reader's attention, I also did not go beyond turkey callmakers. Perhaps others will fill in the gaps. The entrepreneurial explosion fueled by the restoration of the wild turkey spanned many industries. Among those, it is worth pointing out some innovative product improvements that outfitted the turkey hunting boom with better guns, ammunition, camouflage, accessories, and learning tools.

Few today prefer the old-school experience of taking a gobbler with a black powder gun whilst wearing 'skins or dull colors. Gone, for the most part, are the days of shooting turkeys with rifles, and our shoulders are thankful that the best turkey guns are no longer those ten-gauge behemoths that were standard turkey guns in their day. Improvements in guns and loads have driven "size matters" the opposite way. Many now carry a lighter twenty gauge, and even smaller .410 shotguns are currently en vogue. Extra-full and extended chokes, ported barrels, stock configurations, three-and-a-half-inch chambers, red-dot sights, and hydro-dipping technologies are a few ways we can spend our time and money customizing the gun we want. Archery is an additional layer to the onion, with traditional longbows and recurves being primarily replaced by compound bows, which reduce the user's strength to keep the string pulled back, and crossbows make what's old new again through improvements.

Federal, Winchester, and others continued to improve loads in the post-restoration era. Innovations like plastic hulls, shot cups (wads), plated shot, shot buffers, heavier metal alloys, and most recently, Tungsten Super Shot have offered advantages to hunters. As technology changes, one can hope that hunters will strive to make it a game of how close and not how far to honor their quarry and challenge themselves. The experience of sitting inside the spring woods within forty yards of a strutting and gobbling wild turkey is to be in the presence of greatness.

The art of deception required in wars helped drive early innovation in camouflage. Napoleonic warfare that involved outlandish, decorative uniforms and massing troops became poor tactics as weapons evolved. Hand-daubed military camouflage was first utilized in the 1940s as U.S. forces were operating in theatres worldwide. From there, the military regularly refined camouflage before civilian companies had enough of a market to develop hunting camo. [13] Turkey hunters through the 1970s had few options besides getting camo from military surplus stores.

Evolving from military uniforms, concealment for hunting has become a big business. Thus, we have been clothed to have an Advantage® when we pursue our Obsession with the wild turkey. The camo revolution was led by Trebark (Jim Crumley), Mossy Oak (Toxey Haas), and Realtree® (Bill Jordan), resulting in classic patterns like Mossy Oak Bottomland that have made their way onto mainstream products and garments. Old timers who traditionally wore neutral-colored clothing can verify that sitting still is paramount to fooling an ever-vigilant wild turkey. But, for those of us who are squirmy and don't want to sit in a blind, we are thankful for a good camo pattern! There is much more to outdoor attire innovation than camo patterns. These and other companies have brought value-added properties we have come to depend on: water-shedding or wicking ability, thermal insulation, quietness, breathability or air permeability, durability, and many things we don't know but likely appreciate.

Accessories like turkey decoys quickly sprang from the tradition of waterfowl decoys. The decoying of game species has been practiced since our ancestors hunted with spears and bows. The infamous buffalo jumps required young Native American hunters to don tanned buffalo hides to lead animals in the herd to their deaths. In some Plains tribes like the Sioux, there is verbal history that these "decoys" would bellow like a stressed calf, trying to get the herd to follow them (incidentally, that would be one of the earliest historical uses of a "game call" even if produced by the human voice). In Arlie Schorger's comprehensive work on the wild turkey, *The Wild Turkey: Its History and Domestication,* he references witnesses who observed Native American tribes in the Mississippi Valley, Missouri, and Arkansas using turkey heads and skins as hunting decoys. [14] [15] The hunting industry has developed many options for the modern hunter. Buyer, beware that while a decoy might take a turkey's eyes off you, it can attract other hunters!"

Another occupation that was timed well to parallel the return of the wild turkey was that of the outdoor writer. Not a new trade, sporting magazines were popular even in the late 1800s, but several had over 1,000,000 subscribers during the 1960-1990 period as turkey seasons were being created across the country. These pen-wielders provided great material to an eager turkey-hunting public when magazines were how we got our information, and many of those issues were likely read by multiple people in homes, hunting camps, and offices. As someone who enjoys writing and telling the story of wild turkey hunting heritage and history, I stand on the shoulders of those who lived it and wrote about it.

Tom Kelly never set out to write more than one book on turkey hunting, but his timing and material were perfectly met. He is now the most recognized and prolific author of that genre, called 'the poet laureate of turkey hunting' by Jim Casada. [16] Casada will forever be the 'wise man' of turkey hunting history because he researched and wrote about it, even as some of it was happening. Dave Harbour, Dwain Bland, Brian Lovett, Jim Spencer, John McDaniel, Steve Hickoff, Michael Hanback, JJ Reich, John Higley, J. Wayne Fears…there are too many outdoor writers to list that picked up the pen during the post-restoration era. They entertained and educated us through their words and with enhancement through excellent photography by the likes of Tes Randle Jolly, Jami Linder, and many others.

INTRODUCTION

The perfect timing of audiotapes, outdoor television programming, and videotapes cannot be ignored in the growth of game call companies. The technology became available at the ideal time for those companies to advertise and instruct in a manner that also provided entertainment value. Seeing and hearing the people behind the companies built an appreciation for them. Rob Keck emphasized that "In the mid-1970s when you went to turkey calling contests you could hear tape recorders clicking on. That was a common sound and it preceded video as a teaching and learning tool." It continued with CD and DVD technology, only to be disrupted by digital platforms. Some companies have embraced the world of YouTube, podcasts, and social media, but it doesn't appeal to all. Each platform offers something new but has limitations.

The growth of turkey hunting also led to its expansion geographically to include the Gould's turkey in Mexico, which had been primarily extirpated from its original range in the southern U.S. [17]. The same was true for the peacock-like Ocellated turkey in Mexico's Yucatan peninsula, Guatemala, and Belize. [18] Turkey hunters were salivating over hunting in new areas and seeking new experiences. Men like Lovett Williams, a preeminent wild turkey biologist of the time, researched and helped establish hunting camps. Guide services sprang up across the US, including Canada, as the wild turkey population expanded. Turkeys became big business. Towns had festivals, hotels began advertising to turkey hunters, and the future of the turkey and hunter seemed secure. Change is the only constant in this world; some believe these recent "good old days" of turkey hunting have already come and gone.

A recent dip in wild turkey populations has justifiably raised concern, considering nearly losing our turkeys once before. With the development of future technologies, we can expect our equipment to change, and therefore our methods. The changing landscape we live in and hunt on will continue to drive the need for additional changes to when, where, and how we hunt. We hope there will be much to look forward to for future turkey hunters. Careers are waiting to be made as change happens.

The KNIGHT & HALE, PRIMOS®, and QUAKER BOY® stories in the following chapters illustrate the heights of achievement possible when preparation meets opportunity at a singular moment. Further enhanced through the talents of individuals like Mike Battey and Anthony Foster, it is evident that while the competition was fierce between turkey call companies, all shared a greater sense of belonging. The well-articulated turkey hunter of yesteryear, Archibald Rutledge, may have captured it best:

"One of the sanest, surest, and most generous joys of life comes from being happy over the good fortune of others."

Enjoy the story of how these individuals and companies "answered the call" of the wild turkey and, in turn, were "making the call" for the rest of us.

YELP & GOBBLE, INC.

Chapter 1

KNIGHT & HALE

For better, for worse, for richer, for poorer, in sickness and in health… Harold Knight and David Hale have been through it all. Five decades of working together have forged a legendary friendship, helping them navigate their personal and professional hurdles. That span of time is exceedingly uncommon to find in business relationships, given the unique pressures and demands that operating a business puts on individuals. Knight and Hale have not only defied those odds, but they also serve as an example to others. As Knight's stepson and Hale's daughter are married and have kids, they even have grandchildren in common!

The success of KNIGHT & HALE Game Calls, given its humble origins, is the stuff of the proverbial American Dream. When I visited their homes in Cadiz, KY, while researching this book, Hale immediately

Harold Knight and David Hale

gave me a brochure they had done in 2006 that acknowledges the truth of their journey and their ultimate measure of success. "Humble Beginnings; A Common Call to Us All!" is a brief encapsulation of the men and their journey, and as the clever play on words indicates, a call to salvation. Having spent a fair amount of time evangelizing and sharing his faith, Hale has never shown fear of telling it like it is as a man of God and a businessman. Harold is also a man of faith and the innovator behind most calls—a pleasant guy who has a way with words. Two very different men in personality and practice are bonded in their foundation of faith and well-matched to chew on and solve any issue together.

The Knight children in 1953; 9 year old Harold Knight is at right with a baseball glove

Many in the hunting industry have heard about the barber and the farmer who became nationally known hunting celebrities. After a year of barber school, Harold took up the trade at Cadiz Barber Shop, which he would later purchase. Sitting before the former barber, I couldn't help asking Knight if he still recognized a lousy haircut when he saw it (I had gotten a trim a few days before). "Yes, and there are a lot of 'em out there!" laughed Knight. "I was a barber from 1963 to 1984, and I got to interact with many types of people, older and younger. I loved to talk to the older people as they had wisdom. I could comprehend that later in life. Ya had to listen; it was interesting, and I enjoyed it. Anything you do in life, barber, farmer, mechanic…the bottom is filled up, but the top is wide open! That's what I tried to do as a barber and what I tried to do with our game call company. David and I didn't set a lot of goals; we started with nothing, but what we accomplished and got out of it we feel good about."

The two men whose paths were set for a collision course grew up not all that different from one another. As avid gun and bowhunters, they have hunted across the U.S. for almost everything, and Knight is a competitive bass fisherman. Western Kentucky is where their homes and hearts are to be found, as they have lived there for their entire lives. But time changes things, and Knight and Hale have seen that happen at their doorstep. Imagine being in Knight's shoes, where he can't even do a drive-by of the land he grew up on. It is now underwater!

The Land Between the Lakes is a popular National Recreation Area now, but that came at a cost to some locals. The year Harold was born, a dam built across the Tennessee River created Kentucky Lake. Then, in 1963, the process to dam the Cumberland River began. When completed in 1966, it formed Lake Barkley, a peninsula of land between the lakes that gave the area its new name. However, the flooding and the designation of the strip of land as a National area necessitated the removal of over 2,000 families by the Tennessee Valley Authority, including Knight's.

Knight has fond memories of his early days in the outdoors. An introduced population of fallow deer resided there, as did white-tailed deer and a few wild turkeys. Hunting was enjoyable and practical for the Knights, as it was for many rural families. "We were poor, but we had a good life. I killed hundreds of squirrels for us to eat. Shells were expensive, and there weren't any real turkey loads then," said Knight. "I had to ask to split the box at the hardware store and buy two or three at a time. They let you do that then. They were all paper shells, and if they got damp, the paper swelled. Sometimes, I had to sand down the shell where it swelled to get it in my shotgun barrel."

Knight's garage contains a scaled-down model of a copper still. Oddly enough, this is part of his turkey-hunting backstory. "I have a brother that spent a little time in a Federal penitentiary for moonshining," he said matter-of-factly. "It is legal to make 'shine here now; people sell it all over. But it wasn't legal yet at that time," Knight said. Indeed, successful brands and craft companies are sprinkled across the state today, but those looking to squeeze some extra dollars out of a bushel of corn at the time had to be discreet. "Maurice Calhoun was a big farmer, and like a lot of people in that time, he fooled with making a little moonshine. He started me turkey hunting," remembered Knight. I can't help thinking the stealth and cunning of a moonshiner isn't somehow helpful when applied to the art of turkey hunting.

"Maurice would peck on my window early in the morning just once, and I'd be up and ready to go turkey hunting," Harold recalled. "Hunters back then had 'territories' as birds were scarce. You didn't intrude on someone else." Again, the lessons and practices of making moonshine overlay well with turkey hunting principles. Knight was relentless in learning the turkey hunting trade before he finally got to tag along at age 12. He said, "I was picking all these old guys' brains. I would ask them lots of questions, and they let me use their calls. They knew a lot more than I did, but I see things now that I have learned that they didn't know. And some of what worked then doesn't work as good now, like just yelping three times and not getting aggressive at all." When hunting with a moonshiner (the flesh and blood kind, not the friction 'pot' style call that Knight later gave that name!), the ability to hear cars turned out to be an asset. "They didn't get up at daylight to go hunting," remembers Knight. "They got up early, and they looked and listened for cars." The joint pursuits of moonshining and turkey hunting overlap again in the importance of knowing whether you will have unwelcome company!

While Knight hunts many game species, the wild turkey has become foremost among them. As many a hunter experiences, even now, when there are many more turkeys across the country, getting your first solo bird takes effort. It wasn't uncommon at the time for the locals to do some spring turkey hunting, but their restraint had kept native turkeys at a time when the rest of the state saw them eliminated. He got an "incidental" turkey while squirrel hunting at age 11, igniting a passion. He managed to call one up the following year, but the strutting and gobbling bird unnerved him. "I missed by a mile," said Harold. He had to discipline himself to calm down because he would tend to get keyed up and impulsive when hearing an approaching bird. Any turkey hunter will sympathize with that tendency. Harold revealed, "Where we hunted was thick with huckleberry bushes, and you could hear those branches popping as a gobbler was coming through. I can still hear that and those wings dragging now, even though it was sixty years ago."

Harold Knight with a turkey at his Barbershop in the 1960s

Encouraged that he had legitimately talked a gobbler into shooting range, the 13-year-old boy was back at it the following spring. "I called one up and killed my first spring turkey in 1957," said Knight. That was three years before Kentucky declared a season, he pointed out to me. The population of wild turkeys in Kentucky was estimated in 1954 to be around 850 birds. Recognizing they had a huntable population of birds, the state held the first spring turkey season in forty-one years in the Kentucky Woodland Refuge (now part of the Land Between the Lakes), April 27–29, 1960. Without a driver's license, Calhoun provided transport for Knight. Not long after dawn, Knight heard his mentor shoot. Then, the 16-year-old Knight called up and killed a jake; the pair was one of only twelve hunters to take a bird in that first season. Harold said, "All of us were locals that got them, and I am the only one still living." That was big news, and Harold was covered along with the other hunters in a local news article. Now, having hunted across the country, Harold maintains, "The wildest turkeys I have hunted are the ones in the Land Between the Lakes and some places in Alabama. Putting pressure on a turkey is what makes it wild, or maybe wild-er."

This game-rich area drew the attention of hunters across the U.S. for their archery-only deer season. One of the hunters that attended was legendary bowhunter Fred Bear, who at one time gave a youthful Harold Knight four arrows he autographed. "I would shoot 'em at all kinds of game until they weren't any good anymore. Those would be worth some good money nowadays," said Knight.

The first call Knight used was an old cedar scratch box given to him by an old timer. Knight said, "There were few turkey calls commercially available then. Frank Piper had Penn's Woods, and there was Lohman and Lynch. Every serious turkey hunter at the time had one go-to call; for many, it was the Gibson box call. I wish I had one of those now." Henry Gibson of Arkansas is credited with developing the box-style turkey call. He received a patent in 1897 and sold it through hardware stores, where hunters found their wares. A 1921 catalog advertisement listing it for $2.60 would have been a substantial investment for a turkey hunter of the generation that mentored Knight, especially when turkey numbers were so low. "Just seeing or hearing a turkey in the 1950s meant a successful hunt for us," said Knight. "The old hunters saw I had a lot of interest, and that got me in."

Very first Knight tube design offered for sale; it was made of PVC pipe and wood-grained tape

Another call that had likely been around at the time was the 'snuff-can' turkey call. As suggested by its name, it was a metal snuff-can (think of the snorting tobacco popular at the time). Cutting a semi-circle hole in the bottom of the tube allowed a piece of rubber to be stretched over it, and with the lid off, one could blow air across the rubber and through the call to produce a sound like a turkey. Some old examples of those calls exist, as captured in Earl Mickel's book *Turkey Callmakers Past and Present*, where Charlie Bishop of Illinois is referenced as making those by 1939.

Later, this style of tube call would be made from film canisters and pill bottles. Knight had seen a snuff can type call, and he used pill bottles to make his first tubes before he would revolutionize tube calls with his new designs. The predecessor to the tube-style call was likely the 'bird calls' that one can find patents issued for in the 1800s and early 1900s. One

David Hale as a budding turkey hunter

of these calls resembles the tube Knight would design, though its configuration was limited to producing the call of a dove. While he was developing his tube, others were experimenting as wild turkeys spread across the landscape through restoration efforts. One such worth noting was designing a tube of a different design. Kenny Morgan, who, like Knight, began to make tube calls in 1971, received a patent in 1973 for his unique design of a wooden tube with a tin insert that would be recognized as producing the gobble of a wild turkey.

Although Hale grew up hunting small game, there were no flocks of turkeys for him to pursue in his local haunts. His childhood was spent less than thirty miles east of Knight but beyond the range of the turkeys in the Kentucky Woodlands Refuge. His home was near Gracey, in Christian County, Kentucky. Hale's parents were both school teachers, and he was one of three children. He would meet his future wife in seventh grade, where he was eaten up with sports and was on the basketball and baseball teams.

Upon graduation from High School, he chose to pursue college, incented by the likelihood of otherwise going to Vietnam, given that conflict at the time. Hale served six years in the U.S. Army, the first two in the National Guard and then four years in the Reserves. Incidentally, the only turkey season he would miss once he started would be the 1969 season due to his military service. He attended Murray State University in Kentucky, pursuing a degree in Agribusiness. "I didn't see where college was gonna help me," he said. "But little did I know I was going to be in the game call business where that education would help me so much."

He didn't go to the bars or parties during his downtime; he spent time listening to and learning from conversations at the local country store. This is where he first heard the stories from the 'turkey men' who knew of or even hunted turkeys. That was almost unheard of at the time. Hale respected these men and saw others did, too, and set his sights on bagging a bird. He studied as hard on turkeys as on his college courses, diving into everything in print on turkeys he could find. He stealth-hunted them in his early years, given his experience with deer hunting. He also applied the skill of scouting when hunting his first bird. He located a roost tree by 'sourcing' the gobbling, then patterned the turkey's routine. He shot the bird inside thirty yards by putting himself where the turkey wanted to be. It was one of only fifteen turkeys taken in the Land Between the Lakes area that year, in 1967!

The first turkey Hale got made him a turkey hunter for life. The next year, he enthusiastically hit the woods again but never had a chance to kill one. Although he was in the Army in 1969 and couldn't hunt, he reclaimed his spring glory in 1970 as one of only five successful hunters among a few hundred that tried. Game calls would soon become his business, but up to that time, the man who had now become a farmer had never used a turkey call! When asked by a curious friend what call he was using. He had discovered that moving leaf litter around, like walking or scratching like a turkey, was effective, but he sheepishly admitted he didn't use a turkey call. His friend recommended a trip to a barber in Cadiz who made some calls. Following that advice would be life-changing for both men.

Harold Knight with a Land Between the Lakes wild turkey

Every successful game call company has a different recipe for success. In addition to how the two men's capabilities complemented one another, there was a third person they credited with being the secret ingredient, even if they didn't know it then. Hale told me, "Dave Harbour helped us a lot; I was pretty close to him," Col. Dave Harbour was a legend, a talented outdoor writer who became Field Editor of *Sports Afield* magazine and was obsessed with wild turkeys. Hunting turkeys was a passion, and when the NWTF was founded in 1973, he would eagerly become the first Life Member. He published two books on wild turkeys and a journal for hunters to record their hunts and established a scoring system that would become the NWTF Wild Turkey Records program. Harbour would also put Harold Knight and David Hale on the map with his pen.

That story of a chance encounter and the resulting game call supernova it created has often been repeated, but the two company founders know their story can't be told without it. The date of destiny was the spring of 1971 when Floridian Dave Harbour was scouting some ground in Kentucky's Land Between the Lakes. While driving, he saw a man emerge from the woods; suspecting he was another hunter, Harbour drove up to create conversation. Noticing a cylinder suspended on a lanyard from the man's neck, Harbour inquired what it was. He suspected it might be a type of turkey call, and like every turkey hunter, Harbour was looking for that next advantage to use when engaged in a duel with Mr. Tom Turkey. The man stated it was a turkey call, so Harbour curiously asked for a demonstration. The man apologetically said he wasn't very good at it but obliged. Upon hearing the yelps, Harbour earnestly inquired where he might get one. The man, David Hale, replied, "If you'll wait here a few minutes, the man who built this call will come along, and he'll give you one." That other man, Harold Knight, never showed up, so Hale suggested Harbour go by the Cadiz Barber Shop to see him. Harbour did just that; he acquired a tube call and two new friends that day.

Harbour wrote of his hunt in the April 1972 issue of *Sports Afield,* and the article was titled "My Old Kentucky Gobbler." Harbour wrote, "I had the good fortune to run into two other wild-eyed gobbler chasers. Harold Knight, who owns a barber shop in Cadiz, Kentucky, and Dave Hale, a farmer from nearby Gracey, was intimately familiar with every inch of turkey range in Land Between the Lakes. Both had taken big gobblers during two of the last four spring hunts. These congenial young men appraised me for a few minutes, then briefed me on the most promising areas to scout and showed me an amazing new turkey call that Harold had developed."

Harold Knight and David Hale as youthful turkey hunters

I need here to emphasize the kind of men Knight and Hale are. While crossing paths with other hunters in the spring turkey woods can connect people with the same obsession, all too often today, we see the competitive nature that darkens such meetings with storm clouds. I am not casting stones and can admit a bit of guilt myself. All too often, that old territorial nature and establishment of the pecking order surface when we cross other turkey hunters on the battlefield. We would do well to remember we are not at war with other hunters. "I was here first," "I have been hunting here my whole life," and "Where did you park" is the prequel to a one-upmanship to claim a turkey on public ground. I would argue that if Harold Knight and David Hale were that kind of people, few hunters would have been introduced to the calls their acts of kindness earned them.

As a collector of turkey calls, Harbour wrote in the article about his intrigue with how "Knight's invention was radically different from any I had ever seen. It is the only diaphragm-type call I have ever run into which anyone can use effectively with little or no practice." Harbour even tells readers how to use a tube call to make several different and realistic calls, saying it "even gobbles!"

As the story climaxed, he wrote, "Cupping Harold Knight's magic tube in my hands, I queried the forest with a series of four soft, inquisitive yelps." Unfortunately, he bumped that gobbler and sought counsel again with his two new friends. Knight and Hale had located other gobblers, and in a second act of charity, they once again gave up the locations of the birds. Putting his new tube call to work again, Harbour killed one of only eight turkeys taken that year in Land Between the Lakes...and the only one killed by an out-of-state hunter. For Harbour, it was the heaviest bird he had yet taken, weighing twenty-two and a half pounds. "This was my greatest gobbler hunt," he told Knight and Hale, marveling at his luck. Hale demonstrated his future business savvy when he quipped, "It was that new call of Harold's that lured the old bird in."

There were over one million subscribers to that periodical then, so imagine the boost that unsolicited testimony bestowing praise on Harold's call and the character of the two men gave to Knight & Hale's future. It would be directly correlated to the formation soon after of KNIGHT & HALE Game Calls. My friend and fellow KNIGHT & HALE collector, Korby Taylor, said, "This series of events speaks to a few significant things. First, how unknown and revolutionary

The 1972 magazine article by Dave Harbour that lit the fire for KNIGHT & HALE GAME CALLS

Harold's tube call was at the time. And it displays Harold's and David's generosity to help a stranger. Finally, it demonstrates how that act of kindness was a monumental moment for their business; Dave Harbour would open a door for them."

The story Harbour wrote made for good entertainment for hunters and burned into Knight and Hale's minds how important outdoor writers were when it came to affordable and effective advertising. That knowledge would pay big dividends as the company grew. The three men shared the same passion and had much in common. A meaningful friendship developed between them. Their paths would cross again as they became volunteers for the NWTF, all active at the local, state, and national levels. They would continue turkey hunting together; Hale remembered when he and Harbour were stargazing one night and advised Harbour, "You are one of the smartest turkey hunters I know, but you can't call worth a darn!" Harbour was at first surprised, but Hale's comment demonstrates the honesty between the two friends. Knight added, "He was not a world champion caller but was a world champion hunter." It should come as no surprise that Harbour's *Hunting the American Wild Turkey* is Knight's favorite book on wild turkey hunting. Knight and Hale are exceedingly grateful for their friendship with Harbour and credit him with jump-starting their business.

Tragically, Harbour is among a couple of well-known turkey hunters who died of a heart

David Hale and Harold Knight testing one-piece tube calls

attack while turkey hunting (the other being Inman Turpin). When it happened in the spring of 1988, Harbour had just killed a gobbler after an intense physical and emotional hunt. His son Doug perfectly eulogized him, saying it was "a beautiful finale to a truly great outdoorsman's life."

Thus, Knight and Hale were introduced to the public at large. Harold would begin selling calls as "Harold Knight Turkey Calls." Labels on tubes then just said "Harold Knight," as it would be a while before KNIGHT & HALE would appear on labels; the men trace their official start date to that pivotal event with Harbour in 1972. In Hale's newly released book *Adventures In Hunting With Knight & Hale*, he records his advice to Knight to prepare for an onslaught of mail after Harbour's story was published. His statement was prophetic, as Knight received thousands of letters of inquiry. In response to interest from the magazine article, he sold 3,000 tube calls at the modest price of $5 each. Working alone out of his garage, Knight began to find this more than one man could handle.

The first Kentucky State Turkey Calling Contest in 1973; Knight (left) won and Hale (middle) placed second

A few months later, in 1973, while Knight was cutting Hale's hair in his barbershop, he asked Hale about joining forces. Hale was game and began helping, building calls in Harold's basement. Knight was grateful for the help, as his wife had been helping, but it wasn't her cup of tea, so to speak. The men let their imaginations run wild; if they made and sold enough tube calls, they might save enough money for an out-of-state hunting trip to Missouri. It seemed like a stretch to the young barber and farmer. What they would accomplish exceeded all expectations, including their own!

Looking back, Hale and Knight quickly agree that their differences probably made them more successful than their commonality. Together, they yielded more than the sum of their parts. Hale said, "Harold is the idealist, and I am the pragmatist." Whereas Knight has mastered the art of developing relationships, Hale has mastered the art of the deal. His thriftiness is a way of life. Heck, when he and his bride Pam were married, they did it by eloping; The cost was $25! Both men were fortunate to have loving spouses who supported their time in the outdoors and endured the long stretches when the men were working. Hale's wife, Pam, used to call the business "Night and Day," given the commitment and responsibility that kept the men busy. Hale introduced Pam to turkey hunting the first year they were married, and since then, both men have taken their kids and grandkids.

There is a pecking order amongst some hunters- just as in the social structure of turkey flocks. The two men never let egos trip them up; they did things together but retained their uniqueness. Their differences strengthened their business and hunting endeavors. They also learned to brush off the criticisms of others and do what made sense to them. As an aspiring turkey hunter, Hale recalls in an early hunt he made that he was a source of amusement at the game check station. "Early on, I knew the importance of innovation," he said. My shotgun had a three-inch magnum barrel, but I put a three-and-a-half-inch paper shell in it. These guys were amused at seeing my gun, as I had also taken masking tape, put it all around the barrel, and then colored it with magic markers to camouflage it. I had the last laugh when I brought a gobbler back that day!" This is significant for Hale's style as Knight divulged that "David is good at slipping in and getting close. What helped both of us in our hunting was knowing the wild turkey. You can make as much noise as you want walking, but once they see you, it's over."

The innovation happening around them was also helping and accelerating their success. Knight credits technology like the cannon net for allowing the trapping and releasing of turkeys, which expanded and improved hunting. More turkeys meant more hunters that needed turkey calls. Although it ultimately served their business purpose, Knight & Hale loved the wild turkey enough that they became lifelong conservation advocates and volunteers. Knight proudly told me, "David and I started the third National Wild Turkey Federation (NWTF) chapter in the U.S. in 1973, right here locally. We had 800 people come to the first meeting we had!" Hale said, "The fire marshal wouldn't let any more in!" Both men have always been staunch supporters of the NWTF and recognize the importance of having organizations by and for hunters to focus on issues and celebrate success. "I was president of that chapter for seven years," Hale said. Knight said, "Our NWTF chapter goal was to get a biologist for the state of Kentucky, and we did it. We bought a four-wheeler, a cannon net, and other stuff for George Wright here in Kentucky, and they began trapping and transferring turkeys by 1979."

Research at the time indicated that local wild turkeys were not achieving sound reproduction. Infusion of DNA from other wild flocks through the trap and transfer program proved the answer. In a twist of fate, I unexpectedly met some descendants of those birds the night before I interviewed the men for this very book. I was staying at a hotel in nearby Hopkinsville, and when I rose at dawn and pulled the curtains back, a jake flew down that had been roosted in a line of trees following a waterway adjacent to the hotel. Shortly, the jake was joined by another jake and two hens. It seemed like I was meant to be there!

What Knight and Hale accomplished wasn't done in fairy tale fashion. It required an intense and ongoing investment of time and resources. In 1974, they would make their first upgrade, remodeling the back of Knight's barbershop as their new callmaking shop. What helped was the role clarity they achieved to divide and conquer the work, avoiding stepping on one another's toes and making them more efficient. With their natural abilities, Knight continued to oversee production, and Hale was the supply chain guy. The two of them eventually couldn't keep up with all the work alone. "We worked the first twelve years together out of the back of Harold's barber shop," recalls Hale. "I had two daughters that came in, and they would open and answer mail and package stuff up." Knight agreed, "That was hard work when you

The author's collection of KNIGHT & HALE tube call models

worked all day at your job, then worked on game calls 'til midnight, and then had to get up the next morning and do it again."

Up to this time, Knight had been constructing his turkey tube-type calls out of a plastic cylinder (either a PVC pipe or pill bottle) with latex rubber stretched over half of one end of the bottle, nearly meeting up with a 'lip stop' that was glued into the other side. His earliest had consisted of two pieces of plastic, with one slightly smaller piece of cylinder inserted into a somewhat larger one; then Knight switched to a single plastic cylinder.

He continued experimenting with his tubes and noted that thicker latex produced more of a goose call. This call was altered by having no lip stop, and in 1975, KNIGHT & HALE began to make some wooden tube goose calls. Knight informed me that "All of our early wood stuff was made by Jack Thomas. Jack had a lathe, and he was good. I glued in the lip stops and put all the finish on. It's a wonder I'm still livin' after breathing in all the polyurethane! I'll never forget that every time he came to the shop, he brought me the calls in a paper bag and everything just as neat as could be, and every time he'd say, "Do you want any more?" Knight laughed and said, "I said we'd take ten thousand if he could make 'em!" Jack would make many turkey, duck, goose, and varmint calls for KNIGHT & HALE.

Another early figure in the KNIGHT & HALE journey was Jerry Turner. "He was one of our first employees, a Baptist preacher," Harold said. "He come to us when we were workin' in the back of the barbershop, he was diagnosed with cancer early, but lived to be fifty years old. His passion was turkey hunting and ginseng hunting. He had an art of reaching people that served him well. He tuned lots of tube calls and was a jack of all trades. David and I both loved him to death."

The Kentucky boys put on a tube call clinic

For the sake of the chronology of the wooden tubes, especially for collectors who crave such details, it is worth noting that the early wooden turkey and goose tubes were made from one piece of wood. The early ones had no grooves on the bell end, and Knight told Jack to add some grooves on the later one-piece tubes by saying, "Put on some rings to dress it up." Then, for a brief time, they made less than 300 wooden two-piece calls (one cylinder fits inside the other). These are as rare as the proverbial hen's teeth!

During this stretch in the late 1970s, Knight noticed a goose tube that Jack Thomas had thrown in the trash while making wooden tubes. Knight casually inquired why he tossed it, and Jack replied that the tube had cracked as he'd turned the walls too thin. On a whim, Knight took that call out of the garbage can and glued up the crack. Knight stated in an interview with Mossy Oak, "I started thinking of my Dad, who was a bluegrass musician. He built his own fiddles out of very thin wood because he said the sound would be better if the wood was thinner. Dad could take a fiddle apart, tune it, and put it back together. Dad also had a very good musical ear and could distinguish between a good sound and a bad sound. I guess I inherited some of that ability from him. I knew that the thin wood would resonate well and sound good. So, I used that throw-away wooden tube in the World Goose Calling Championship that I won in 1979."

Knight would like to have done more competitive calling but found it hard to find the time when you are in the game call business. But his guidance and KNIGHT & HALE products would allow others to have success at call competitions. Knight spoke of one such example in an interview with Mossy Oak. He said after his 1979 Goose Calling Championship, "I met this young boy – I think his name was David Coleman – a goose guide in Maryland. He asked, "Will you show me how to blow that tube call?" I told him sure. So, I taught him everything I had learned about the tube goose call. The following year, in 1980, I went back to the World Goose Calling Championship to defend my title, and that young man beat me like a drum. The next two years, he won that championship with that same tube call, and I heard that he won the World Goose Calling Championship this year with that same tube goose call."

"After I won the World Goose Calling Championship, David and I invested in an injection mold to make tube goose calls, and we sold a heck of a lot of them," Knight recalls. "We discovered we could modify the tubes for gobbling and for elk calls. We made tubes for Ben Lee and at least one other manufacturer." They had purchased and moved an injection mold company, Ethridge Plastic, into their new shop and are still making calls for other manufacturers. This investment required a twenty-four hours seven days a week operation and a more extensive staff.

Along with their tube calls, they started giving away lanyards, "We were one of the first; we originally bought them from H.S. Strut for one dollar apiece," said Knight. "Eventually, we had a tool and die man make the part that made the crimp, and then we started doin' them ourselves. We built six machines and made one million lanyards a year! We made a bunch for others, secondary business. We put a lot of competition in business and took 'em out too." For someone who cares, one can determine the make of the lanyard. As Knight said, the H.S. Strut lanyards were a little thicker rope. The first handmade lanyards that they did, before having the machine crimping, were all handmade by Hale and painted with green John-Deere paint by Eric Mitchell; hence, they refer to them as "the John Deere lanyards."

KNIGHT & HALE had expanded their tube call offering to include a new species and leveraged new technologies. This was merely the beginning of what the fledgling company would achieve. Realizing that new hunters needed help understanding how to use calls, they offered instructional cassette tapes and released a 45 rpm record titled *Original Knight Tube Turkey Calling.* Along with Mike McLemore, a World Goose Calling Champion, they also made a 45 rpm record featuring goose calling. These weren't gimmicks, as Harold Knight and David Hale used those calls, and plenty that hunted with them can vouch for their effectiveness. Knight relished telling me, "I'd take that tube goose call out into a cornfield and blow it at high-flying geese, and they would come in and almost land on my head!"

"We were innovators," said Knight of their reputation and impact in the industry. They had started with the one-piece wild turkey tube, first made from plastic in 1971-1972. In 1973-1974, several hundred wooden one-piece (hand turned on a lathe and then drilled out) calls were made from walnut or cherry and perhaps less than thirty from maple; other woods would be uncommon. From 1974-1977, they made two-piece wooden tubes, and then in

1977, they discontinued the wooden calls and commissioned a two-piece call made in an injection mold. They called this the Combination Hen and Gobbler Call, as the outer tube could be removed, producing two different sounds when used with or without it. Applying learnings as they went, Knight shortened the lip stops, which allowed the user to get their lip under the rubber reed. He shared that "this enhanced the sound it produced. We found out later that the end piece on the two-piece call didn't serve much purpose." All later tubes would revert to one-piece tubes...the original design was hard to beat.

One can see the pricing going up through following their ads, as demand increased and they had to increase their assets and add people to keep up. From the original $5.00 Knight charged, the first ads in *Turkey Call* in 1973 show a price point of $5.50, and the first wooden tubes offered

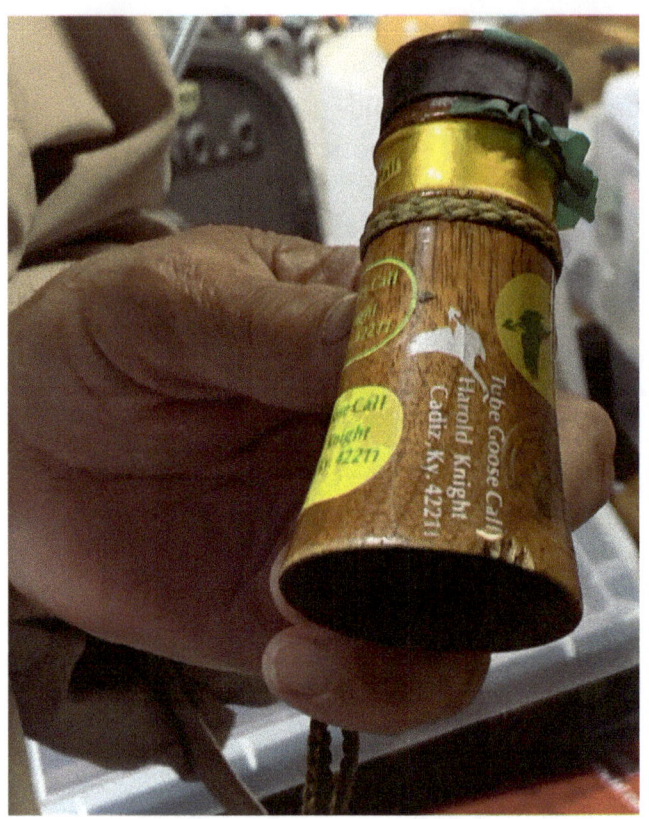

Knight's championship winning goose tube

in 1974 were nearly double that price at $9.00. By 1976, the earliest plastic tube was no longer for sale, and in 1977, the price was up slightly on the cherry or walnut tubes to $9.50, plus a dollar for postage. 1978 saw the introduction of a wooden version of the two-piece, or Combination Call. That sold for $13.95 (and would go to $15.00 the following year...they weren't offered for long given the time to hand-make them), whereas the plastic tube two-piece was $8.95. All these tubes are now collectible items, with the handmade wooden two-piece calls among the rarest. 1984 was the year they launched the one-piece molded tube with the flared bell that would be called The Widowmaker and be part of their lineup for years. It took only ten years to achieve over one million dollars in their wholesale business.

With their momentum, Knight said, "A day came in 1984 when we realized we had to go full time." He set down his shears (though he still cuts Hale's hair), and Hale set aside his thoughts of expanding his farm for good. "I try to keep a positive attitude as much as I can," intoned Hale. "I truly believe the glass has to be half full instead of half empty. I tried to farm full-time for myself; over time, there were three farms I bid on, and I didn't get any of 'em. I had prayed "Lord I want to farm." But Hale finally realized it wasn't all about what he wanted. Although he had 300 acres of cropland at that time, it became clear to him that there was a different path he needed to follow.

They moved production out of Knight's barbershop that year, in 1984, to a building in the

CALLING ALL TURKEY HUNTERS

Harold Knight and David Hale were quick to leverage the NWTF's new bi-monthly publication, *Turkey Call*, which had a rapidly growing circulation.

They were among the few early advertisers and placed ads in nearly every issue for years.

Note the introduction of new products and price hikes as KNIGHT & HALE grew. Selling copies of Dave Harbour's book was a nice way to help the man who put them on the radar of many turkey hunters. The following ads were taken from *Turkey Call* magazine issues as referenced below.

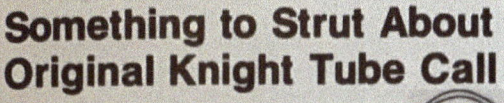

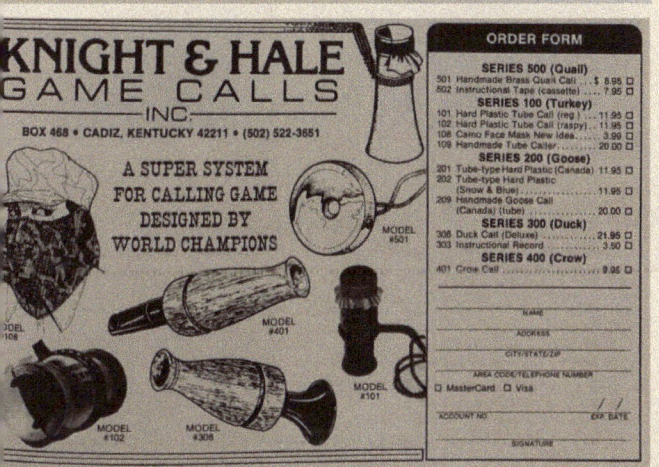

Top Left: Dec 1973-Mar 1974

Right: Number Two, 1976

Middle Left: Sept-Oct 1978

Bottom Sept-Oct 1984

Commercial Park in Cadiz, Kentucky, and beefed up to ten full-time employees to make game calls and help run the business. Jim Strelec was brought on as their Sales Manager, increasing their time to promote sports shows by giving seminars nationwide. Strelec recalled, "After we built the first building, David and his girls, Harold and myself would work there all day. When we built it, I convinced them to put in bedrooms, a bathroom, and a kitchen to be able to host outdoor writers and friends. We didn't have enough money to put 'em in hotels, and this way, we could stay close to 'em."

Similar to the evolution of other game call companies of the time, they grew from their initial offering of turkey calls to many other products. That expanded their consumer base, helping make KNIGHT & HALE a household name. By this time, they had greatly expanded their game call lines to include turkey, goose, duck, crow, and quail calls. The handmade brass quail call is very scarce, and chances are you didn't even know about it. The Double Clucker goose call was introduced in 1987 and was a good seller for the pair. "I loved that name," said Knight. "The logo has a double goose head on it, and that call won three World Championships!" KNIGHT & HALE made several calls that would win National or World competitions, including the Double Clucker (three), Tube Goose Call (five), Inhale/Exhale Deer, and the Fighting Purr Turkey Call. This is not an exhaustive list, as many other calls were used by ProStaffers in calling competitions. Some may have been prototypes or had slight modifications. KNIGHT & HALE regularly sponsored calling contests, helping to carry on a tradition the two founders had been part of.

Despite not having marketing backgrounds, the men were creative and understood their target market. They knew they needed a catalog to reach potential retailers. They also knew they would have to spend money to make it, but Hale told me, "We didn't have much money given the reinvestment in the business." Through the resourceful Jim Strelec, they were introduced to a publisher in 1986 who might be able to help them. Given the lack of funds, they got creative. Hale said, "Harold offered to take the publishers duck hunting for a solid week." It was a good swap, and it worked. Strelec told me, "I went to my friend's house in Chicago, and we took photos of products from every angle. I had to do writeups on how every call and product worked. Well, he produced us a full-blown color catalog; we were the first ones out with something like that."

They also needed to create demand with consumers, so Hale contacted an acquaintance, Peter Matheista, from the LaSalle Group in St. Louis, who was a marketing whiz, saying he had $8,000 to spend on advertising but "wanted to tell the world about his calls. Peter laughed, saying, "I can't even tell the people in St. Louis about it for that!" Hale challenged the response, saying, "Well, that's all I got, so take it or leave it." After thinking about it over the weekend, Peter got together with Hale and presented him with a wrapped package, saying, "Before you open this package, I want you to sign a disclosure." Hale obliged. The package contained what was to be one of the most successful promotions the budding company would enjoy: "You Make The Call," or as Hale calls it, the "Sexy Deer Call Ad."

Deer grunts were a best-selling product for KNIGHT & HALE

At the time of printing of this book, there may yet be some hunters who remember this campaign and phoned in after seeing the "You Make The Call" advertisement. KNIGHT & HALE placed an ad in ten magazines that advertised a toll-free 1-800 number that hunters could call and then listen to a forty-second recording of a call being demonstrated, followed by ordering information. There were three numbers listed: one for turkey (tube), one for goose (tube), and one for deer (E-Z Grunter). Hale explained, "These were landlines at that time. A user would dial the 800 number at our expense and listen to a world-renowned caller do these calls; it was cutting edge at the time." The enthusiasm was newsworthy, and newspapers noticed it. Hale said, "The Memphis paper put it on the front page, and they had a huge circulation. A radio station called us. We were charging $9.95 as the suggested retail price for the E-Z Grunter. We were hearing that people were standin' in line at work just to hear it. Deer people hadn't been calling deer much yet. They would call back again and again and again. The people from Bell (the phone company) called, wondering what was tying up all the lines!" The first month, we paid for 7,000 calls that came through, but there were 47,000 calls that didn't come through 'cause the lines were so busy."

Building on that success, they continued to invest, diversify their business, and innovate. In 1991, they built a 12,000-square-foot production plant to manufacture KNIGHT & HALE products. The pair hired Tommy Aiken from Greenfield, TN, as he had a good rapport with outdoor writers from newspapers and magazines. "We got Tommy to find us a sporting goods store, and we began to place products," said Hale. "We also made deer grunts for M.L. Lynch: we sold 30,000 units through them."

Knight, ever the innovator, remembers thinking about goose calls while lying in bed. He reflected on how to make a goose call sound like multiple geese with rapid calling and wondered, "How can I make a call that calls quicker?" He decided to make one that could run on both the ingoing and outgoing breath and did so. Ever the businessman, Hale remarked, "I was not impressed, but I said make a deer grunter like that." Knight did, and Hale exclaimed, "This is it!"

The Fighting Purr was sold for years; shown is the author's packaging variations of those calls over the years

Hale told me, "We called it the E-Z Grunter Plus and had it patented; it cost us $14,000 to do that then that we didn't have. But that E-Z Grunter Plus is our number one all-time selling call. It lasted over twenty years...and Walmart bought 15,000 a year. We sold over a million. That gave us a new number one call, relegating EZ Grunter to our number two seller. It should not be ignored that the growth of 'big box' stores like Walmart, Cabela's, and Bass Pro- all of whom KNIGHT & HALE got contracts to sell calls through were strategic growth enablers. Again, their timing was fortuitous, as it had been 1981 when Wal-Mart opened their southeastern US market and saw nationwide growth in that decade.

Other than the iconic tube call, KNIGHT & HALE might next be recognized for their line of 'pushpin' calls. Terry Hall, a well-known call maker of the time, made the earliest pushpins (and first box calls) for them: first wood, then plastic. They are easily recognizable, longer at five inches than the later four-inch length calls. Knight told me, "The Dueling Hen call was next and was the original fighting call." They made two different 'variants' of this call. Both are standard pushpins but come with a striker. Each plastic paddle has a conditioned area to use the striker on. This allows the user to operate the pushpin with one hand and use the striker on the conditioned area, producing the sound of two turkeys, hence the Dueling Hens. I guess fights amongst all species attract interest within that species! Of the two variants, one has a conditioned trough on the paddle, while the other has a more open surface across the paddle. Knight said, "I like the one that has more open space for runnin' the striker, as I can make better calls with circles than straight on the trough."

Next would be another of their heavy hitters, The Fighting Purrs. These consist of two sleek, black plastic pushpins, which can be run by holding one in each hand to simulate a gobbler fight. That certainly plays to the base instinct of gobblers during mating season, when the fight for pecking order has genetic implications: the winner takes all! Turkeys are not monogamous and form a sort of 'lek,' where two or more males of a species perform courtship displays to compete for mating rights. Hale is a self-proclaimed pushpin fan and had excellent results with them. Hale recollected, "I lived out in the country and had a turkey flock that I hand-raised. They were wild enough you couldn't approach 'em." Knight chimed in, "Our 'test' turkeys!"

Hale told me the rest of the story. "One day, I had a hot hen, and wild gobblers were tryin' to get through the fence to her. I was standin' right there, and the wild gobblers were ignoring me! They were making this aggressive purring noise, and I didn't say anything but wanted to test it. So, I made the same call they were making back to them, and them turkeys came to it wanting to fight! Not focused on me. But on the nearest turkey to whip his butt! I told Harold, "Let's go hunting," and we went to a tough place for turkeys. Now, he hadn't seen the purrs yet. He was using his tube and got a shock gobble, but the turkey wouldn't answer again. We got close enough we heard them struttin' and drummin'.' Two of them. And they started to fade away; we never could see 'em. I said, "Let's try something," and pulled out the purrs. They started double and triple and gobbling at 'em! We got one, and Harold said, "In forty-some years of turkey hunting, I've never seen anything like this!"

The Kentucky country boys knew they had a tiger by the tail with the Fighting Purrs. The fortuitous engagement with Harbour resulted in a magazine article, and the newspapers that had picked up the "You Make The Call" phenomenon had provided KNIGHT & HALE with a promotional model that worked. Outdoor writers held the key to a vast public consciousness about what was new and trending. "Magazines and newspapers were more popular then than they are now," recognized Knight. "Nick Sisley, Lee Marks, John Trout...people like that right there were a big help. We worked hard at it." Hale added, "You have to invite the writers to go turkey hunting and genuinely show them a good time." It wasn't a secret, as others were feeding stories and guiding hunts to provide outdoor writers with material to whet the appetites of hunters during the heyday of hunting magazines. This was before the turkey hunting content we can pull up on social media today in a few keyboard strokes, and magazines enjoyed record subscriptions. Hale even advocated a competitor to use this approach, "You'll be twiddling your thumbs while we are turkey hunting and getting coverage. He didn't listen." The proof is in the traction that Harold Knight and David Hale got, building a multimillion-dollar business along the way. Others were not twiddling but had been busy innovating and leaning into the new opportunity created by the growth of turkeys and turkey hunters.

So, Knight told Hale, "I am going to talk to some outdoor writers. All the magazines then had turkey stories, so I told them I had a story about these new Fighting Purrs. One he contacted was Tom Fulgham with the NRA magazine *American Hunter.* I told him I needed some help getting a story in the February issue on hunting using a fighting purr as a tactic, and he said,

The evolving KNIGHT & HALE logo and color schemes over time can be observed in mouth call packaging spanning much of the company's lifespan

"I can't help." Knight appealed, "You are the Editor; can you give it (the story) to (Michael) Hanback?" The editor replied that Hanback had a story already, but perhaps if they could have an exclusive, it could be reconsidered. Knight informed him they couldn't do that, as others were already aware. The intrigue of the story won out, and the story appeared in the February 1992 *American Hunter* with a cover splash saying, "NEW TACTIC! Fight-Calling For Spring Gobblers."

The new call would ride a wave of publicity. Knight said, "Fourteen publications came out with articles! We got so many responses we had to hire three ladies just to answer all the mail, and there was a $24.95 check with each one of 'em." Hale added, "We had to make 85,000 units, and a unit has two calls in each." They would make that same number of Fighting Purrs each of the next three years. Knight said amusedly, "We had so many calls we didn't have places to put the boxers." Hale was amazed when he heard people were renting out the calls they bought. "That was a good testimony to the use of those calls." Knight said, "They were one of the most challenging calls we made; they had a lot of parts. The plastic parts were made by our in-house molding guys. The first ones sold were in the old black and red KNIGHT & HALE package color scheme. By this time, they had built their 15,000 square-foot production facility, and Hale said, "We ran the mold twenty-four-seven until April 10, when sales were made for turkey season."

Anyone who knows Knight and Hale knows that giving back is in the two men's DNA. They maintained a Nature Center for years, which would close when the company sold. Knight said, "We had thousands of kids a year come to that; they still talk about it. We never made a cent; we were trying to give back. We had the best naturalist in the United States, Scott Schute. We had everything there, from mountain lions to wolves to every kind of snake you could think of." Both men have been stalwart ambassadors and volunteers for the NWTF. Hale has been active in all roles at his church, and Knight coached sports for local youth. Offering local youth an opportunity to get work experience and earn some money was something they enjoyed. This was especially important after the demand for the Fighting Purr calls was creating demand. No one could have foreseen how this would also lead to the most tragic moment either man has faced.

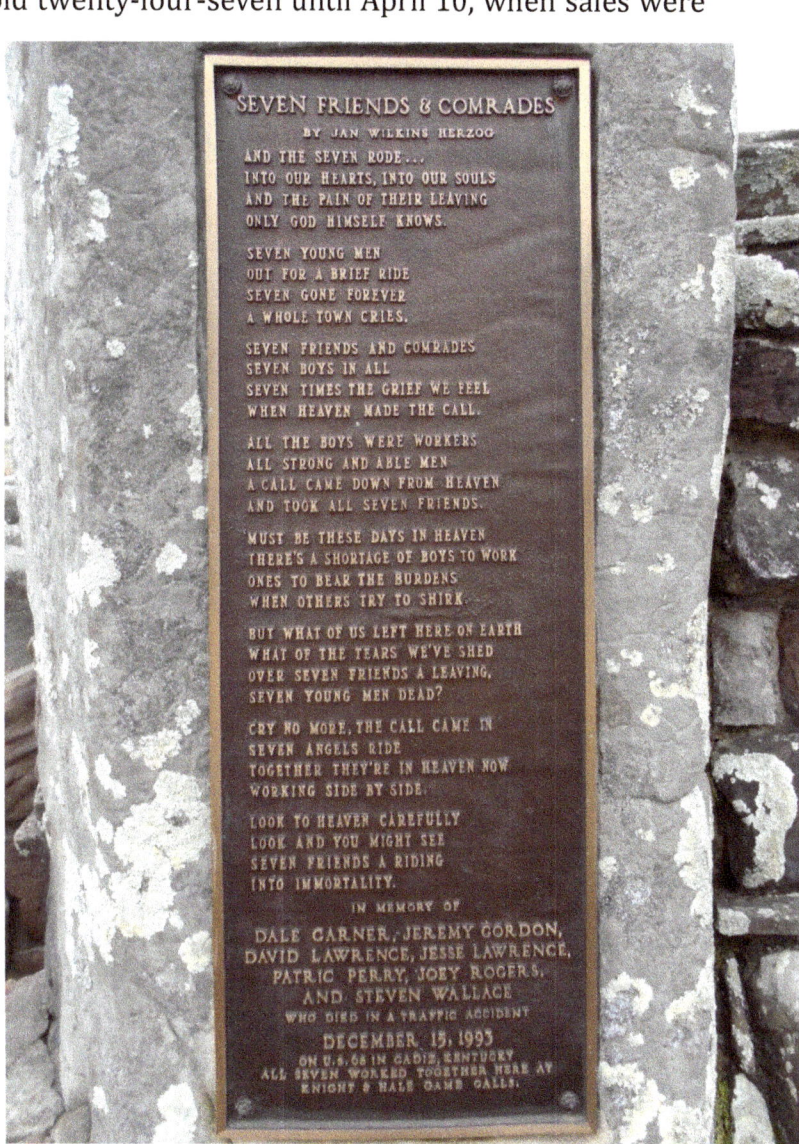

KNIGHT & HALE erected a memorial to honor the youth who worked for them that were killed in an automobile accident

A few days before Christmas 1993, several young men in their teens working at the plant, one of whom was Hale's nephew, left for an evening dinner break. They were crammed into a small car, a Honda Civic, and on the way back, there was a loss of control of the car. Striking another vehicle, all seven of the youth were instantly killed. The loss for such a small community was staggering. "They were all good kids, good students, obviously responsible students holding down part-time jobs to make a little extra money," Sheriff Randy Clark was quoted in a news story. "Some

Harold Knight and David Hale worked with many outdoor companies; Bill Jordan who founded Realtree® (right) was one of the Ultimate Hunting show Sponsors

Adventures in Hunting with Knight and Hale by David Hale; released 2023, available on Amazon.com

were athletes, some I had on my Little League baseball team." Hale said, "These boys were working here because they were the top kids in this county. Their parents had taught them a work ethic, and they wanted a job, so we gave it to them. They were pretty much hand-selected." Jim Strelec added, "Part of the criteria to work for us was their grades in school. They were the cream of the crop. We hurt for the families of these fine young men. We lost the best there was." KNIGHT & HALE erected a memorial to the young men at their manufacturing plant, which bears a touching poem by Jan Wilkins Herzog of nearby Lone Oak, KY. Knight and Hale still sponsor an annual fishing tournament called the 'Seven Friends Fishing Tournament' that raises money for college scholarships for local high school graduates.

There were other unexpected bumps in the road. In what they can laugh about now, Knight told me with a sparkle in his eye, "We had a cat get in our building once, and it crapped all over a bunch of calls!" Early on, their packaging bore a cross emblem, professing their Christian faith. Hale said dejectedly, "We had some folks that didn't want the cross on there, so we took it off just theirs, where they sold it through and took their money. But we left it on for others!" Another time, a new employee they hired thought he was helping to clean up, and he ended up burning a bunch of their old stuff...that was particularly hard for this author to hear, given his interest in such items!

Like other successful business people, others sometimes imitated or copied them. "95% of the owl calls have copied our throat piece," claimed Knight. Later, after they were acquired by PRADCO, the Hale Fire gobbler tube was a flash in the pan due to a patent dispute. And then they had an issue when a company was going to buy 100,000 grunt calls from them, amounting to $350,000 in sales, but backed out. "So, then we had to go elsewhere," said Hale. Given that they were sitting on inventory, creating cash-flow issues, this was a problem. "A year rolls around and they hadn't bought anything from us. A writer, Kathy Etling, wrote an article on grunt calls in *Outdoor Life*." The attention resulted in Walmart putting in an order for 12,000 calls, but Hale requested they place a minimum order of 100,000. Hale smiled and said, "They said OK, we will take 12,000 immediately and the rest later. Hale said, "If you are going to pick them up, bring a certified check." They had it in two weeks.

The market penetration KNIGHT & HALE got at Walmart was tremendous, but it also introduced new issues to overcome. In Hale's new book, *Adventures In Hunting With Knight And Hale*, he brings to attention the double-edged sword of supplying such a large company. It reduced their need to spend advertising dollars but increased production pressure. It also over-indexed the company's overall market share with Walmart, as at one time, over 50% of its capacity was sold there, meaning losing the contract would be crippling.

In 2016, KNIGHT & HALE resurrected a popular friction pot called Ol' Yeller. They learned the hard way about shoplifting at such stores. Since their inception, they and other game call companies have sold products in a 'clamshell' package, a molded plastic package hinged to open at one end to remove the contents. Knight said disgustedly, "People would take our expensive call out of our package and put in one that was cheaper and buy it, then put the cheap call in ours. We got 3,300 back like that, so we had to come out with packaging when selling at Walmart so it couldn't be removed." Theft even hit close to home at times, as Knight recalled, "I killed a turkey with three spurs on each leg in the Land Between the Lakes. Someone stole those legs from our building." Thankfully, the memory will never fade.

There were more ups than downs for the growing game call business. The 1990s were a whirlwind for the pair. In addition to all their other ventures, they wrote a book. A nationally known outdoor writer, Wade Bourne, partnered with them to write and publish *Harold Knight & David Hale's Ultimate Turkey Hunting* in 1994. It is an excellent how-to book on turkey hunting, full of tactics and advice, with some good hunting stories to help illustrate their points. They were constantly giving interviews, traveling to sporting goods shows, developing calls, and working with ProStaffers. In addition, the onset of outdoor television and home video were other trends that offered opportunities, and KNIGHT & HALE were on top of them. Some may remember *The American Sportsman*, the first hunting show aired on television (TV), aired by ABC, and hosted by Curt Gowdy.

David Hale and Harold Knight would win a Golden Moose from the Outdoor Channel in 2015

For my generation, which grew up watching such shows in our formative years of turkey hunting, KNIGHT & HALE were both entertainers and educators. They first appeared on the show *Woods and Wetlands* in the late 1980s, then moved to the Outdoor Channel in 1989, hosting *Ultimate Hunting*. Seeing another way to do what they love and stay ahead of the competition, they took an enterprising approach that paid dividends; as Hale recalled, "TNN was the number one channel on cable TV at the time. "We had a guy that went into towns with 50,000 people and bought airtime. It was country people who were our base and supported us, and this helped us bring our show to hundreds of thousands of people. The bad thing about it is we couldn't tell how many people watched; there was no Nielsen's. But we had no problem getting sponsors! We had Mossy Oak, Matthews, Browning, Sheffield Financial, and more." All along their journey, Knight and Hale owed part of their success to those who helped them and worked for them. When they started doing the *Woods and Wetlands* television show Knight said "we were fortunate to be able to use Bill Dance's film crew. We then got our own studio and hired people like Chuck Jones (formerly with PRIMOS®) to help. Hale was a cameraman. A good hunter knows how to capture stuff." KNIGHT & HALE would bring the outdoors into homes through TV for twenty-five years.

One of those who was part of KNIGHT & HALE's on-screen presence was Bill Jordan of Realtree®. He told me, "I have always been thankful I came through when I did and with who I did. None of us had any money, no backing in our particular businesses, but we all invested in and helped each other. In 1986, when I was starting Realtree®, I was at SHOT show when Harold walks up to me and introduces himself." He recalled Harold then inquiring, "Hey, Bill, tell me what you're doing." After Jordan told him about the camouflage he designed and was marketing, Harold said, "Well me and David, we all are really interested."

The *Realtree® Outdoors* show that aired on Sunday nights often featured guests. Jordan said, "We had a way to showcase people like KNIGHT & HALE and their products, along with ours; we needed each other. They'd come down here and hunt, and we'd go up there. While filming, sometimes we'd take a break and sit down and record some turkey hunting or deer hunting tips to help paint a picture for people. Harold and David played a big part in the education side, sharing their knowledge. Like the timing of when to call and when not to call; I learned so much from those guys." Jordan emphasized how special those early days were. He said, "We all get older, but they have always been a big part of my life, a huge inspiration for me. One day next week I'm gonna call Harold, and I can assure you that we'll pick up conversation from thirty years ago like it was yesterday!" The two companies would work together, on-screen and off, over the years. A friendship was formed. When KNIGHT & HALE decided to put out their first VHS tape, Realtree® was one of the sponsors.

Home videos allowed people to rent or buy content that could be watched anytime and were powerful advertising tools. As an avid collector of wild turkey audio and video, I can tell you that twenty of the over 400 wild turkey hunting VHS titles I have are KNIGHT & HALE titles. The first turkey hunting videos released I have noted were introduced in 1985, and by 1988, KNIGHT & HALE entered that market, becoming one of the first twenty-five turkey hunting

VHS tapes (by release date) that I know of. That initial entry was named "Productive Turkey Hunting" and was presented as an instructional video. Series like KNIGHT & HALE's "*The Ultimate Spring*" video (later ones were released on DVD) became wildly popular as new turkey hunters yearned to learn, and all hunters craved hunting during the off-season. They marketed sixteen seasons of "*The Ultimate Spring*." The first one featured hunts filmed in 1994 and was released to video in 1995. The narrator's opening line is, "Each year throughout the United States, a special breed of outdoorsmen labeled as spring gobbler hunters yearn for the first signs that represent the arrival of the spring gobbling season." That hasn't changed, but rewatching those old videos and seeing the featured calls and products is fun.

The Dueling Hen, their earliest pushpin call, was featured, as was the outrageously successful Fighting Purr. I was intrigued that they were promoting a permethrin spray to repel ticks even then. The years since they announced that product has seen an outbreak of Lyme disease carried by deer ticks and the more recent Alpha-gal syndrome passed on by Lone star ticks (in which the infected person develops a meat allergy, which can last up to years). It is a shame that more people don't treat their clothes with permethrin; it kills ticks on contact and is labeled as safe for the user when applied to clothes (not to the skin). Hale said, "My brother was influential in that product. The outdoor writers and press are not doing enough to advocate using it. I have three in my family with Alpha-gal. Half of the Fish & Wildlife people at a meeting I went to had it. That shows they are not educated about it. First, you have to educate yourself and be responsible for yourself. I see people every year wearing shorts and all bit up; it just shows they don't know or care enough to learn."

What does fish bait have to do with KNIGHT & HALE? In 1997, Knight recalled, "We got approached by this guy in a necktie who said, "I am here to buy your company." Knight retorted that they weren't for sale. "You'll have to come to Cadiz if you want to talk about that," Knight told him. He said, "Then another guy approached us from PRADCO (a subsidiary of EBSCO), one of the biggest fish bait companies. A year later, we sold to them." PRADCO hired Knight and Hale to continue to represent their former company after the sale of their company in 1998, but it made life a bit more complex in some ways. "Billionaires don't think like we do," said Knight. "We had good relationships with the owners and had good hunts with them." There have been times the pair have regretted selling, but when sitting with them while researching for this book, they both agreed that hindsight is a good way to judge things, and they sold at the right time." No sale or transaction is 100% right or wrong, acknowledged Knight. "A lot of things I didn't like, but a lot of things I did. You could tell that the upper echelon of those companies are real smart. We made lifelong friendships. They also acquired Knight Rifles, Summit Tree Stands, Code Blue, and Moultrie."

It turns out that you can have too much of a good thing. Knight informed me, "Sometimes we had a tendency to bring out too much new stuff at once, which could take away from it." Keith Wahlig, a ProStaffer for KNIGHT & HALE, told me he remembered getting that exact advice from Knight as they worked on developing diaphragm calls, which would be another great seller for the company. Knight and Hale have pointed out that while there are fewer

Knight and Hale after being acquired by PRADCO

turkey hunters than deer hunters, turkey hunters utilize calling much more as a tactic and buy various types of calls to find an advantage.

So, KNIGHT & HALE added about every type of turkey call one can imagine over time. In addition to the kinds already mentioned, they made all manner of box calls. They learned along the way, which improved quality. Knight credits former NWTF CEO Rob Keck for showing him how grain on a box call must be aligned. Knight pointed out, "You can note on our earlier calls the grain isn't all oriented right," which affects sound quality. They had several box calls that were great sellers, including the Wet Willy, a box made to run wet by adding a material to the calling surface.

The talented Anthony Foster helped design and then manufacture their popular Kentucky Longbox. They wanted to hire Foster to design calls and run their production lines. By this time, Foster was doing call designs for several companies and manufacturing their calls on his production line. He was also active in the Foster Millworks cabinet shop he had with his Dad: Foster Millworks made the cabinets in the KNIGHT & HALE hunting lodge! While Foster would end up later working exclusively with PRIMOS®, he is very fond of Harold Knight and David Hale (see the chapter on Anthony Foster).

They developed a full line of locator calls designed to induce a wild turkey tom in the Spring to "shock-gobble," a hormone-induced response to loud noises during the breeding season. These include crow, hawk, owl, woodpecker, and calls that produced a gobble. Designing and manufacturing so many types of calls for numerous species required an intimate knowledge of the vocalizations they were recreating. Knight explained, "What always fascinated me is

After PRADCO acquired KNIGHT & HALE, Mike Battey was hired in 1998; Respectfully named "The Call Dr." he would design many products in his time there through 2004. Included in this 1999 catalog were several items Mike was behind: the new Ol' Yeller pot, the Spit'n Feathers audio series, the diaphragm cases, and the strikers pictured.

that animals have a reason to make the sound they do; they aren't gossipers. Knowing what they say is part of the art of game calling, not just running a call good." In the case of a turkey, knowing which turkey is saying it and to whom is important. This understanding would be critical to Knight and Hale's success in the woods and their business venture.

They also knew that using a game call was no guarantee. Hale recalls hunting a pressured bird in South Dakota. "Harold killed a bird, but I was running the camera, so I hadn't got one and decided to go out the next morning. I arrived an hour early, and every fifteen minutes, I'd get out and hoot. Finally, one answered." Hale went on that he thought, "Good, there is one there. And in fifteen minutes, I hooted, and there was a gobble further away, so now figured there were two turkeys." Another fifteen minutes went by, and he hooted again, this time hearing a gobble even further out. He said, "I thought that place was full of turkeys! I then heard other cars coming in, so I knew it was about time to get going." For the fourth time, he hooted and got a response, "But the gobble was almost out of hearing, and I knew then I was dealing with a pressured turkey." The cars coming in were a testament to the number of owl hoots and yelps this bird had likely been plied with. "So, I went after him. It was one of the toughest turkeys I ever killed...pressure can do that to any turkey," David stated.

Pot calls were a significant line for them, and there was one name most game call companies who wanted to market one had on speed dial: Mike Battey. KNIGHT & HALE introduced its first pot call in 1995 under the 'Ultimate Series" name, which was a nod to their Outdoor Channel TV series. In 1998, they upgraded this line by going to a new pot designed by Battey. Their big break with pot calls would come via the relationship with Battey in 1999 with the release of Model KH158: the Ol' Yeller Sla-Tek. The author gets misty-eyed when recalling the number of memories made with this call over the years. And I have plenty of company, as that call is one of the best-selling production turkey pot calls of all time. The yellow ceramic disc that comprises the calling surface earned the call its name.

Battey recalls, "I produced the first ceramic disc on the project I called MTF (Molded/Tuned/Formulated). The result became the trade name Sla-Tek. The project was to get a disc with sound quality on par with the best slate and crystal calls and not affected by moisture or cold. Not to mention easy to run and produce more volume if desired. Sla-Tek ranks up there with the top products I ever designed. The color is part of the formulation process. It's not just one bag of material used in the injection mold; there were two that were blended or mixed that gave it that yellow. No one has yet figured out what and how to reproduce it. Or failed?" He is doubtful it will be reproduced and qualified, "There really was a rather taxing process to get it all just the way I wanted it for sound. A lot of work and testing. But it paid off." Sla-Tek is thinner than other ceramics, but the special blend helped tune it to a specific pitch. The pot was Battey's "competition cup" and included a graphite material, contributing to the sound quality. "My graphite material vendor went out of business in 2002, and that I could not reproduce. Those pots have a unique sound and are my best callers," said Mike.

Knight praised Battey, saying, "He was a genius with calls, pot calls, and crow calls. The Battey pot is as good as anything made." Hale added, "We sold 80,000 of them the first year and the same the second and third year. We made a commercial with a big yellow dog; he came around a corner and ran off with a call." Knight delivered the punch line used in the commercial, "So easy even a dog could use it!" I can still remember kneeling on mine by accident and hearing the crunch of the ceramic surface as it broke. I was devastated; it was a call I trusted that had served me well. The printing on the surface had long since been rubbed away by my conditioning of the surface (to 'rough up' the surface to create more friction with the striker). That sent me to eBay, where I made my first purchase on that platform...then I bought a few more so I would never again be without one of my 'go-to' calls. The first three "variants" of the Ol' Yeller call all have the word "Sla-Tek" printed on the call's surface. Of those three calls, the first had a black pot, the second green, and the third yellow. None of the later models of Ol' Yeller had the word "Sla-Tek" on the label because that unique material was no longer being used to make the ceramic disc, nor was the pot itself of Battey design. "Ol' Yeller wasn't as good of a call when we got away from the Battey pot," said Knight regretfully.

Always looking for that new thing that made life easier for the customer, Knight recounted how their popular Power Tip striker was conceived. Any customer solution starts with a problem that needs to be solved, and any hunter knows that in the early morning, dew is a problem. When using a pot call, the surface develops condensation when the dewpoint is right, and that wet surface reduces friction, and the call won't call...and with a porous

*KNIGHT & HALE ceramic-surfaced calls in author's collection;
the calls with Sla-Tek indicate original release*

material like slate, it doesn't dry well (yes, slate is a rock, but it is porous). Knight told me, "A guy in Florida told us that he put JB Weld on the end of his striker tip. That created better friction against a wet calling surface. We had to figure out a way to produce it. So, I took regular Scotch Tape, wrapped it around the business end of the striker, and then put JB Weld on the tip of it. I made thousands."

Because of the hands-free operation of the mouth diaphragm call, they are wildly popular with turkey hunters. Of that, Knight told me, "Looking back, I wish we would have started that business sooner and brought it in-house. Chris Parrish and his wife did many for us. One of the biggest sellers was the Half Moon Cutter, so named 'cause when I cut diaphragms, I made a half-moon to give it a different sound. It is hard to duplicate diaphragms 100% due to how rubber thickness can vary, frame variances, stretch/tension, and more."

2009 ProStaff included (top) Rod Petit, Kerry Terrell, Keith Wahlig and (bottom) Mark Prudhomme, Chris Parrish, and Steve Stoltz

KNIGHT & HALE made all manner of accessories for hunters, some of which were consumable items like chalk to apply to friction calls to increase friction, lanyards, and turkey decoys. Historically, there are accounts of live domestic turkeys serving as 'Jezebels' to lure in wild gobblers. Turkeys are wary, given just about everything, walking, crawling, and flying, knowing they are good to eat. They can be reluctant to approach a hunter calling to them, and decoys offer a visual confirmation of another turkey. As flocking creatures, they are predisposed to such visual aids, and during the breeding season, even more so. A decoy also can focus a turkey's attention elsewhere than the eager and anxious hunter concealed nearby. While not a tactic all hunters endorse, it is an effective one.

Knight and Hale had proven the effectiveness of decoys and developed one they called the Peeping Tom (clever), as it had the head of a second turkey attached to a life-size turkey decoy, making it appear as two turkeys together. Hale said, "The Peeping Tom was a good idea, but business folks didn't like it." After they had sold their company to PRADCO, the decoy company Carry-Lite was also acquired by the owner of PRADCO (EBSCO). With that company, EBSCO inherited 4,000 gobbler decoys to sell. Knight hand-painted a gobbler decoy and added a beard and fan. They called it Pretty Boy, given how they spruced it up and sent it to Dixon Brooke, a relative of one of the head people at EBSCO. Knight said, "He killed a turkey with it, and Dixon said, "It is a go!" Knight continued, "But then one of the head business guys took offense to being passed over on naming it. I called Dixon back and told him this boy was upset, and he said as far as I'm concerned, you did the right thing. A call from Dixon to the man moved things forward!"

Along their journey, KNIGHT & HALE assembled a team of top-notch ProStaff to extend their reach across the U.S. and Canada. Some of the ProStaff were competitive callers who called in competitions for various species. Success in calling contests for those sponsored by or using KNIGHT & HALE calls helped strengthen the brand. Knight said, "I think we had the best ProStaff in the U.S.: Walter Parrott, Chris Parrish, Mark Prudhomme, Steve Stoltz, Kerry Terrell, Shawn Right, Keith Wahlig, Mark Grieco, Rod Petit. There are too many to name and no one worth leavin' out."

At one time, they had around one hundred ProStaff, and Hale's daughter, Amy, managed them. I talked to several former ProStaff who highly complimented Harold Knight and David Hale. Mark Prudhomme told me, "They were innovators. When Harold started goose-calling on a tube, people had never heard that. After that, others started doing it. The timing of everything was perfect for them: the return of the wild turkey and the videotapes. I used to go to a local sporting goods store and rent those things and watch 'em. They got good exposure and kept coming up with something new. When they did it, it wasn't gimmicky. Just two real people who were good hunters, and you could relate to them."

The production game call world is small, and people's character is no secret. Several other game call companies failed, some due to poor business practices or illegal activity. Knight and Hale are highly respected and greatly admire many of their competitors. Of the man who owned the Penn's Woods game call company out of Pennsylvania, Harold said, "Frank Piper, I knew and thought a lot of him. Had he been younger or lived longer, he would have had one of the top companies. There was no one I disliked." Knight also developed a close relationship with Mr. Fox Haas, the father of Toxey Haas, Mossy Oak's founder. It forged a strong bond between KNIGHT & HALE and Mossy Oak. In 2017, Knight participated in a successful hunt with the 87-year-old southern gentleman the hunting public has endearingly known as "Mr. Fox." At the time, it was the remarkable seventieth season the elder Fox had taken a turkey!

In 2016, Knight and Hale partnered with Michael Waddell's Bone Collector. L-R: Travis "T-Bone" Turner, Mark Prudhomme, Nick Mundt, Michael Waddell, David Hale, Chris Parrish, Harold Knight

Those at Mossy Oak greatly appreciate Harold Knight and David Hale. Cuz Strickland shared his sentiments with me, saying of them, "Man, the legends! When we got started with Mossy Oak, everyone already knew who they were. I remember the first time I met them. The first turkey calling contest I was in was the Gulf States Classic. I was apprehensive; I felt like I was out of my league. I went to the caller's room, saw Harold, and was thinking, "That is Harold Knight; why am I even here?" He chuckled and continued, "But Harold just walked right up to me and began talking about calling." In Strickland's view, KNIGHT & HALE, Penn's Woods, and Ben Lee helped teach others in the hunting industry how to do public relations. "We got to work with Harold and David; they were on our team for a while," shared Strickland. Then he added, "Although I never got to hunt with them personally. But the spring before last, I finally got to do something that had been on my bucket list: hunt with Harold Knight."

Strickland enjoyed telling me of his time in the turkey woods during 2022 with Knight. "The spring before last, I finally got to hunt with Harold. We were trying to get Bill Sugg, a turkey; I wasn't there to shoot a turkey; I was filming and just loving it." Sugg hunted the day prior with Knight, and on the video, they start with a gang of four gobblers roosting, which Knight had seen the day before. The videography captures the sheer delight of the men just being together (the video is available online at Cuz 411).

The turkeys are characteristically uncooperative, but off-camera, Strickland strikes a turkey with his tube call at 10 AM. As the men formulate a plan, Knight eagerly walks, prompting

2022 hunt with Ronnie "Cuz" Strickland on left, Harold Knight on right, and Bill Sugg

Strickland to inquire, "What's going on?" Knight replies with a smile, "We're gonna head him off. If we can't call him up, we're gonna head him off." After they re-position, Knight points and tells Sugg, "He's liable to come up right there," displaying woodsmanship earned over sixty-five seasons dueling with gobblers.

The video presented is raw, unedited footage showcasing Knight's pleading yelps on his favorite pot call: the KNIGHT & HALE Moonshiner. Knight's yelps and soft cutts trigger a constant cascade of gobbles as the flock comes into view across the hardwood bottom. The gobbling is so frequent and intense that the woods ring with their reverberation. When Sugg finally pulls the trigger, Knight doesn't take long to cover the distance to the camera. Beaming, Knight says to Strickland, "It never gets old, brother! To see someone kill a turkey just excites me to death. I hope to the good Lord that I never lose that." Knight's playfully pleasant personality shines in the post-hunt chatter as he ribs Sugg for having three different makes of shells in his gun. Out of a handful of green, red, and black shotshells, he picks up one with the labeling worn off from years of riding in a pocket and quips with comedic genius, "Ronnie, that 'un right there is old enough to draw social security!"

After this hunt, Knight tells Sugg, "We got ole' Ronnie here, with that tube call. Did you notice what got 'em started? They got started on that tube call! They answered it. Don't tell me the tube call don't still work!" Minutes later, Knight is chafing to help Strickland have his turn and says, "Ronnie's got a tag; let's go kill another one." He is instantly out in front of the men, a picture of fitness at age 74. The following day, after a quick camera tutorial, Sugg is filming, and Strickland is set up on chain-gobbling turkeys. Strickland told me, "Harold again got back behind us one hundred yards and started calling. His timing and the little things he did on a pot-and-mouth call was like a flock of four or five turkeys behind me for nearly an hour. It was a natural, subtle calling. I was enjoying it so much, I almost forgot to watch out for the gobbler!"

Strickland kills one of the toms that Knight calls up, thus checking off a significant bucket list item. He hefts the turkey and tells an elated Knight, "He's as old as he's gonna get," a nod to one of David Hale's favorite lines. Knight again credits Strickland with "getting out the microphone," referring to Strickland's use of a tube call to locate the gobblers. "It was exactly what I expected it to be," Strickland told me about the memorable experience. "Harold is one of the best callers and woodsmen I have hunted with. He just got the biggest kick out of me killing that turkey since most of the time I am filming someone else."

It is the men themselves that have most impressed Strickland. "I never heard them say one unkind word about anybody while I was there," he divulged. "Harold made me start crying as he was talking about David's illness." As I witnessed, the two old business partners get together daily for breakfast. Strickland's tears were prompted by the men's bond and commitment, making him think, "I hope I have a friend that good."

Without fail, Knight and Hale were revered by those I talked to as being willing to help others.

Will Primos told me about his respect for the men, saying, "In the early days of my business, I learned what I was doing wrong by seeing what they did right." Preston Pittman said, "Harold and David were so good to me, they helped anyone. Once, I called and told Harold that I couldn't afford a mold to do some calls I wanted." Knight replied, "No problem; what do you need, Preston?" Pittman explained that he wanted to make some crow calls and will never forget what Knight said graciously, "It's fine. I'll shoot ya the components, but you have to figure it out and assemble and tune 'em yourself." A grateful Pittman would return to KNIGHT & HALE and buy owl hooter components and diaphragm call boxes.

The sign on Harold Knight and David Hale's lodge; the building is full of memorabilia and memories

A blemish on their sterling reputation is a hunting violation related to their hunting guides in Utah. When retrieving a bull elk Knight had killed, they took a four-wheeler (ATV) through a marked gate, indicating no motor vehicles were allowed. The guides assured them it was no problem, but it was. They paid $1000 in fines for operating an off-highway vehicle in a closed area. This unfortunate incident resulted in more caution when making plans for hunting trips. That gut-wrenching day for them was compounded by tragic events known now as 9-11; it was the same day terrorists struck the U.S. using hijacked airplanes.

Where it all began is still relevant, as Knight is recognized as an expert tube caller in the industry, regularly doing seminars and podcasts. While KNIGHT & HALE's brand is still owned by EBSCO, the new owners are not currently putting out new turkey calls. The last tube call released was a figured wooden tube called Grandmaw's Snuff Tube. Knight believes, "It would have been a big seller if done right." Knight has been working on turkey and goose tubes with the multiple-time World Champion, former ProStaffer, and dear friend, Mark Prudhomme. Harold said, "Mark reached out and wanted to learn the tube goose call. You gotta put time in to learn, and he did. And, I have learned as much in the last few years working with him on tube call technique that I am going back to the tube, where I'd been using a mouth call more lately. The cutting I do on the tube I can't do on a mouth call, and neither can the average person. He is a super person and very talented."

Hale, now in a battle with Parkinson's, has lost none of his fire for the outdoors. The two men are the model of friendship, spending time together daily. "You can't imagine how important it is to have someone to talk to," Knight said about the advantage of having Hale as his business partner. Neither has their love of the outdoors diminished. Hale passed on to me, "I love the fact that people have opportunity to hunt turkeys now, but I fear that disease is going to wipe our turkeys out. We've got a problem with a declining population we need to face. Predators, disease, and a few other things." Knight agreed, "We now have the resource. It's too bad kids now think they are defeated if they don't go out and kill one. To see and hear one is a success to me. Too many times I went and didn't see and hear nothing." Hale nodded, "Being outside is a success to me."

Although the new owners of KNIGHT & HALE are not putting out new products, there is no lack of appreciation in the hunting community for the impact that Harold Knight and David Hale have had and continue to make. Many people are part of their legacy, whether those who

2020 NWTF GNCC Hall of Fame presenters (P) and inductees (I); Pat Strawser (P), Tom Stuckey (P), Chris Kirby (P; accepting on behalf of inductee Dick Kirby), John Brown, Jr. (P), Ernie Calandrelli (P), Paul Butski (I), Denny Gulvas (I), Ron Jolly (I), Harold Knight (I), David Hale (I), Matt Morrett (P, accepting on behalf of inductee Walter Parrott), Mark Prudhomme (P), Will Primos (P), Preston Pittman (P)

worked for them were on their ProStaff, watched and learned from them on TV and video, or used their calls and products. Among the recognition they have received, the two men were inducted into the Legends of the Outdoors in 2009. 2015 brought them the coveted Golden Moose from the Outdoor Channel, a Lifetime Achievement Award for their *Ultimate Hunting* show. In 2020, they were inducted into the NWTF Grand National Calling Championship Hall of Fame.

What is in the future for Harold Knight and David Hale? Knight contemplated, "If you add up all the days I've hunted spring turkeys, it would easily be five years. I have LIVED turkey hunting. I would just like to ease out. I will be 80 years old on April 19, 2024. My goal is to kill a turkey and win a fish tournament at 80. As long as I have my health, I'm happy. It ain't about me and David anymore. We want to help others and teach them what we can. We have got to do every kind of hunting across the country, and turkey hunting is still our favorite. We haven't got 'em figured out yet!" Hale enjoys memories of days in the woods. "One of our tricks was hearing a jake "keouk" and we knew he was honoring a silent, strutting bird." Hale has just published his memoirs, including content on and by Knight.

Hale has just penned his memoirs in his new book, *Adventures In Hunting With Knight & Hale.* It captures much of his journey as a hunter and businessman. He shares that story through the many artifacts he has collected, everything from animal mounts to recovered bullets, game calls the company built, and his priceless memories of people and places. Harold contributed to it as well. It is a gift to all of us who appreciate the legacy they will leave behind. It is also for those future generations to learn and enjoy the ingenuity and success of two boys from Kentucky who built and sold a game call empire that started with a pill-bottle tube call.

C. Special thanks

To the many people who helped make *Knight & Hale Game Calls, Inc.* successful.

OUR LOYAL STAFF:

Amy Edmonson	my elder daughter, was in charge of *Commonwealth Productions*, the video department of *Knight & Hale Game Calls, Inc.* She also managed our Pro Staff
Christy Hale Millay	my younger daughter, was the CEO and CFO of *Knight & Hale Game Calls, Inc.*
Derek Edmonson	created *Edmonson Technologies, LLC* to camouflage paint products
Tommy Akin	coordinator of our writers
Max Baer	media buyer for our TV shows
Bill Bynum	magazine writer who was also an employee
Tammy Cherry	our secretary
David DeHart	purchasing and general oversight
J. T. Ethridge and family	mold and design development
Butch McElwain	Harold's brother and cameraman was in charge of prod development on elk calls
Rachel Hamby	head of shipping
Chuck Williams	IT department, and R and D
Glenn Hester	handmade box calls
Jack Thomas	our original hand carver, who handmade turkey and goose calls
Dr. Jim Head	family doctor in Nashville, TN
Tim Kiser	"fly boy", friend and pilot
Mo Lynn	farm manager
Gary Mitchell	tuner and life long friend
Dale Heflin	mold builder
Tony Hurt	editor and cameraman
Forrest Jones	our first sales rep
Roger Kennedy	helped us do field work
Jay Lee	tuning specialist, primarily for owl calls
Wayne Lovely	mold maker
Rick Martin	plant manager
Maria Plymale	Harold's niece, was our receptionist for all those years
Jeff Pryor	tuning specialist, primarily for goose calls
Jim Strelec	sales manager and seminar specialist; one of our first employees
Lisa Sumner	our first receptionist
Jack Thomas	master wood designer and carver
Fred Troball	delivery specialist for PRADCO
Jerry Turner	long term co-worker in call development and general operations

A Special thanks from KNIGHT & HALE to some staff who helped make the company a success

YELP & GOBBLE, INC.

KNIGHT & HALE TIMELINE

(* = approximate date)

1944 – Harold Knight was born on April 19 in Kentucky.
1946 – David Hale was born July 3 in Kentucky.
1955 – Harold Knight opportunistically kills his first wild turkey while squirrel hunting at age 11.
1956 – Harold Knight goes on his first wild turkey hunt with Maurice Calhoun at age 12.
1957 – Harold Knight calls up and kills first wild turkey in the spring at age 13.
1960 – First spring turkey season in Kentucky in 41 years; 16-year-old Harold Knight is one of only 12 successful hunters.
1963-1984 – Harold Knight becomes a barber at Cadiz Barber Shop.
1964 – Land Between the Lakes completion displaces Harold Knight's family.

1965-1968 – David Hale attends, then graduates from Murray State University with a degree in Agribusiness; the business degree would later be of use as he helped run KNIGHT & HALE.
1967 – David Hale kills his first turkey; he is one of only 15 successful hunters taking turkeys in the Land Between the Lakes that year.
1969 – David Hale misses his only turkey season due to his military service.
1970 – David Hale meets Harold Knight after someone mentions Knight's turkey calls.
1971 – Harold Knight begins to make tube calls. Dave Harbour hunts wild turkeys in the Land Between the Lakes; he meets Knight & Hale and kills a turkey using Knight's tube.

1972 – Dave Harbour's article "My Old Kentucky Gobbler" appears in *Sports Afield*, introducing Knight and Hale to the hunting public; 3,000 orders for tube calls start KNIGHT & HALE.
1973 – National Wild Turkey Federation is founded; Knight and Hale start the third chapter in the U.S. in Kentucky. 800 people attended their first meeting. While cutting David Hale's hair, Harold Knight asks him for help with his turkey call side business. The first Kentucky State Turkey Calling Contest was held; Harold won first place, and David won second place.

1974 – KNIGHT & HALE make their first upgrade by remodeling the back of Knight's barbershop into a callmaking shop; Hale's daughters begin helping with managing mail and phone calls.
1975 – Goose tube calls are first offered by KNIGHT & HALE.
1977 – KNIGHT & Hale discontinues wooden tube calls and commissions plastic tubes to be made using injection mold technology.

KNIGHT & HALE

1979 – Harold Knight wins the World Goose Calling Championship with his goose tube call. George Wright, a wildlife biologist in Kentucky, begins a wild turkey trap and transfer program.
1984 – David Hale puts aside his dream of expanding his hog farm and Harold Knight lays down his barber shears; the pair go full-time into the game calls business. They moved their callmaking operation to a Cadiz, KY Commercial Park building.
1986 – With the help of Jim Strelec, the first KNIGHT & HALE catalog is produced.
1988 – "Productive Turkey Hunting" becomes KNIGHT & HALE's first VHS release.
1989-2015 – KNIGHT & HALE features a hunting show on the Outdoor Channel: *Ultimate Hunting*.
1991 – KNIGHT & HALE expands to a 12,000 square foot production facility
1992 – The Fighting Purr calls launch to great fanfare.
1993 – Tragedy strikes KNIGHT & HALE as seven youths working there are killed in an auto accident.

1994 – Wade Bourne joins Knight and Hale in writing a turkey hunting book: *Harold Knight & David Hale's Ultimate Turkey Hunting*.
1995 – The first of 16 seasons of "The Ultimate Spring" VHS (and later DVD) series is launched.
1998 – KNIGHT & HALE sell their company to PRADCO (a subsidiary of EBSCO). The pair stayed involved in the business for many years. Mike Battey, "The Call Dr." is hired to help design calls.
1999 – KNIGHT & Hale introduces the Ol' Yeller pot call.

2009 – Harold Knight and David Hale are inducted into the Legends of the Outdoors.
2015 – The Outdoor Channel awards Harold Knight and David Hale a Lifetime Achievement Golden Moose award.
2017 – Harold Knight participates in a hunt where his 87-year-old friend, Fox Haas, gets a gobbler.
2020 – The NWTF inducts Harold Knight and David Hale into the Grand National Calling Championship Hall of Fame.
2022 – Ronnie "Cuz" Strickland lives out a dream by killing a turkey that Harold Knight calls in for him.
2023 – David Hale authors *Adventures In Hunting With Knight And Hale*.

Author's KNIGHT & HALE collection

YELP & GOBBLE, INC.

Chapter 2

PRIMOS® HUNTING

Will Primos and Brad Farris with a bull elk taken by Primos. He was using a .54 caliber flintlock he commissioned to be reproduced

Amongst many other things, Wilbur "Will" Rivers Primos is a historian. Don't conjure up images of a stuffy professor delivering monotone lectures full of dates and places you can't remember. Nor a snobbish or bookish know-it-all. In his signature hunting products business, Primos has fused what worked from the past with what could be improved upon and has had fun doing it. Gleaning lessons from the past have influenced the direction and decisions in his life. He embraces the cautionary statement, "Those that fail to learn from history are doomed to repeat it." That is sound advice for a business model and applies well to turkey hunting and life in general.

Primos has snuck a bit of history into his callmaking while leveraging more modern materials or methods. If you have held in your hands The Revival box call by PRIMOS® HUNTING, you may know your call is very purposefully based on the Gibson box call that was invented well over one hundred years ago. If you have schooled a gobbler with the outstanding PRIMOS® Tall Timber Gabriel box call, you should know that is the title of the first book published dedicated to spring turkey hunting, written by Charles Whittington in 1971. The PRIMOS® Wing Bone Yelper is a plastic representation of a turkey call style traced back to the Native Americans.

Our homes tell The Truth (pun intended!) about what we love, as we tend to surround ourselves with what we value most. Primos' home is not full of the awards he has won, nor does he possess the thousands of magazines containing articles and ads featuring him and his company. Instead, his house is a testament to his respect for others. It contains many items that hearken back to Native Americans and the time of the mountain men. He has carefully preserved cherished correspondence with friends and fellow outdoorspeople and many personal tokens of appreciation he has received from admirers.

Those who have watched Primos hunt on TV and video will have heard him mention his love of the movie *Jeremiah Johnson*. Primos has a particularly keen interest in mountain men. Though a brief period in our nation's history, spanning between the 1804 Lewis and Clark expedition through the mid-1800s, the appeal of how those men sought freedom, took calculated risks, and showed industriousness is yet relevant.

Primos told me, "In 2003, I wanted to commemorate the 200-year anniversary of Lewis and Clark. I had a reproduction made of the .54 caliber short-barreled flintlock carbine they had ordered to be made at Harper's Ferry Foundry, but the guns weren't yet ready when they left." So, the gun was not used during the Lewis and Clark Expedition. Primos took that gun on a hunt in Colorado with Brad Farris, who recorded the hunt on video for "The Truth: Big Bulls" series on elk hunting. Primos enthusiastically told me of the resulting hunt, "What an experience, using a flintlock, understanding what those Mountain Men had to do using a flintlock. The Corps of Discovery, the guns they had to survive with, protect themselves with, and gather food with. What a great experience." Primos killed his elk on the last day of the hunt with twenty minutes of daylight left. The entire experience is preserved on the "Big Bulls 6" DVD by PRIMOS® and is worth watching. "I can remember that sunset, that gun on my shoulder, and I'm humming that theme song of the *Jeremiah Johnson* movie," Primos wistfully remarked.

Primos has a deep admiration for the story and screenplay based on the man who was Jeremiah Johnson. "His real name was John Johnston," he quipped. Fittingly, he has an actual copy of the original movie script that was handed to all the actors and even the original hand-typed synopsis that was used to solicit interest in writing the screenplay, along with several original black and white photos from the movie set hanging in his home. The story of how he came to get the original hand-typed synopsis and photographs speaks to how Primos has influenced others and illustrates the power of the platform PRIMOS® HUNTING has in its outdoor media productions.

"One day, I got a call from a man named Ronnie Smith from Alabama," Primos said. "What he told me, it hit me hard." Will was reticent to tell me the private details, so he suggested I should talk directly to Ronnie. With contact information from Will, I left Ronnie a message, which he quickly returned. Ronnie shared that years ago, at the age of 25, his younger brother was killed. His brother had been his best friend and hunting buddy, and he struggled with the loss. "I was so delusional and distraught; I really thought I could cut a deal with God to let me die and go visit my little brother. I was in a bad place. My buddies would come over and see me and knew I was takin' it rough." His friends decided to leave him VHS hunting videotapes they thought he would enjoy and raise his spirits.

This happened in 1988, and a new video, the first in what would become a PRIMOS® series phenomenon, had just launched. That tape, "The Truth About Spring Turkey Hunting," was one of the videos Ronnie's friends happened to leave him, and he recalled, "I popped that tape in, and while watchin' it, I went into a zone. I mean, it was like I was there in that swamp in Mississippi, and when they were talking, it was like they were talking to me. I realized that I had to live, to make and share such moments and memories with my own family. Will was so convincing and adamant. I knew then I was gonna have to get me another huntin' buddy."

With a renewed vigor for life, Ronnie wanted to do something for Primos to show his appreciation. Ronnie said, "The Truth" did something to reactivate my outlook and life. So, I found out something that meant a lot to Will, which was that he was an admirer of the movie *Jeremiah Johnson*. So, I figured that was the ultimate gift, to give him something back that would put him in a special place." Having a well-connected network across the country, he got to work, tracked down, and gifted Will the amazing items, to his utter astonishment. "That was a God thing. That was me needing to give back to Will, and God knew how important that was for me. Later, Ronnie would be a guest on the DVD "Big Bulls 8" on an elk hunt. At one point, Will said, "Ronnie is so.... full of life." Ronnie pointed out to me just how much Will is responsible for that.

```
From:    Warner Bros. Studio
         Burbank, Calif....843 6000




                        "JEREMIAH JOHNSON"

                             SYNOPSIS



          Soured on civilization, Jeremiah Johnson (ROBERT REDFORD)
     is determined to find a different way of life.  This yearning
     prompts his decision to become a mountain man, a decision common
     among daring individualists in the mid-1800's.  With supplies and
     a smattering of hunting and trapping advice from French shopkeeper
     Robidoux (CHARLES TYNER) he rides off toward the Rockies.

          Although he manages to bag a huge grizzly bear, other attempts
     to get food and furs are relatively unsuccessful.  As winter sets
     in, so does discouragement.  One sub-zero day while desperately
     attempting to catch a trout by hand, he looks up to find his ama-
     teurish efforts being observed by a Crow brave, Paints His Shirt Red
     (JOAQUIN MARTINEZ) on horseback with a rifle.  He glances hopelessly
     at his rifle on the bank and realizes he is at the Indian's mercy,
     but the brave merely stares at him and slowly rides off, exposing
     a string of freshly caught giant trout draped over his horse's mane.

          As Johnson and his starving horse continue on their way, he
     discovers a frozen man, Hatchet Jack, with a death note bequeathing
     his expensive .50 caliber rifle to whomever finds him.  The acquisi-
     tion of the rifle heightens Johnson's spirits somewhat, and shortly
```

An original synopsis of Jeremiah Johnson gifted to Will Primos by Ronnie Smith

I love the film *Jeremiah Johnson* for how it captures the extraordinary man and the period in which he lived and portrays a powerful message of forgiveness. But I consider myself a rookie compared to Primos; "I have watched it 5,000 times, and that is a conservative estimate," Will Primos told me. It may be due to Primos having some of the same quintessential, rugged American individualism Johnson had. Primos told me about the most challenging part of building his company: "A lot of what I did was a lonely journey, leaving my bride and staying in places I didn't want to stay. I saw the insides of planes, taxis, and convention rooms. It wasn't like I could take a day off just because I had worked fourteen days straight."

As consumers of the brand, we see the fun and adventure that is part of the PRIMOS® journey, but not the intense periods of sacrifice and investment of time and energy by those on the inside. I believe that is why Primos can escape into this movie. I asked Primos what he thought the meaning of the film was, and he told me, "It was about searching for a better life, getting away from things that brought pain. We go to such places to get away from it all." Primos said he is most moved by the lesson Jeremiah Johnson's life teaches us. In Primos' words, "Johnson realizes at the end of the movie that an Indian, Paints His Shirt Red, he encounters is the Crow Indian Chief he traded with before the incident that resulted in the Crows killing and scalping his bride and adopted son. In an act of forgiveness for Jeremiah's role in what became the war with the Crows, Paints His Shirt Red raises his arm and extends his hand out in the sign for peace. Jeremiah realizes what this moment is; he can't return the gesture strongly enough or stretch his hand out far enough in acceptance of Paints His Shirt Red's offer. It's all about forgiveness," and then during the interview Primos pleasantly surprises me by softly and reverentially singing a part of the "Ballad of Jeremiah Johnson."

An original Gibson box call (bottom) and the PRIMOS® reproduction of that historical call for the NWTF

His knowledge of history also has breadth. The proof is in the naming of some PRIMOS® calls and the dialogue recorded on their hunting show. Recorded on Season 18 of "The Truth" in 2018, the episode "The Gibson Legend" is an excellent testament to what Will refers to as "the call that started it all." That refers to the first patent for a box call, which was granted to Henry Gibson in 1898. Will told me," The technology that Gibson used is still with us today. The tools and machines we use are more precise, but the basic box call design and attention to detail remains the same."

During that episode, Primos tells the

story of the octogenarian lady, Miss Vivian Latta, who would visit the family restaurant often during the years he worked there. She knew of Primos' callmaking and shared her late father's love for turkey hunting with the young restaurateur. In 1981, she gifted Will something of her father's. "She handed me this brown grocery bag. I opened it and took out an a o-o-o-o-old leather case! And in that old leather case was an original Gibson box call. I couldn't believe what I saw!" Primos promised her that he would cherish it and share it with others, and as a man of his word, he did precisely that.

Primos made a shadow box for the call and case and displayed it at PRIMOS® headquarters for all to see, later gifting it to the National Wild Turkey Federation's (NWTF) museum. Primos and Anthony Foster (who runs the PRIMOS® CNC shop) worked with the NWTF to make a Limited Edition of 1,641 Gibson box call replicas. According to Foster, only minor modifications for better sound were made; the printing on the paddle ensures it can be distinguished from the original. There was one call for each NWTF local chapter to auction off, raising hundreds of thousands of dollars for the conservation organization. "Master callmaker Anthony Foster and myself have done extensive research and testing to bring you a real authentic reproduction of the Gibson box call," Primos said in the episode. Primos demonstrated that the calls work by filming a successful hunt using one to call in a gobbler. Raising his arms triumphantly after the hunt, Primos exclaimed, "I'm talkin' 'bout Gibson box all day long!"

Will Primos as an aspiring hunter in 1954

Understanding the success of PRIMOS® HUNTING requires knowing the founder's sense of stewardship and discipline. Born on March 2, 1952, to Kenneth and Mary Ann Primos, his family roots included a robust entrepreneurial work ethic, a deep Christian faith, and a connection to the land. "The family business wasn't always game calls," said Will's cousin and business partner, Jimmy Primos. "The Primos family is a big one. In 1946, our Grandfather, Angelo "Pop" Primos, who was a Greek immigrant, bought fifty acres of land near Jackson on which to raise his family. He had four sons and a daughter, all of whom built houses across the farm. We were fortunate; we had a pond, a horse pasture, and a love for the outdoors."

Faith and family would be a foundation that Primos relied on both personally and professionally.

Looking back on life and his journey at 71 years old, Primos reflected, "Someone told me recently I was a blessed guy. I told him that he had no idea how true that was. My mother has prayed for me every day of my life, including before I was conceived. When you have a full-time guardian angel livin' on earth with you, you are blessed. I haven't had a lot of tragedy; I've had some orthopedic surgery along the way, shoulders and a knee. I'm currently dealing with an eye issue, but I truly am the most blessed guy in the world!"

Pop Primos' life demonstrated to his family that one can achieve the American Dream. As an aspiring restauranteur, he started in Jackson, MS, opening a small bake shop in 1929 with his wife, Mildred. Through his tenure, it grew into five restaurants, where many of the family were employed. Will Primos said, "The work ethic is the main thing, and then the entrepreneurial spirit rises. We were held accountable as a family. I had four sets of aunts and uncles, and when I was across the street talking to my Aunt, and I would reply, "Yes," to her, she corrected me. It was, "Yes, ma'am!" Primos continued, "Everyone was on the same page. Everything about PRIMOS® starts with family: if it doesn't support the family unit, it doesn't work. That's one of the things that concerns me about the world today: the loss of the family unit."

The restaurant business also allowed Will and Jimmy Primos to gain appreciation for their customers. "Owning and running restaurants helped us learn people," Jimmy told me. Another lesson from the restaurant is the importance of being early adopters of new technologies. A visit to the Primos Café website (www.Primoscafe.com) provides the following insight into how Pop Primos showed them the way:

Pop was a dreamer. He liked to travel to different cities to get new ideas. At the Roosevelt Hotel in New Orleans, he discovered an electric eye door, which he soon put into his location. The "Electric Eye" is an old-fashioned term for photodetector, an electronic circuit activated by light. First developed in the 1890's, the common application here is an automatic door.

He had elevated, round sitting booths built and installed, which he first saw upon his travels. He also designed his kitchen so customers could see the cooks cooking and preparing dishes. He always had a big display of his bakery items next to the cash register. When Pop opened this 2nd location, he installed air conditioning; Primos was the first restaurant in MS to have it.

Pop knew his business, and he acquired many patrons. He always had fresh ideas and slogans for his business. A few popular sayings he used to market Primos were:

"Taste the Difference," "Meet Me At Primos," "Stay Healthy, Eat at Primos"

Much like the wrap-around advertising we see today on some bakery and catering trucks, Pop wanted to have his advertising not only on the sides but on the top of his truck so all the businesses in the buildings downtown could see it when looking down from the tall buildings. Pretty genius for the 1930's.

Just as Pop found and used new technology and business practices to enhance the appeal and performance of his restaurants for customers, Pop's grandsons Will and Jimmy kept their eyes fixed on who their calls were for and pursued excellence in the user experience. They rigorously sought continuous improvement and leaned into new technologies.

An unknown sage left us the quote, "Blood makes you related. Blood means a connection from birth. But loyalty makes you family." The Primos family lives this principle. Primos credits several people, not least Cousin Jimmy, for inspiring his ultimate path to hunting and manufacturing game calls. Indeed, anyone who has seen the two together, whether on camera or at a sports show, can see that blood binds these men. Looking back on our youth, we know what it means to have older kids give you the time of day. Don't underestimate your impact as a mentor, as you never know what the potential of that youth will turn out to

Young Jimmy and Will Primos

be. In Will's case, Jimmy made a sound investment. And, in the end, Will gave as good as he got, as together they would take what Will started in 1976 as a garage-based startup and build it into a multi-million dollar hunting company!

Primos also appreciates what his late father, Kenneth, did to shape him. "My Daddy was in the U.S. Army Air Corp; he was a First Lieutenant and served as a navigator on a B-24 in WWII in the Pacific Theater. And when he got out, he wanted to go fishing. He got him some bamboo flyrods and also a sixteen gauge Fox side-by-side shotgun. I remember him taking me squirrel hunting as an observer at six years old. I was taught first to listen; you could hear 'em gnawing on hackberries. I was in love with the woods." Laughing and enjoying the memory from 1958, he said, "Dad killed a squirrel on that hunt. He helped me cook it, and I mounted the skin. I was on fire!" The seed for Will Primos' future had been planted.

Throughout his childhood, Primos was eager to spend time outdoors and learn how to hunt. Will was keen to tag along on hunts with Jimmy at every opportunity. Jimmy recalled, "Will had a passion for hunting and would get my hand-me-down pellet rifles and such. He is my first cousin and is five years younger, but we grew up more like brothers, hunting and fishing together," Jimmy said. Will reiterated this, "My cousin Jimmy lived down the road on the same property, and when you're 6 and had an 11-year-old cousin who would take you huntin', he was your hero. Those were wonderful, great years!" Will enjoys telling the story of when Cousin Jimmy taught him not to waste the animal whose life is given to the hunter. "Back when I killed my first blackbird, I was 6 or 7 years old; I was so proud of it. Well, Jimmy made me cook it over a fire and eat it. I thought it was good!"

It wasn't about the killing for Primos; even then, it was more about the sacredness of life and our relationship with the creatures whose lives became part of ours. He learned wing shooting with doves and how to clean game like the "big cane cutter" rabbits they hunted. Will told me, "Going back and thinking about quail hunting with my Uncle Gus, he had some good bird dogs. I was 8 to 10 years old; I wasn't even carrying a gun back then and had to run to keep up. I just remember putting that warm body, that quail, in my hand. Man, that lit a fire under me! I then got to go on duck hunts with my Uncles. Daddy was not a duck hunter; he was working hard to save money to send his three kids to college, so time was limited." On one of these duck hunts, he became transfixed by how the duck calls worked. "It all started with duck calls in 1963," Primos told me.

Like any pre-teen, the correct course of action was to tear it apart and see how it was made! His father had some woodworking equipment in his shop, and Primos sketched out the call and then turned some wood on the lathe to fashion his inaugural game call. Although there were design specifications and subtleties beyond his ability to comprehend fully, this first introduced him to the principle of how air-operated calls worked.

The fire was further stoked as he transitioned from being the greenhorn observer to a full participant in the hunt. "Back then, there weren't a lot of deer in Mississippi, but there were some in the river bottoms, especially the Mississippi River bottoms. There were clubs there on land owned by timber companies, and my Uncle Billy and Uncle Aleck, Jimmy's Dad, were members of Ten Point Hunting Club. I got a .30-.30 lever action rifle with open sights as a Christmas present. I couldn't wait to break it in."

Primos recalled, "Around 1961 to 1963, I remember going out with that gun and sittin' on that stand. The dogs were released to stir the deer around and just to hear the deer walk through the leaves before you could see 'em. Man, I can remember how incredible that was. Those were memorable times." He recalled, "The first buck I shot at, I missed, and it was a good ten point. I know 'cause the next guy on stand killed it. But I shot a spike

Will Primos' first deer in November 1965

that showed up a couple hours later. It was great to be part of it, be part of the skinnin' room. Everyone that killed a deer got their name called, and when I got my name called, I was so proud."

Will Primos said Jimmy became the master hunter in camp. "Jimmy was going and consistently killing six and eight-point bucks." Jimmy also pioneered turkey hunting within the family. It may surprise some that turkey hunting was not something the iconic Will and Jimmy Primos learned and grew up doing as a family tradition. It had to start somewhere, and they were up to the task.

Jimmy told me the story of when turkey hunting first became part of the Primos legacy. "I killed my first turkey in 1973 in Pike County, MS. There were not a lot of turkeys or turkey hunters back then. What turkeys we had were along the river and mostly inside the levee. My college roommate at Ole Miss had some family property that held turkeys, and he had been hunting them with his father. It was he who introduced me to turkey hunting. To get to his property, we went through Liberty, Mississippi, which was home to Lynch box calls at that time. That was the only real turkey call around that was widely available. There was no internet, videos, or turkey hunting shows to learn from, so hopefully, you had someone to teach you. Turkey hunting was reserved mostly for those who knew or had them. I didn't know anything! The first time I went, I climbed up into a tree stand. The first time I actually got one, I used an M.L. Lynch Fool Proof to call while sitting up against a log. I called in and killed a jake, I couldn't have been prouder… I just knew I had killed a turkey, and I was excited. It was all luck and no skill."

As with many starting in pursuit of turkeys, they hunted them with the equipment and methods they knew. "We deer hunted them, basically," explained Will. Jimmy added, "One thing people probably don't know, and I'll admit it, is that you could hunt with a rifle for turkeys in Mississippi at that time. I love guns and shooting rifles, even as a kid, and now I own a gun shop, The Range, in Gluckstadt, Mississippi. So, early on, I hunted turkeys with a rifle. Some parts of the Mississippi Delta had a larger field of view. Regardless, I quit it even before it wasn't legal, as I discovered it was much more fun to call them into shotgun range." Before video and audiotapes, if you didn't have a hunting mentor, books and magazines were essential sources of information and inspiration, and Will endeavored to learn all he could. In 1973, a new book on turkey hunting, *Tenth Legion*, by Tom Kelly, was released. It will likely be the best-selling turkey hunting book of all time, as it has remained in print, which is remarkable for a hunting book. Primos instantly connected to the idea of turkey hunting as a lifestyle and of the commendable characteristics of the wild turkey that create a quality of hunter set apart within the hunting community. He later praised and promoted the book on a PRIMOS® audiocassette, *Primos Wild Turkey Talk*, even offering it in his first-ever company catalog.

Primos regretfully told me, "I had a copy of the original printing of *Tenth Legion*. I loaned it out to a guy and never got it back." That original printing now fetches thousands of dollars!

Primos, a self-described book lover, and an avid reader, eventually bought later book printings. He told me what an honor it was to receive the National Wild Turkey Federation's 2018 Tom Kelly Communicator of the Year Award. The trophy is one of only three proudly displayed on a table at his home. The award recognizes a "long-standing commitment to sharing the wild turkey conservation success story and support of the NWTF mission." Receiving the award spurred Primos to reach out to Kelly to get one of his books inscribed. The full text of Primos' message to Tom and the patent cheeky response of turkey hunting's poet laureate is worth sharing here in full:

Will Primos managed to kill his first turkey around the same time he started making turkey calls, which were only for his personal use. His esteem for wild turkeys, his obsession to learn about and to hunt them, and the drive to make turkey calls for himself now perfectly aligned the stars to navigate his future. More and more of his mental and physical time would be given to this new endeavor.

"His second turkey was with me," Jimmy said, "in a camp on the Mississippi River, on the next to last day of the spring season. I had been walking around with my lab looking for turkey sign, which I found and told Will about. He coaxed me into going the next morning, and we had to use a ferry to get across the river to, where we heard a turkey cackle. We sat back to back by a tree, with Will on my left side using one of his mouth calls. Soon, Will's calling was getting a gobble in response to every call. Later, I realized he had been throwing the calls around to his left side, so the turkey we were working had to come around a thicket to his side, where he could get the shot," laughed Jimmy. "I saw him aiming his shotgun, but I couldn't see the turkey. However, I did see him flinch, as in his excitement, he hadn't taken his safety off! He managed to get the safety off and killed it, a beautiful gobbler with a ten to eleven-inch beard and one-and-a-half-inch spurs. We drove back to downtown Jackson as he wanted to show his wife. About noon, we arrived and pulled out that turkey, and right there in the middle of the city at high noon, two game wardens pulled up. At that time, turkeys had to be tagged…and thank the Lord we had had the presence of mind to do that!"

As with many architects of successful companies, the road to get there wasn't paved for Will Primos, nor without bumps. "I didn't want to go straight to college after high school," he shared. "When I was 18 years old, I joined the Air Force. I took an aptitude test and became a Marksmanship Instructor. Like his father before him, the outdoors became an escape for him in his leisure time. He learned, quicker than most, to measure a successful hunt by the quality of the experience. Primos said, "I would just go and love to squirrel hunt. I'd just sit and wouldn't even shoot one; I just loved listening to all the sounds. One day I watched a king snake crawl by at five yards, I was enthralled with the noise it made scuffing on the leaves, and amongst all the other sounds it was such an incredible peaceful moment."

Upon graduating from college in 1974 with a business major and biology minor, Will Primos' hunting roots were strongly calling to him. "I was struggling out of college; I was recently married and not making a lot of money. I tried to get an outdoor job managing properties, but

WILL PRIMOS

mailed to Tom on
March 9, 2018

Tom Kelly
5101 River Road Apt 1109
Bethesda, MD 20816-1569

Tom,

Will Primos here. I sat with you at the NWTF Banquet awards on Saturday evening February 17 in Nashville.

I was honored to be called on stage to stand by you and receive the Tom Kelly Communicators award. The bigger award for me was just having the opportunity to be with you for a brief time.

I have admired you for a long time and as I told you I drove to your house in 1976 and knocked on your door hoping to meet you. You were not home but I got to thank your wife for your writing the Tenth Legion.

Prior to that I had bought a copy of the Tenth Legion from you and you had written a note to me encouraging me in my pursuits and signed the book. That was in 1975 if I remember correctly. I loaned the book to a friend and it was lost.

I purchased a copy of the latest printing and am sending it to you with a request that hopefully you will write a personal note, sign it, date it and re-send to me.

I have included a self-addressed stamped envelope for you to return the book to me. If this is not possible, no worries as I have another copy.

My prayer and wish for you is that you continue to plot, plan and dream and that all your dreams come true!

God's speed to you and thank you for all you have contributed to encouraging many to love and protect Ole Gabriel!

Will

Will Primos
601-750-7504

103 CHENAL COURT
MADISON, MISSISSIPPI 39110

"To plant a tree whose shade you may never sit is a gift to all those who may travel your path one day."

Will Primos

Will, thanks for the note that you sent one on the $6500. You ought to try to find top or cap. I saw one on the web for $425 which is not too bad a price for an oak that will out live us all, but I sold them for abilities practically in one sentence.

Tom

Amicable correspondence between Will Primos and Tom Kelly in 2018 it wasn't working out, so I entered the restaurant business with my family." It must have been a bitter pill, given Primos' hopes and dreams. Like many others in the family, he had worked there as kids after school, making salads and cleaning dishes." I didn't like it; it was confining, but I understood why my granddaddy did it. Coming from Greece and building it with hard work, it was his life. There was no play; it was all work. We went on vacation once, and one of the grandkids asked him to play, and he really didn't know how!" Although grateful to have obtained work in the family restaurant business, he knew it was not his calling.

Primos received precious encouragement in honing his callmaking abilities, which he now credits as pushing him towards that destiny. "One of my Uncle's hunting buddies, a guy named Buck Dearman, wanted me to make a mouth call that would last for more than a few days. Buck was my instigator and encourager!" While some hunters had traditionally used leaves as mouth calls, they had to be carefully selected: Smilax, Peach, and other leaves may have been used. They were carried in a container with some water to keep them wet and supple and, of course, would not last more than a day in the woods. Furthermore, it took both hands to get the correct tension when blowing across a leaf to reproduce a turkey's "yelp." Occupying the hands required movement that could expose a hunter to the scrutinous gaze of a gobbler, leaving the gun lying useless on his or her lap.

The first person to receive a patent for a hands-free mouth call that specifically targeted Meleagris gallopavo was W.P. "Henry" Bridges. It is worth noting that he was better at predicting the future preference of turkey calls than that of game management practices. He was one of the staunchest proponents of game farm turkeys, which would prove to be a misguided effort to

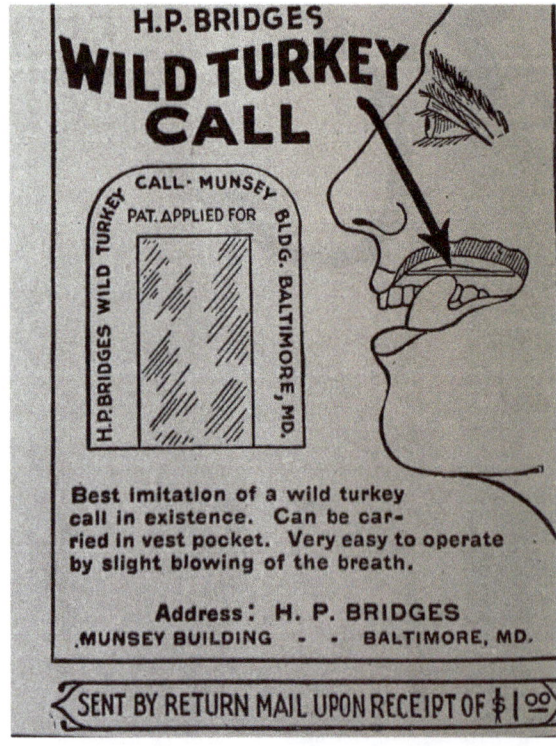

Will Primos with one of his first wild turkeys

The 1923 Henry P. Bridges advertisement for his patented "Wild Turkey Call" in Field & Stream

establish huntable turkey populations. Bridges wrote a book that is an interesting read, The Woodmont Story, which is an excellent story of the Maryland hunting club he helped manage that would host turkey hunts for six U.S. Presidents and Babe Ruth. *Field & Stream* magazine even recorded a wild turkey hunt on film featuring Bridges, advertising it as *Field & Streams Movies of Turkey Shooting*.

In any case, his 1921 patent was for "A Sound Producing Device," which he advertised in *Field & Stream* magazine. It consisted of a single reed, or membrane, of a supple material like rubber stretched until taut within a metal frame. This could then be inserted into the mouth and held between the tongue and upper palate. It reproduced sounds akin to the voice of a wild turkey when the air was huffed between the call membrane and the tongue. Bridges was not the only one at the time that was experimenting with mouth calls. Primos has oft told the story about the origin of the mouth yelper familiar to him. "A turkey hunter from Andalusia, Alabama was walking the streets of New Orleans and a guy was selling a tiny bird call, a third of the size they are now. This hunter stood there and thought, "Dang, I can make it sound like a turkey."

My friend and fellow wild turkey historian Jason Worley wrote an article for Mossy Oak (obtainable on their website) titled "The Earliest Known Diaphragm Calls," and he elaborates more on that story.

"It was also sometime in the 1920s when a hunter from Mobile, Alabama, traveled to New Orleans to receive treatment for rabies. Jim Radcliff, Sr. spent his time in the French Quarters while waiting to complete the 21 shots in 21 days that were necessary to treat rabies in those days. While there, he ran across a ventriloquist who made bird songs with what was essentially a diaphragm call made with a lead frame and thin rubber reed. The ventriloquist made Radcliff a call, and so began his story of bringing the diaphragm call to turkey hunting."

Jim Radcliff and the Mossy Oak connection

In 1926, Radcliff partnered with friend Fred Stimpson to form the Bull Pen Hunting Club on the Tombigbee River in Alabama.

Mr. Fox Haas would join another of Stimpson's three hunting clubs: Choctaw Bluff.

Choctaw Bluff is where Mr. Fox's son, Toxey, would have the vision to form Mossy Oak. That name originated from an old post oak heavily covered with moss on the property.

Bridges' and Radcliff's ideas were good, but their timing was off. Due to excessive hunting, lack of game laws or enforcement, and habitat loss, there were few turkeys during their time, thus few hunters to buy such inventions. The wild turkey restoration across the United States was well underway by the 1970s, with wild turkey populations growing fast and newly established turkey seasons creating new hunters across the country. The local population of turkeys in Mississippi was no exception, and there was now a new demand for that old tech.

In the fall of 1974, Primos met a local turkey hunting camp owner, Eleanor Roessler, who showed him the triple-stacked framed mouth calls she made for hunters. Another fellow named Brossie Dantone was making a similar call with two frames stacked. He quickly noted the merits of both the construction and sound quality. A stacked frame design allowed multiple reeds to be built into a call, one above the other with only a slight separation. The result was a more complex, raspy sound like a mature hen turkey. Even then, those hand-made diaphragm "mouth calls" of the time were crude compared to today's slick calls and didn't last long given their materials of construction.

Primos was, among others, in the right place at the right time and picked up Buck Dearman's challenge to make a better mouth call that lasted. His first mouth diaphragm had a frame cobbled together from beer cans, but it worked! "Beer cans were made of tin then," said Primos. It was a tiring and time-consuming process. "I had to figure out how to make them faster; I was using tin snips to cut the beer cans. So, I had a machinist make me a die that could punch out the center of it, and the next step was the outside of it. I figured out how to slide an aluminum strip across it, and it took two whacks with a sledgehammer sitting on a concrete floor to cut them out!" Thus, Primos would begin to have calls not just for himself but for which to supply friends.

An enterprising young man who knew the value of his work, Will Primos charged a friend $20 for the first one he sold. "It took me hours to make it," he recalls. Primos remembers a few production companies making turkey calls at the time in addition to the well-established M.L. Lynch. Some private individuals also made calls for themselves and sold a few. "P.S. Olt had been around awhile, and there was QUAKER BOY®, Lohman, Ben Lee, and Penn's Woods, to name a few." Others, too, were sensing the onset of demand: the timing was now right for Primos to step up his game call game.

"When I started trying to market my calls, I had a local dealer here, then a guy from Pennsylvania came down here huntin' and bought some calls and took 'em back and told some dealer in Pennsylvania. So, then I had a dealer there," Primos recently shared on Clay Newcomb's excellent outdoor history podcast Bear Grease. "When I'd get time off from the restaurants, I'd travel the state of Mississippi and call on different sporting goods stores. He originally priced calls sold by his dealers at $7.99 but then raised the price to $17.99 to slow down demand, given how hard they were to produce. Imagine his frustration when he got a call one day to come and take home the whole jar (Will used a glass Jack's Cookie jar to house his calls in the dealer's store) as some customer had popped in a mouth call to try it, didn't

The die Will Primos had made before he started his company. He used a sledgehammer on it to cut mouth call frames from strips of aluminum on his garage floor

like it, and put it back with the others!

On a trip to Greenville, Mississippi, Primos visited a sporting goods store where he introduced himself to the owner, Clyde McGee. "A great guy. I told him what I was trying to do, showed him my call, and I had him listen to me run it. This was actually during turkey season. I'd just killed a turkey and had taken a little recorder…. a cassette tape recorder, and I set it on the ground. If I remember correctly, I cackled at the turkey eleven times. And finally got the turkey up there, and it didn't take long, and I killed him! I was just hammerin' him, BAP-BAP-BAP-BAP, BAP-BAP-BAP, and he Garrroobble-obble-obbled." That style of calling aggressively to a turkey, called Cuttin' and Runnin', was pretty new at that time for most hunters. Skepticism about Will's call demonstration was voiced by an old man who was sitting there in the store. The old timer told Primos, "You called TOO MUCH, and you called TOO LOUD!" Primos responded, "Sir, the turkey's dead!"

If you are fortunate enough to own a call, catalog, or accessory bearing the PRIMOS YELPERS name, you have an uncommon piece of PRIMOS® history. That earliest name for Primos' company is based on the fact that he was only selling mouth "yelpers" at the time. "It was around '75 or '76 when I first sold to a dealer. All I was making was three different yelpers;

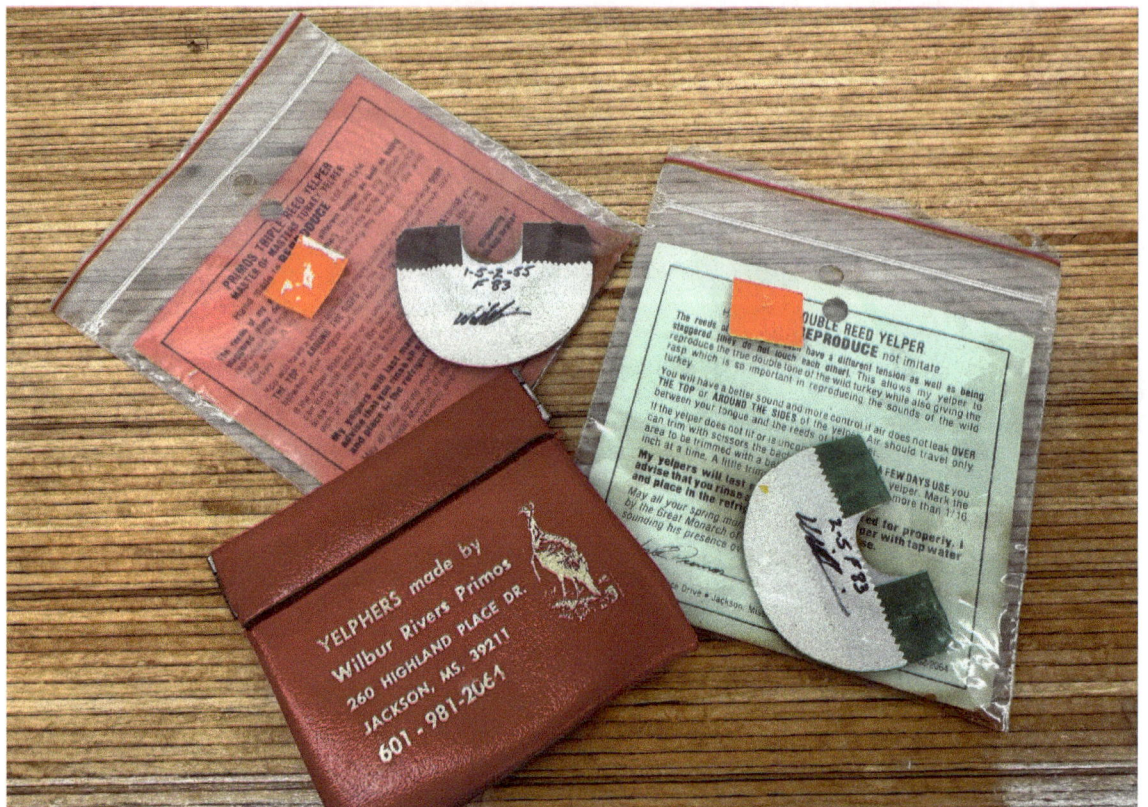

The infamous "Yelphers" mouth call case and some handmade calls by Will Primos from 1983

that's what the old guys called them," Primos said. "My stacked frame calls were all handmade, stamped out of aluminum, and made one at a time with non-lubricated rubber reeds."

"Rubbers are what we called condoms then," Primos said, chuckling. Jimmy would help Will when he could, and he elaborated, "Most people would make mouth call reeds out of a dental dam, but we started with condoms. We bought them by the case! And they had to be non-lubricated. We had a board we stretched 'em out on to cut to make reeds. Once, I went to a drugstore to get my case of Trojan non-lubricated condoms and got a big smile from the lady behind the counter."

Primos said his side business of making yelpers "grew little by little, and I went to the SHOT Show when it was in Atlanta. I could get the whole display booth in the back of my Bronco after 1984." Walking away from a show with hundreds of orders to fill was evidence enough for Primos that there was a future for him in the game call and hunting industry. For the next few years, he would continue to expand the distribution of his calls.

"I wasn't advertising then," said Primos. "Finally, in 1983, I decided to do an audiocassette tape and hired a guy to follow me around in the woods." To fully appreciate this, you must realize that this was not a handheld or a digital recorder. This was a large, reel-to-reel recorder! It did the job, in any case. "It had a parabolic mic. You can actually hear the woods come alive on the tape. Then, you can hear me calling, shooting, and running to the turkey," he proudly recalled.

"We then went to the studio; I had two friends helping me, and I organized all of the call sounds for the instructional part of the tape. I can teach; that's a gift." With so many new turkey hunters, he realized, "I had to teach them how to put a mouth call in their mouth, how to make a sound, how to begin to put it all together," said Primos. The tape was titled *Wild Turkey Hunting with Wilbur R. Primos and the Southern Boys*, which Will now thinks is a stupid name. "I placed a business card-sized ad in a local newspaper for less than $100, and it was a huge success! I would come home from work at the restaurants and have five to fifty orders. I had to figure out how to do a Cash On Demand (COD) payment, but we got it done."

Primos realized he needed additional advertising as he started selling at sports shows. His first product lists were just product inserts for items sold at such venues. "It was an 8 ½ inch x 11-inch piece of stationery in 1983 and had every call we made on it," recalls Primos. He doesn't remember the specific year, but it was 1986 or before when PRIMOS YELPERS put together its first product catalog. As a collector, the author has one from 1986. It is a simple eight-page affair, black ink on cream-colored paper, with sketches of the products. Featured

The first audiocassette Will did in 1983, *Wild Turkey Hunting* with Wilbur R. Primos and the *Southern Boys*. Also pictured is the second audiocassette Primos Yelpers did

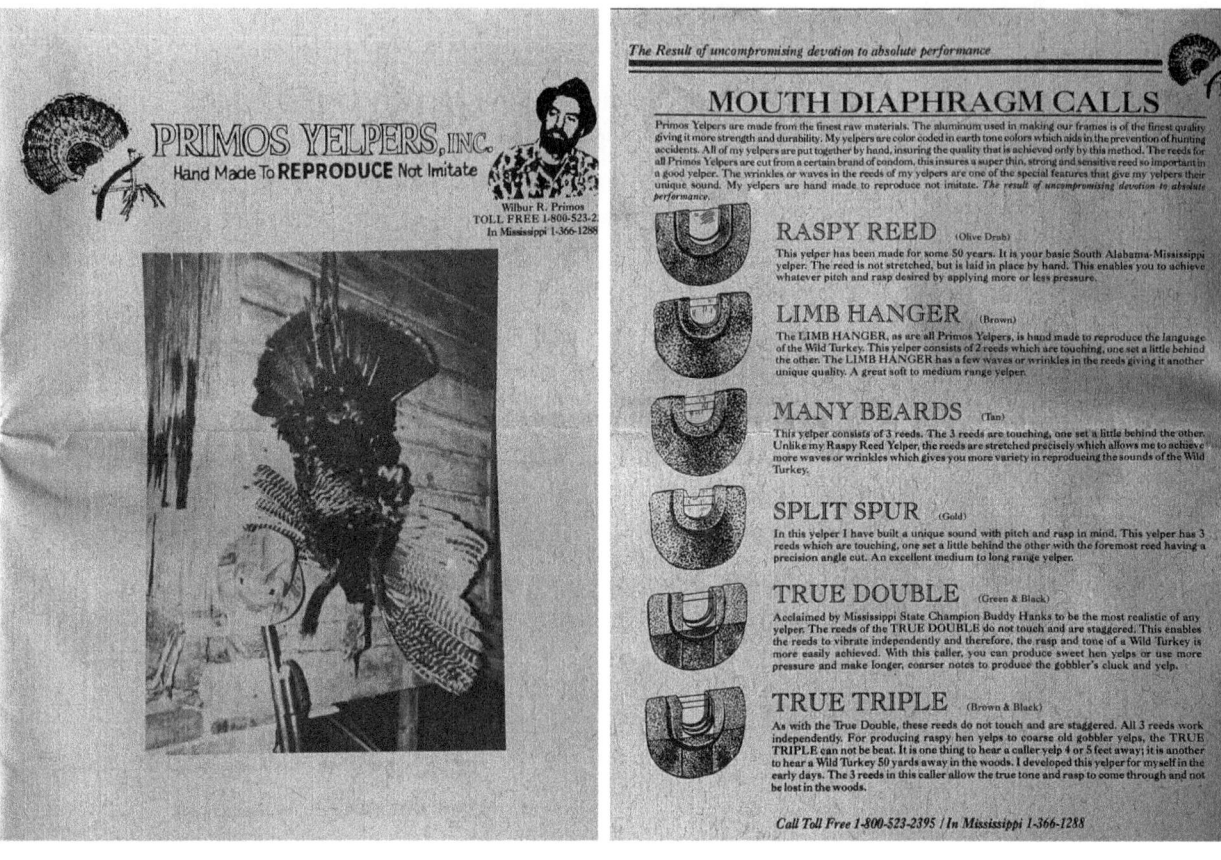

1986 Primos Yelpers Catalog

are six diaphragm call models and the first audiocassette tape Primos had recorded.

Also advertised are calls and accessories made by third parties for PRIMOS YELPERS. By expanding offerings, Will Primos widened his consumer base and increased revenues. Incidentally, all the products in the catalog are now collectibles. Look closely, and you'll see there are no model numbers for PRIMOS YELPERS calls yet, and one of the items is perhaps the rarest of all PRIMOS® products: the infamous red PRIMOS YELPHERS diaphragm case.

"The Yelper Case was inspired by my friend Vernon Phillips," Primos said. "His nickname was Dirt, and around 1975, he came over one day and said, "The Bank of Canton, MS is giving these coin purses away for loose change. I think it would make a perfect yelper case." Primos saw the practicality of a way for customers to carry his mouth yelpers and "found a supply place for promotional products and ordered some." He placed the minimum order for 250 and had "Yelpers made by Wilbur River Primos" screen-printed in gold onto the fire-engine red case. The instant he received them, he was dismayed to see "Yelpers" misspelled as "Yelphers." I obtained one from a former PRIMOS® ProStaffer, but I have never seen one for sale. So, I asked Primos what he did with the misspelled cases. "I sold 'em!" said the business-first Primos. "I think they were $4.99 each."

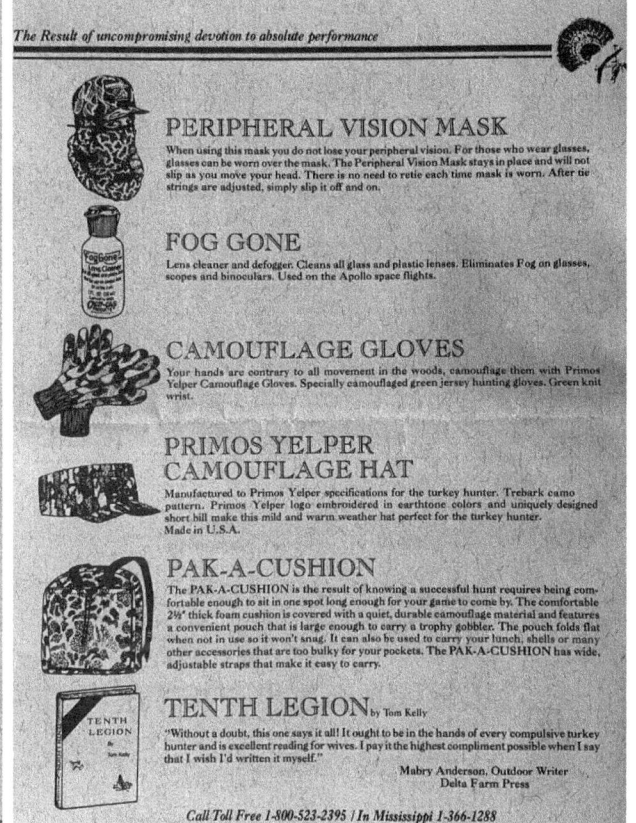

Another facet of the "Yelpher" story illustrates Will's personality. He said, "When I got 'em, I used a hole punch to give 'em some air. Otherwise, it would make a perfect petri dish for bacteria." That is true, given a call would go back and forth between the case and the user's mouth, often in hot, humid conditions. There is Primos' biology training surfacing! He was right to be considering the health and safety of his customers, which is also personally important to him. Some might even consider him a health nut, given the discipline he maintains with his diet. It is to his credit, as he rigorously maintains his health and fitness.

I had to know where the classic sketch of Primos on his early products came from. In it, he wears a close-cropped black beard and dons a Fedora hat. Primos laughed, "There was a company started by Don Norton, a champion bass fisherman, called Brell Mar. It was a takeoff of the words umbrella and Marine. He liked to hunt in the rain and made this umbrella that fit to a tree to shield you from the rain. They hired a guy to head it up and make it big, but it never did get big. They were gonna make a turkey blind, one with stakes that you put around you to hunt a turkey. I went to visit and didn't like the product that much, as it flapped in the wind. They said, "You need to have a character to advertise yourself." So, Will had the likeness made by Mr. Sherill Nelson. I also had to know about that Fedora hat. Primos laughed again, "Russell Davis, he made it for me. He was a friend of mine. With him, you took your hat, put it on the bedside table, and put your yelper, YAWK BOX, gloves, and whatever, and put it in the hat. And that is where you started in the morning, putting it all back in the pockets of your hunting pants."

A YAWK BOX displayed by Rev. Wiley Reid's (who made them for Will Primos) grandson, Brad and great-grandson, Zach

Will Primos is shown signing author's 1980s Primos Dual Reflector at the 2019 NWTF Convention

The YAWK BOX would be one of the first calls Will Primos would contract to be sold under his banner. He had a good eye for quality people and calls, which was vital as he sought to expand his business. "I would travel and see people and didn't have funds and capital but had to start somewhere. So, I found those that would sell to me so I could resell 'em." The "YAWK BOX" was a scratch box made up of two shaped pieces of wood that reproduced a turkey sound through friction when rubbed together. The late Rev. Wiley Reid (a Baptist preacher) from the Brookhaven, MS area made the calls.

Primos had seen Rev. Reid's calls and admired both the man and the call. He contracted Rev. Reid to make the calls and Rev. Reid's wife, Miss Katie, to sew the camouflage carrying cases. These cedar calls were produced from 1977-1984 and were succeeded by two additional cedar scratch boxes, the Hen Yelper and the Jake Yelper (1985-1992). Rev. Reid and Katie's grandson Brad is a friend of mine, and I was touched when he gifted me a rare and valuable "YAWK BOX" made by his grandad for Primos. It included that carefully hand-stitched camo case by his grandmother. Such is the quality of the people in the turkey world. After Rev. Reid's death, a man named Boetler made some for Primos before that call was retired.

Another notable person whom Primos obtained calls for resale from was the late Kenny Morgan of Louisiana. "Kenny helped me learn to call on his Morgan tube," Primos told me. On the next audiotape that PRIMOS® would release, *Primos Wild Turkey Talk*, Will Primos demonstrates what purrs and gobbles on one of those tubes. He credits Morgan's tube as making the best gobble he has heard. This would later inspire the well-received PRIMOS® plastic tube call or Snuff Can-style call line. Of his initial foray with making tubes, Will told me, "I turned some prototypes out of wood myself, then some out of metal. We used everything, putting it to the test before we sold it; man, that metal one was cold in the morning!" chuckled Primos. Many people know Cuz Strickland's affinity for the tube call; he won't go hunting without one, but fewer know that it was Will Primos using a tube of Kenny Morgan's that led to PRIMOS® making Cuz's future favorite call!

Paul "Poke" Forney told me, "Will saw an ad we placed in Turkey Call magazine that we ran for a year or so, and he contacted us." Paul and Joe Forney of Forney Brothers Game Calls made The Dual Reflector glass-over-slate pot call. The legendary D.D. Adams and Lewis Stowe are recognized as being pioneers in plastic mold pots. D.D. Adams is the namesake for the National Wild Turkey Federation's top pot call award and was a school friend of Forney's father. They spec-ed out a mold to make him pots, but D.D. ended up going with Dick Kirby of QUAKER BOY®, who licensed his call. Instead, the Forney Brothers made a deal to supply nearly 200 pots to PRIMOS YELPERS.

Other notable items in the first catalogs include a Red Wolfe Gobble Call, a Smith's Game Calls Easy Squeeze-O-Matic pushpin, Tom Kelly's book *Tenth Legion,* and audiotapes and the book Voice & Vocabulary of the Wild Turkey by wild turkey expert Lovett Williams. "I appreciated Lovett Williams, what he was and knew, and I wanted to help expose him," said Primos. This is another excellent example of the best folks in the world of the wild turkey helping one another.

Meanwhile, Jimmy attended Ole Miss (the University of Mississippi), graduating in 1969. He then entered the Marine Corps and served as an officer (2nd Lt.) in Vietnam from 1970 to 1971. Even a world away, family and hunting were always near his heart. Jimmy obtained a set of Woodland (or Leaf) camouflage, which had been developed in 1948 by the U.S. Army. Jimmy saw its utility for hunting and sent a set to Will. "He wore it 'til it was falling apart, and even after one sleeve fell completely off, he had his Mama sew in some material to reconnect it," Jimmy told me amusedly. The innovation in camouflage for turkey hunting was soon to come, and the relationship that PRIMOS® would make with Mossy Oak would benefit both companies.

When his Marine Corps service ended in 1972, Jimmy became a broker with Merrill Lynch. "The New York money man," Will once referred to him in jest. Jimmy then got into real estate but was also chafing about his future career options. Jimmy told me, "Will came to me in 1985 as I had just sold my real estate company, and said he thought we could make something out of the PRIMOS YELPERS game call business he had just started. It sounded like fun! We had always enjoyed turkey hunting together and becoming his business partner in 1986 is one of the best decisions I ever made in my life. We made a good team and had a lot of other folks to help along the way."

"In 1984, the NWTF Convention was held in New Orleans," Primos said. He set up his booth at that show, and PRIMOS® has had a booth every year since, other than 2021, when no physical convention was held due to the COVID-19 pandemic. Primos recalled, "My booth at the New

Cuz Strickland, Barry Fincher, Will Primos, Gene Anderson, and Jimmy Primos at an NWTF Convention in the late 1980s

Gene Anderson and Barry Fincher attend the PRIMOS® booth at a late 1980s NWTF Convention

Orleans Convention was next to a guy's there named Marvin Killingsworth, an architect from Alabama that loved to turkey hunt. He had one of these new video cameras from Walmart and had videoed a turkey hunt sitting up against a logging and loading site trash pile, a wood pile. There was a line seventy-five yards deep to his booth, and everyone was watching. It showed how badly people wanted to learn. Since my booth was next to his, it was a great draw for me. I sold out!" Primos realized the potential of the home entertainment platform and recalled thinking, "That's what I'm gonna do." Like his grandfather, Pop Primos, Will Primos instantly recognized something new the customer wanted.

Jimmy believes Will is a visionary, always thinking five years ahead, whereas most people think only one to two years ahead. Yet, this was not a simple decision but a carefully weighed investment. "The video equipment cost over $40,000," Will told me. There were limitations compared to recording options today. "It was heavy and could only record twenty minutes of film per tape, then they had to be switched out." Battery life was no better. This would also require more staff. Primos continued, "So, in 1986, Boyd Burrow helped me get one hunt on camera. We called it "Spring Turkey Hunting with Primos: A Video Textbook." In 1987, this first PRIMOS® VHS tape was released, presented in a format that taught turkey hunting basics and was anchored with the hunting footage.

Boyd Burrow and Will Primos after a successful hunt in the 1980s

As an ardent collector of all things wild turkey, I have over 400 wild turkey-hunting VHS titles in my library. The first ones I know of came out in 1985, putting the PRIMOS® video among the first twenty I have seen. This was to be a significant driver of growth for PRIMOS®. Primos said, "Cuz (Ronnie Strickland) was our first full-time camera guy. He came on board and helped with our first all-hunting video, "The Truth About Spring Turkey Hunting." I bought him a truck and told him not to wait on me, as I had a day job, and to record whoever he could get to go, and he recorded twelve kills during 1987." As the video was going through production for the eventual release in 1988, they decided to present themselves honestly. Primos did not want to be doing re-shoots and re-enactments, which some companies didn't avoid. He tried to connect hunters to the experience, warts and all. Those bungled birds, the misses, and all the unexpected occurrences humanized Team PRIMOS®. Viewers loved it!

"The Truth" video series began in 1988

The story of how the PRIMOS® video series ultimately got named is legendary. Will Primos asked his inner circle, "What are we gonna call it?" Cuz replied to this, "All I know is it's the truth." Primos said, "That's it!" People may not know that the following year after the hunts were complete and they were working on the second release of their hunting chronicles, it was Cuz who asked, "What are we gonna call it?" Primos replied, "Are you crazy? It is "The Truth II!" Some may notice two titles for the first PRIMOS® videotape in "The Truth" series. The original release from 1988 was titled "The Truth," but after The Truth II" was launched, the original was re-released as "The Truth I."

"The video series really helped take us to the next level," Primos told me. Initially, the company made just enough tapes to sell to sporting goods stores for $44.99 each. The stores, in turn, would rent the tape out. Remember that this was during the early days of home video, and many people didn't yet own a VCR player and had to rent one along with the tape.

Video technology invited Will, Jimmy, and the growing PRIMOS® team into people's homes. The way they authentically presented themselves resonated with viewers, and the business prospered. Jimmy again credited their approach to their Grandfather Pop and said, "He taught us to treat people right, to be honest, and to "do unto others," and that came through on our videos. People liked us and identified with us." People would tell the PRIMOS® team, "Y'all are just like us!" This is a great example of how powerful it can be to connect to viewers through the screen. There are many who find more than entertainment value in productions like "The Truth." For some, it is how they get education and inspiration.

Will, Jimmy, and their ProStaff team modeled how hunting should be fun and enjoyable. Jimmy maintained, "It is not a contest and about egos and killing the biggest or the most. We would take 200 to 300 videotapes to shows we attended and sell them out by midday at $40 apiece. It was expensive to do, as besides the filming equipment, the machine to make copies was $1000." It turned out to be a sound investment, and by my count, there are forty different PRIMOS® wild turkey hunting and instructional titles between VHS and the more recent DVD format. There are dozens of other releases as they eventually expanded into game calls for different species and began making videos for those as well.

Going beyond turkeys into the production of other lines of game calls led to PRIMOS YELPERS being renamed PRIMOS® WILD GAME CALLS in 1987. This was the first of several naming tweaks as the business evolved. The physical growth of PRIMOS® required continuous re-investment. Jimmy told me, "Our first production office was a 700-800 square foot extension off Will's garage. It was just word of mouth and advertising. Getting placement at retailers now offering turkey and game calls nationwide required making larger minimum quantity orders.

The first deer call PRIMOS® made was in 1986-1987, a grunt call. Jimmy recalled, "I had read an article on deer calls and told Will we needed to get us a deer call, and he looked at me like I had lost my mind. Haydel's had one. Hicks, Inc. in Alabama was our only distributor, and they asked us to build one. We built and hand-tuned every one of them." Using multimedia technology and advertising gave the new PRIMOS® business a leg up. Their first print ad may have been in *Turkey Call* magazine, though they advertised in several. One of the most successful print ads they ever did was for their hardwood deer grunt call. "Deer calling back then a lot of people didn't believe in, so we advertised a free instructional audiocassette on how to use it with the purchase of the grunt call," Jimmy said. "People loved "free," and it was a good deal. We had trouble keeping up with demand."

After turkey and deer calls, waterfowl calls came next, followed by elk calls. "We continued with calls and videos for deer and elk, and here from Mississippi, we became number one in elk calls. How? By commitment," said Will Primos. "We always had goals, even back then," disclosed Jimmy. "Even back in 1988, one goal that Will and I would talk about when going to outdoor sports shows was to be first in some major call categories: turkey, deer, and elk. We would set up our booth on Fridays, sell all weekend, then drive home and make calls." Through the work of all at PRIMOS®, they would succeed with that goal in a few years. Jimmy told me, "*Bowhunting* magazine did an annual survey where writers and readers chose the best products, and PRIMOS® HUNTING got all three categories, turkey, deer, and elk, around 1995, and have been winning ever since. It really made us feel good that our customers recognized our commitment, but then it is easy to get lazy and soft, and we never did that. We kept that passion alive and instilled it in our employees. It was a neat time."

While producing, advertising, and selling the increasing number of products were essential to the company's prosperity, they emphasized quality control, reliability, and customer service the most. In Jimmy's opinion, "A lot of calls being made in those years were poorly made or poorly serviced. Some companies did an excellent job creating a great story about a call, but it was just marketing; it wasn't grounded in truth or reality. We built a better product, including the packaging. The PRIMOS® green package pops...it stands out. I can walk into a store to this day and spot the PRIMOS® products from a distance. Will and I were involved in every step, every facet, making sure everything was done the best way we could do it. If somehow a customer had an issue or got a bad call-which can happen-as the bigger you get, the harder it is to keep quality control; we'd always make it right."

"I can remember mailing out replacement calls or parts with a handwritten note," Will Primos said. "I got good at hiring the right manufacturers; I borrowed a lot of innovation and technology from the automotive and medical industry. In the medical field, they are reproducing precise instruments that are within hundreds of thousands of an inch; these get used in surgeries. I learned it the hard way and didn't know you could get that precise. I used to have to hand file some of the old Wench duck calls until I figured that out." The ability to make such precision parts allowed for the development of The Hoochie Mama elk call. Primos said this is how they were able, "to make the same thing that happened in your mouth with an Elk open reed call happen in your hand."

Those call names! I must admit that I'd love to be in the corner of the room when vetting names for calls was taking place. Looking at the PRIMOS® lineup of hundreds of turkey calls and accessories over time, some are named to inform the user of their utility; The Wet Box, Classic Crow, and the No Lose Call Case are such examples. The "Lefty" Box Cutter is another, but more of an unknown for many. "Ten percent of the population is left-handed," Jimmy told me, "and we had enough hunters asking about it that I talked to our call designer, Anthony Foster, and he worked his magic. A call made specifically for left-handers was another way to separate us from the competition. I'm not sure how many we made, but it satisfied the needs of those who asked." That is now an example of a rare and sought-after PRIMOS® call, regardless of whether you are a southpaw.

When the utility of the call is combined with a clever tongue-in-cheek name, it has some marketing sizzle. Jimmy said, "We put a lot of effort into naming products. You can't imagine how important that is. We spent hours and hours debating call names. And when you came up with a name like Hoochie Mama for an elk call, and everyone grins, you knew then that you had it!" They were creative. Consider the Chick Magnet (three interchangeable magnetic lids to go on a box call), the Drag Strip (trough call), and The Karen (diaphragm call). Some product names changed as they were developed. PRIMOS® call designer Anthony Foster told me that The Lil' Hotbox was originally going to be named The Mojo, and Foster still refers to the Super Freak as The Stretcher. That was a pot call with a stretchy strap to attach it to your leg, similar to the earlier call, The Freak.

The innovative and best-selling Hoochie Mama Elk Call

The ability to use and demonstrate calls on videos and TV shows as products were launching was a clever way for game call companies to inform and influence hunters, always seeking that new advantage. Cue the theme song, and in 1999, PRIMOS® introduced their own show on the Outdoor Channel, *PRIMOS® Truth About Hunting*. Jimmy concedes, "We didn't truly know what we were doing, but we noticed a thirty-minute deer hunting show would feature only one or maybe two hunts. A turkey hunting show would be one hunt and one kill. We offered something different. We started with the rocking chairs on the porch introducing the hunt, then we'd put three or four hunts into a show." PRIMOS® made the show more about the people and experience than the product or the kill and brought in a storytelling aspect with broad appeal.

What they did appealed not only to target customers but to the entire industry. Jimmy validated that, saying, "The Outdoor Channel holds their version of the Oscars, the Golden Moose awards, at SHOT Show. After the first year of our show, PRIMOS® won five Golden Moose awards. We had the benefit of so many hunts and an honest presentation of it. No one was showing the misses or screw-ups. Those are the best parts! People remember that more. It blew everyone's minds; we were tickled to death." That level of success from a company new to television had likely raised some eyebrows. The show is still in production.

When it came to competition, PRIMOS® had plenty. As turkey numbers grew, so did the number of hunters that needed calls. "Most game call companies are very honest, and if there was a problem, we could call and say "you are stepping on us," or we'd get that call, and they or we would make a change. As fellow hunters, we had a lot of common ties," said Jimmy. I am impressed with the mutual respect among the innovators and company founders of that time. Will Primos said, "David Hale and Harold Knight, I learned from them; I learned some of the things I was doing wrong. I love where they came from and who they are." Jimmy stated, "There was competition, but what helped us was having a combination of calls, and people getting to know who we really were through audio and video."

Intellectual property (IP) was something PRIMOS® determined was important in a competitive space. Jimmy recalled, "The first year we did one million dollars in sales, we thought we'd be rich, but, in a sense, we were broke. We had people working all across the country, and protecting our innovations was expensive. We believed in IP; we had many patents on different products, plus trademarked names." The importance of IP was reinforced through a patent they obtained in 1994 for the "Palate Plate Elk Mouth Call" invented by Rockie Jacobsen. "Essentially, it was an extension or plate on the top of the mouth call that served as a backing plate for the reed to come in contact with to help create a smooth and consistent transition from a high to a low note, and it helped fit and hold the call in the user's mouth," said Jimmy. Jimmy is too respectful to name the infringing company. He said, "IP is one of the most expensive and complicated things, but we had a great law firm and fought for five years, and despite the appeals, we won in front of the Federal Circuit in Washington, D.C., in the end. Our final legal fees were 2.3 million dollars. This company had been so flagrant that in an unusual

YELP & GOBBLE, INC.

United States Patent [19]

Foster et al.

[11] Patent Number: Des. 415,054
[45] Date of Patent: ** Oct. 12, 1999

[54] **BOX CALL**

[75] Inventors: **Anthony A. Foster**, Brookhaven; **Wilbur R. Primos**, Jackson; **James A. Primos, Jr.**, Madison, all of Miss.

[73] Assignee: **Primos, Inc.**, Jackson, Miss.

[**] Term: **14 Years**

[21] Appl. No.: **29/096,908**

[22] Filed: **Nov. 23, 1998**

[51] LOC (6) Cl. **10-05**
[52] U.S. Cl. **D10/119**
[58] Field of Search D10/104, 116, D10/119, 121; 446/202, 203, 204, 205, 206, 207, 208, 209, 210

[56] **References Cited**

U.S. PATENT DOCUMENTS

D. 231,927	6/1974	Shoemaker	D10/119
D. 279,461	7/1985	Zafreniere et al.	D10/119
D. 347,399	5/1994	White, Jr.	D10/116
D. 360,160	7/1995	Morningstar	D10/119
D. 393,810	4/1998	Richardson	D10/119
2,511,403	6/1950	Fleener	46/189
2,833,086	5/1958	Johenning	46/180
3,583,094	6/1971	Tribell	46/178
4,041,639	8/1977	Funk	46/189
4,343,108	8/1982	Lee	46/189
4,606,733	8/1986	Willis	446/397
4,662,858	5/1987	Hall	446/397
4,932,920	6/1990	Hean	446/397
5,484,319	1/1996	Battey	446/397

Primary Examiner—Marcus A. Jackson
Attorney, Agent, or Firm—Foster & Foster

[57] **CLAIM**

The ornamental design for a box call, as shown and described.

DESCRIPTION

FIG. **1** is a top perspective view of a box call design according to the present invention;
FIG. **2** is an exploded isometric top view of the box call design of FIG. **1**;
FIG. **3** is a front elevation view (which is identical to the rear elevation view (not shown)) of the box call design of FIG. **1**;
FIG. **4** is a bottom view of the box call design of FIG. **1**;
FIG. **5** is a right side elevation view of the box call design of FIG. **1**; and,
FIG. **6** is a left side elevation view of the box call of FIG. **1**.

1 Claim, 2 Drawing Sheets

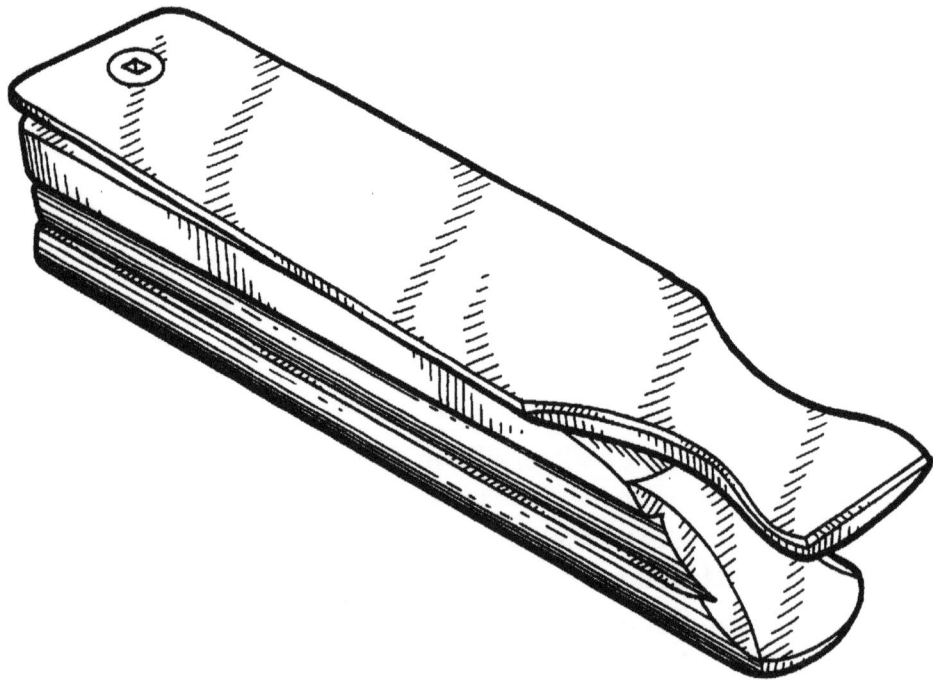

Anthony Foster, Will Primos and Jimmy Primos received a patent for the Heart Breaker box call

move for an IP case, the jury awarded us triple the damages. We prevailed in the end and protected our Intellectual Property."

A statement at the time of the jury verdict by PRIMOS® was, "Although Primos was pleased with the findings of the jury, they would have, of course, preferred not to have fought one of their competitors in court. Primos feels strongly about its patents and trademarks." Primos continues to invest in IP and has over four dozen filings and awarded patents to date.

Though technology theft may be rare, there is a lot of imitation of ideas in game calls. "We weren't always first with ideas," Jimmy acknowledged. "We sometimes had to react." Some of the best PRIMOS® turkey calls, at least in Jimmy's (and my) opinion, came through their business relationships with true industry innovators. One callmaking talent they tapped was Mike Battey of North Carolina. "The Call Dr." was his well-earned nickname at the time, given how he had revolutionized production game calls through his materials research and grasp of sound. The first collaboration between the parties was in 1991 when the PRIMOS® Two-Hole Slate and PRIMOS® Two-Hole Glass models launched, including a mold-injected graphite plastic striker top Mike designed.

Jimmy believed, "When it came to friction calls, there was no one better, and one of the critical things in business is to know your limits. We had seen a plastic pot Mike made, and it was an unbelievably great pot! I would love to claim credit for what he created, but it was his creation." One of PRIMOS®' most successful products ever was the result, the PRIMOS® Power Crystal. "Mike got a twenty-five cent royalty for every pot that came out of the mold. At first, that was a couple grand a year, but then we got placement of the Power Crystal at Walmart. There was a clause in Mike's contract for a $25,000 buyout, which we offered him. He thought we were crazy for that; it was so much money, but we wrote him the check. With the success we ended up having, he would have made that amount and more every year for years...and he still reminds me of that to this day," Jimmy affably remarked. Then, he adds playfully, "Of course, I remind him that he wrote the contract."

Many other calls developed by Battey followed in the PRIMOS® lineup. The Battey World Class slate and glass pot calls were launched in 1995. Today, the used calls by that original name are eagerly snatched up when offered for sale secondhand. It is not uncommon for them to sell for over $100 and double that for a new call in the package. "Using the name Battey for that call is a double entendre," said Jimmy. "Not only is it Mike's last name, but it also drives gobblers batty!" The Battey World Class Slate lives on at PRIMOS® and is sold under the name Ol' Betsy.

Another callmaking wizard PRIMOS® leveraged was Anthony Foster. Of Foster, Jimmy acknowledged, "Towards the beginning, we had seven primary calls in-house that we could control steps and quality for. Anthony, another Mississippi native, was a very smart guy and had an ear for tones and sounds, one of the best I have ever been around. He had a woodworking shop, and I got hooked up with him. He began making some of our products, and we saw an opportunity. Will and I wondered if we could keep him busy and fill all his capacity. It was a concern, but in a leap of faith, we bought him out in 2002 and brought him on board."

That was a pivotal moment for PRIMOS®, as they found a skilled technical talent that has since made some of their most successful calls and accessories, including the wildly popular The Heart Breaker box series and the Trigger Stick shooting rest (invented by Nate Young of Utah). The Lil' Heart Breaker single-sided box call that Foster designed was one of the first calls the author used with great success…and I still do. "Those boxes sound get better as they get older, like a violin or musical instrument," Jimmy said admiringly. Anthony Foster and Mike Battey have made waves across the production turkey call industry as innovators. Those two individuals get their own chapter later in this book, which is an acknowledgment of their and others' underappreciated contributions in production game call manufacturing.

Foster has some excellent business sense as well. He told me, "One of the things with PRIMOS® is that it has always been a large-scale production company, and we didn't get the credit we deserved for our amazing and consistent quality. People didn't have a clue, but perception is reality." While a company may have the best technology and employees, consistency and efficiency aren't guaranteed. Lorena Lipe was the executive assistant to Will Primos and saw how his approach made a difference. "Will is one of the most disciplined people I have ever known," she said. "He set up systems and had manuals put together on how to build things because we do seasonal products. You work six months in advance, switching from turkey calls to elk calls you haven't made in half a year. The process is on record, which helps make it like muscle memory; customers can consistently get the same sweet call they like. So, you become efficient by taking out guesswork or recreating what you do."

Foster wanted to help connect customers to the discipline and quality of their operations. He said, "My concern was that we weren't telling the story correctly, so I convinced the company to do some special calls that demonstrated our capabilities." The limited edition Grand Slam box and pot call series is an example. A box and pot call were released each year for four consecutive years, from 2014-2017. Each year, the box and pot would feature one of the four subspecies of wild turkeys hunted in the U.S. that are part of a hunter achieving a "Grand Slam" when harvesting all four. These are the Eastern, Osceola, Rio Grande, and Merriam's wild turkeys. Limited to 1200 boxes and 1200 pots each year for those four years, they have appreciated nicely from the original price point. They are now worth multiple times the MSRP, with the Eastern pot bringing an average of nearly $200 and the boxes closer to $500.

"That success eventually led to our PRIMOS® Custom Mill Shop," said Foster. The Custom Mill shop has that small batch feel, like that within the bourbon industry. Foster informed me, "We've only touched the tip of the iceberg with it. The idea is to build a product for

The PRIMOS® Power Crystal is one of the longest running production pot calls. Shown are several "variants" of the call's printing and packaging over time

NEW "BATTEY" WORLD CLASS SLATE
Model No. 215

Graphite is the highest composite conducer of musical vibrations, so it was logical when we asked Mike Battey to engineer the creation of our slate and glass calls that he use graphite. When we first heard the sound test, we knew it was "world class". The "Battey" World Class Slate comes complete with an abrasive pad, a perfectly balanced hickory striker and a waterproof acrylic striker. For the turkey hunter who wants to own a slate with a superb, honest and mellow tone, you will be proud of the "Battey" World Class Slate.
SUGG. RETAIL $19.99

NEW "BATTEY" WORLD CLASS GLASS
Model No. 217

Graphite is the highest composite conducer of musical vibrations, so it was logical when we asked Mike Battey to engineer the creation of our slate and glass calls that he use graphite. When we first heard the sound test, we knew it was "world class". This call comes complete with an abrasive pad, a perfectly balanced hickory striker and a waterproof acrylic striker. For the turkey hunter who wants to own a glass with a superb, crisp and raspy tone, you will be proud of the "Battey" World Class Glass.
SUGG. RETAIL $19.99

The PRIMOS® Battey World Class premiered in 1995 and is still sold as the Ol' Bestsy

Pictured are Limited Edition box calls made for Mossy Oak by PRIMOS®: 2007 Tribute to Bob Dixon "Battleship" call (for Dixon Vest), and 2023 Fox Haas (for Mr. Fox Vest)

someone where they can be involved in it, and they end up with a work of art. It demonstrates what PRIMOS® is capable of." Most recently, the shop was used for a joint project with Mossy Oak, of which Foster said, "We are friends with Toxey, and they reached out to our Marketing Department with a tight timeline. We ran those Mr. Fox box calls, called the Fox Hass 1944 box call, for them to be ready to sell alongside their limited edition of 1,944 Mr. Fox vests at the 2023 NWTF Convention. Of the Fox Haas 1944 calls we made, 200 sold at the NWTF Convention, 200 at the Mossy Oak vest event, and 350 for online sales." It was the second limited series the two companies had done; in 2007, 1,986 Dixon Vests were released by Mossy Oak to commemorate the life of Bob Dixon, who was an early contributor to PRIMOS® as well. The first 100 vests had a set of numbered calls, including a Bob Dixon Tribute Battleship.

As with any company, lessons are learned from what worked and what didn't. "The name, usability, durability, and packaging all matter," said Jimmy. But there are failures even from the best people and companies, especially those on the cutting edge. "One flop we had was when we got Mike (Battey) to do an injection molded box call, The Prospector. We didn't keep it in line very long; it sounded like a squeaky barn door!" Mike has pointed out to me that there may have been some alterations to the original design from the original graphite material. The devil can be in the details! During call development, learning from failure does lead to future success. Jimmy shared, "We had a family of calls we used the word 'Power' in. What turned out as The Power Cow was originally supposed to be an elk call but became a crow call when we were working on tuning it."

Success can also be fleeting, as they learned with The Real Wing, put on shelves in 1999. It consisted of an injection molded base to hold primary wing feathers sourced from white domestic turkeys and painted to resemble the familiar black streaking on a wild turkey wing. Used by hunters to simulate the sound of turkeys flying down from roost or fighting, Jimmy said, "We created a big story behind it, and if you hadn't killed a turkey yet to get a wing, it was a useful product. That first year, we sold a ton of them, but it ended up being a product that didn't sell through as people could easily duplicate it after they saw it or harvested a turkey. They either made their own or just used their hat, flapping it against their leg. It was a one-year product. I don't know how many hundreds of thousands of white turkey wing feathers I had left in our warehouse to dispose of!"

Any callmaker has calls they particularly favor for their use. Will and Jimmy are both fond of the True Double diaphragm. The call is proven in the field and is one of the iconic early calls on which they built the company. Jimmy was nostalgic in telling me about it. Among Jimmy's other go-to calls are the boxes in The Heart Breaker series, the more recent Tall Timber Gabriels single-sided box, and for pots, the Power Crystal, Power Slate, and Ol' Betsy slate.

Until I started collecting calls in earnest, some of the subtle changes in the PRIMOS® company name, logo, and slogans escaped my attention. At the end of this chapter is some information about PRIMOS®, including an approximate timeline with the various company names and slogans. Some may recognize "For The Woods" appearing on PRIMOS® calls and packaging from 1997 to 1999. I asked Will Primos for the story behind it.

Will Primos and his domestic turkey Loretta back in 1977

"I had a hen and gobbler from 1977-1984 that I hatched from a nest that a Bush Hog destroyed. I named them Conway and Loretta," Will told me. "I got to listen to 'em, and I'd sit down and tease Loretta with crickets, and she'd cackle at me to get the cricket while standing on my leg. I watched her and observed her closely." Primos said it was through observations of these turkeys and his passion for the sounds of the woods that he chose "For The Woods" as the company's first slogan. He continued, "Then one day Jennifer Bricknack, who worked for us, walked into the office and said, "I got a perfect slogan for ya…Speak The Language." Primos said he wasn't crazy about it and told her, "I will think about it." He bounced it off a few others at PRIMOS®, and they enthusiastically said, 'We love it!' Will finally recognized a good thing, and that slogan is still in use.

I also asked Primos about the familiar "PRIMOS® green" that we correlate with their packaging. Primos started using that color soon after launching the business, though the color scheme was later updated. He told me how that happened; "Boyd Burrow, VP of Marketing and who had ran a camera when we produced our first turkey video, said the green needed a little something to accent it, so we added the orange." Again, it is something that has aged well for PRIMOS®.

Indeed, I'm not the only one who associates the PRIMOS® theme songs with good memories. Primos divulged, "The original song was part of a library of music you could get by paying a yearly fee, and you could use it for video productions as background music. Cuz was listening to music from one of those libraries and found it. That became the theme for "The Truth" series." Just as in game calls, a form of flattery is copying, which unfortunately others did. Primos confirmed that "others started using it, so we said, "We're out. We are getting something uniquely ours. My wife, Mary, and I reached out to John Baranco. I grew up around Johnny in Jackson and he had a band in High School that perfectly reproduced the Chicago band's music, they were called "The Cracker Jacks. Johnny went to New York and became a jingle singer, doing ads for Fortune 500 companies like Dr. Pepper and Coca-Cola."

Primos told Johnny he wanted him to produce a song, and even though it was not the type of work Johnny did, the persuasive Primos got his agreement to make a song that PRIMOS® could own. "Mary and I played the original theme song music for him, and then he calls me a couple weeks later and he said, "I will get all the instrument players there, and you can listen and make comments on the spot so we can get it right." Will and Mary sat down with the band and did just that. Primos recalled, "As we listened, I urged Johnny to think about the Allman Brothers, music that gets you involved." Johnny said, "Ok, I got it." Primos continued, "Then, my wife Mary said, "Yes, but think about "Chariots of Fire," and Johnny said, "Now I really got it!" Primos said, "Johnny walked over and talked to the band, and they nailed it on their next take." That is now called the "PRIMOS® Victory Song," which is still part of their TV and YouTube show.

So many contributed to the success of PRIMOS® HUNTING that it is simply not possible to mention them all in this chapter. Primos reminded me several times as we worked on this, "It is important that it is not about me. Yes, I lived the life, but there are so many people that are part of it. I got to be a part of their lives in a positive way and got to see 'em have families; that is what it's really all about. I love business more than just about anything, even more than hunting; I love putting things together to make them work." As my friend and fellow PRIMOS® collector Alex Lee White told me when helping edit and add to this chapter, "PRIMOS® was the perfect storm at that right time with the visionary drive of the founders and the talent they tapped into. It is staggering to think of the impact of all the incredible people in play both locally and externally to the company that are part of their story."

While Primos started out doing it himself, he is quick to share credit. "You don't realize what skills and attributes God has given you," He said. "But along the way, I selected people who were like-minded. My cousin Jimmy came around 1986, and Anthony Foster and the people that worked for him, the vendors...policies and procedures were written, and you tried to teach them that culture. I don't know what I would have done without my assistant, Lorena

Lipe. You go back to Boyd Burrow, who was the cameraman before Cuz. Boyd was the guy stuffing bags with calls, and he became the Marketing Director! Each person: Cuz, Chuck Jones, Bob Dixon, Ron Jolly, Jeff Sherwood, Slade Reeves, Brad Farris, Troy Ruiz, and others; they had ways they shared their love. Ron Jolly captured it well in his book *Memories of Spring* in the chapter Rattlesnake, Mississippi."

If you want a finger on the pulse of a company and its people, I have found no better source than an executive assistant. Few have such access to the span of the company across function, level, and role. Lorena Lipe spent thirty years of her life with the Primos family. Her first three years were at the family restaurant managed by Will's brother, Don, where she met Will. Then, she spent twenty-seven years with the PRIMOS Hunting family, serving as Will's assistant for much of the time. Will expressed his appreciation when I talked to him for someone who had been his strong right hand for so long. He said, "Lorena did just about every role in the company at one time or another. She was essential in what PRIMOS did."

"I joined about 1993 when there were thirty-five or fewer employees," Lorena told me. "We, the team that built the company, all wore multiple hats. We – even Will – did whatever it took to make things work. No job was too big or small, whether cleaning the bathroom or taking out the garbage. All the work made the business grow. I actually started out answering the phone and doing some accounts payable; I became the Graphic Designer because I was the only one who knew how to run the Mac at that time.!" She worked within Sales and legal and even became the IT Manager when the job needed to be done." Taking the initiative, she got on the internet to figure out how to put Cat 5 (data) cables through the roof. She became Will's assistant around 1997 and quickly gained Will's confidence.

As demonstrated by Lorena, such resourcefulness allows companies to navigate challenges quickly but requires a high degree of trust. She said, "Will was gone a lot making videos and doing sales, and he empowered all of us to take care of customers and vendors. He taught that if we took care of them, they would take care of us. If a customer service rep is on the phone with a customer who received something damaged, we didn't have to go to Will to get help. He supported us to do what was right; it might cost the company some money to send out a replacement, but a happy customer will return and help us grow. Will made sure we made ourselves easy to do business with."

Lorena's comments helped reinforce and crystallize what others touched on regarding Will and the company's culture. She has told many people, "With Will, what you see is what you get. He was always genuine. He wasn't acting for the public. He really was that great guy that fans were drawn to on TV, video, and at industry shows. In all that Will does, whether it is personal or professional, he is led by his faith. He wasn't afraid to share his faith with those who were open to it, but he led with it. He treats everyone like his family and does what is right for them." Primos had an open-door policy, and she said "Employees could go to him for help with any problem. It didn't have to be work-related. If someone had a medical issue and couldn't get in to see a doctor, he'd drop everything; more than likely, you'd have a doctor's appointment the next day."

Summing up three decades as part of the Primos and PRIMOS families, Lorena said, "They formed so much of who I am, Will, specifically. I've been so blessed to have been a part of it and to have him and Miss Mary in my life. They doted on everybody's children; my kids have had the pleasure of knowing them. He was not only a boss, he's my friend and was my mentor. Both personally and professionally, he taught me how to do life and business right; for that, I'll be eternally grateful."

Primos is especially thankful for the contributions of Brad Farris at PRIMOS®. He shared, "Brad had an innate sense of what to do. We tried once to hire him, and then he came two years later and said, "Now I'm ready." He watched people and learned how to, and how not to, treat 'em. He's a great relationship guy. In life, we need people who will look out for each other, and that's what we did," Primos said respectfully.

"There were two things I wanted to do in life: fly a fighter jet or hunt for a living," quipped Brad Farris. While I'd not care to ride in a fighter jet with Brad, I have yearned to hunt with him. He has fulfilled that goal of hunting for a living, but there is much more to what he does than people see on *The Truth About Hunting* television show. "I worked at Indian Archery, where I met Will in 1987 when he came in to get some bows tuned, and we hit it off." Farris continued, "I was 17 years old and green as a gourd. I just loved doing something with hunting and thought, "I should be paying to work here!" Farris knows it was late summer or fall, as the shop had advertised a pre-season bow tune-up for deer.

Friends Brad Farris and Will Primos

Farris said, "I looked up to Will so much. I used to sit in my Uncle's truck, listening to him shoot a turkey on a PRIMOS® audiotape. I was shy, and when he came in, I didn't say much. When his turn at the counter came, he had two bows he wanted set up identically. He saw me working hard to set them up perfectly, even if it required taking something apart more than once. I was kind of a perfectionist: I didn't like being hurried. My Uncle used to say, "Dig the best ditch you can dig; don't cut no corners." Brad continued, "As the line behind Will grew, I told him, "I feel rushed working on your stuff. Can we meet later so I can do more?"

The young man's persistence made an impression on Primos, and in a few short years, he offered him a job as a shop foreman. Farris was thrilled to get the offer, but the newly available video cameras that outdoor companies were using to film hunts had captured his interest. He now had his heart set on making videos for Indian Archery. "The first hunt I filmed was their very first deer video, in October 1990," Farris said. "Back then, just getting deer in focus on a camera was something you showed someone as you had it! After several videos with Indian Archery, I went to work for Tara Wildlife in 1994." There, he would run into Will when team PRIMOS® was there hunting.

Primos would keep his eye on the young talent, and in 1997, Farris accepted the second job offer Primos extended. "I went to PRIMOS® full time as a videographer when Jeff Sherwood became the video manager," said Farris. "It was Jeff, Kenneth Lancaster, and myself. My daughter was born that fall, and it's the only elk season I've missed at PRIMOS® since. After Jeff left, I took over in 1998." Farris wanted to do a television show but told me, "Will wasn't ready. He knew it would help us grow, but he wanted to pace us. Our business was getting call orders out. Mossy Oak had a show called *Remington Country,* so Will agreed to become a Sponsor. In about 1999, he had us start looking at the Outdoor Channel, and we started filming for that. We came out with the first episode of *The Truth About Hunting* in 1999. Next thing you know, we were doing twenty-six episodes a year. And we had *The Truth About Whitetails* show for a few years, too; doing thirty-six episodes a year with five or six guys was a tremendous effort! At the same time, we had to navigate making the videos and then go from videos to DVD."

It was evident to Farris that Will had something special, and he said, "Will's always had a unique eye for marketing and being a step ahead. I've thought many times since then about how the timing of PRIMOS® and *The Truth About Hunting* was perfect. But that is how Will is different, as he could see that perfect timing then! He was so good at aligning himself with people like Paul Korn. Paul had an injection molding company; he was an avid hunter like us. He understood an elk call and a turkey call. Without Paul Korn, we'd have had a much harder time perfecting the Hoochie Mama elk call. Paul was great at making those molds and getting the preciseness in the final product. If you are off by a minute amount, something in the thousands, it just won't work. He taught us a lot about those types of products."

"And then you had Jimmy," Farris said lightheartedly. "He was a Marine Corps officer. He had that leadership ability; there was no grey area, and you knew where you stood, but in a good way. If you didn't give 100%, Primos wasn't for you. If you wanted an eight-to-five job with a paycheck at the end of the week, you didn't make it long. Will is the most demanding person I know in this world, but also the most giving. If you want to win, you have to work hard and give it your all. He created a heckuva team! He was so good at getting the right people in the right seat on the Primos bus. Will and Jimmy are brilliant."

Primos and Farris told me they became best friends through their work together. The commitment they showed each other was selfless. Farris demonstrated his friendship through dedication and hard work and embraced Primos' values. He told me, "It took five years working for PRIMOS® before Will fully trusted me enough to turn me loose. He wanted to be sure. We had a rule that if anything we produced didn't look positive for hunting and our outdoor lifestyle, we would not put it out there. If we can do something in a learning way, that was the idea." Primos reinforced his part of the friendship by supporting what was best for Farris. "I left PRIMOS® in 2012," Farris said. "I had developed a passion for the land, wildlife management, and making things better. I sat down with Will and shared that with him. He was so understanding, and he said to me, "Listen, if you need to stretch your wings, you should do it." The show continues to be a fan favorite, with Farris still on the PRIMOS® team as a host along with Will and Jimmy Primos, Brad Farris, Troy Ruiz, Lake Pickle and Jordan Blissett.

In our professional lives, we spend as much time with coworkers, maybe more, than with our family at home. Along the way, we experience a roller coaster of ups and downs. Primos speaks fondly of sharing a seat on that ride with Cuz Strickland. "Cuz is just naturally good, and making sure people knew him as "Cuz" is an honor; I nicknamed him that. He is called "Cuz," because one day we were walking into a grocery store in Natchez, and someone sees him and yells "Hey Cuz! He yelled back at 'em, "Hey Cuz!" And I asked, "Who was that?" And Cuz said, "I don't know, that is just what we all call each other around here." Will said, "That is what we are gonna call you: "Cuz!" Will was sorry when Strickland made the decision to leave but understood and supported him. He even went one step further, advising his new friend starting a camo company that the young man would be a good one to hire. You know the rest of the story; Strickland became one of the industry icons and strengthened the ties of two hunting industry powerhouses along the way.

Strickland helped give me perspective on his time with both PRIMOS® and Mossy Oak. "When I met Will, he was still building calls out of his house at night. He finally got an office on North State Street in Jackson. When I left PRIMOS®, Will was really just getting started," Strickland said. His decision to leave was unavoidable at his stage in life, yet difficult, nonetheless. "When I was doing video and making *The Truth*, I was driving back and forth from my home in Natchez, where I was born and raised. Over time, the job became bigger and then it became every day." Even though Primos had bought him a truck, this was a stretch for Strickland's time and family life. "I'd work in Jackson a week at a time, then go home for the weekend; It was a two-and-a-half-hour drive one way." Strickland was married with two little girls and had to follow his heart. "I loved working there, but it just became too much," he shared. Strickland appreciated the time and experience and made friends for life but had to find work closer to his family.

Toxey Haas had started Mossy Oak by this time, and through Bill Sugg, Mossy Oak and PRIMOS® had become connected. Strickland later learned Primos had urged Haas, "We need to keep Cuz in this loop." Haas promptly hired the young talent. Strickland continued, "Toxey had me cover the local Mississippi area, and I kept on filming with them. We even gave the footage to Will when we got something good. My relationship with Will continued to grow even after I left. He was the first one to promote Mossy Oak, and we promoted them right back. My connection did strengthen the relationship of the two companies."

Mossy Oak and PRIMOS® ad from 1987 March-April *Turkey Call* magazine

Strickland is nothing if not humble, which is a massive part of his appeal to the outdoors community. "I still have trouble thinking I am a part of all this," he admitted. "I've just been blessed; it was a God thing." He admires those who built companies from their love of the wild turkey. "I've been around a lot of people, and Will and Toxey are absolute visionaries. They could see stuff I couldn't see. It was fun to watch that, watching the birth of the outdoor industry."

Many of us have put PRIMOS® and Mossy Oak into the same sentence, given their similar values and impact on the hunting community. Jimmy told me that while "we had sponsors for our videos and TV show, we didn't really work with other companies. We liked to stay lower on the radar and do our deal, but Mossy Oak was an exception. Bill Sugg came to see us in 1986 with a pair of original Bottomland pants and a shirt and asked us to wear it on video. We had been building PRIMOS® for ten years and had a little understanding of how to build a hunting products company, so we helped them out of the gate." Will Primos had recently instructed Bill on how to master a mouth call, and upon seeing how the clothing hung on pine, red oak, and pin cherry trees vanished at forty yards, he became a believer in this new innovation in concealment.

One of the first promotions that Mossy Oak did was an ad featuring Mossy Oak founder Toxey Haas and Will Primos shaking hands. It was accompanied by an incentive for anyone purchasing a pair of Mossy Oak pants or shirt to receive a free PRIMOS® turkey call. Jimmy told me that "Mossy Oak was a lot like PRIMOS® in finding people to work for them that shared their obsession. It is hard to be upbeat all the time. Everyone keys off the leader, so if something had Will or me down, we'd remind each other we had to be upbeat for our employees. Toxey, Bill, and Cuz, they were the same way. They inspired."

Will and Jimmy Primos had an eye for talent and helped launch many along the way into successful outdoor careers. After Cuz, they brought in Chuck Jones for work on the sensational show *The Truth*, and Chuck connected them to Ron Jolly, known to all now as "Jolly." Jolly shared, "In 1988, I was offered the job, and I was thirty-seven years old when I started; I always considered myself that old quarterback that had one more year in him. I knew I started late, but I gave it all I had: I pushed the envelope. I was raised on the farm, and my Dad said, "When the ox is in the ditch, you gotta get him out!" He continued, "We did what it took to get the job done. When I first came, Will was still workin' at restaurants, borrowing money; nothing was handed to him. I was still farmin', so my Dad took care of the farm, and I paid him what Will paid me."

Jolly was a Videographer and a Publications Director for PRIMOS® for several years. He was behind the camera every day of the season and attended consumer, buyer, and distributor shows every weekend between seasons. "It was hard on relationships; the videographer job came with telling everyone up front, "You are here to do one job, and that is to pull the trigger when I tell you to; if you do it before or after that, you are wastin' our time." Jolly continued, "It took three years to do the first elk video; we learned as we went. The first two years, we shot elk butt's runnin' away, but we got educated. It was all worth it, and Will was brilliant here as he justified the expense of videos as a sales tool for the line of calls. But we had what we said was a "hokey-meter," and if it got too oriented on products or marketing, we'd say the hokey-meter was going off." The growth of Primos and popularity of the video series prove that the visionary Will and Team PRIMOS® got it right.

The quality of the people involved was directly correlated to the quality of products the company was putting out. Jolly's trip down memory lane helped surface some people who built on the company's initial video success. "The Truth II About Spring Turkey Hunting" included some of my footage, and I did episodes three to eight. Chuck Jones did "The Truth Big Bucks 1," and I did episodes two to four, as well as the first elk video," recalled Jolly. And in between, he would help do many instructional audiocassettes and videocassettes. He acknowledged many whom he appreciated who were a part of it: "The late Bob Dixon and Jeff Sherwood were great contributors. We were lucky to have guys like Mike Lingo and David Vinson who were excellent deer hunters and willin' to get deer figured out and get me in there to film. Three people who really helped make my life easier were Will Walker, David Cardin, and Coates Head, excellent hunters who were willing to "play the game" to help get good hunts for the camera. Those guys are all still best friends to this day."

Regarding what people might not see or understand in the videos, Jolly said, "Wilbur was always very passionate about turkeys, not just about killing them but about conservation. We were a lot alike in that the way we were taught was to do things the old-fashioned way. It was about calling a turkey to you. It was about how close and not how far. For deer, we never got lost in the fog of monster bucks. We hunted the biggest we could find, but Will and I would about pee our pants with a reasonable eight-point," he laughed.

Appreciation for what Will Primos and those at PRIMOS® did is widespread in the outdoors industry. Another company that is no stranger to the on-screen world is Realtree.® "I know Will well. We are friends, and we have a connection to each other," Realtree's® Bill Jordan told me. "We both attended the University of Mississippi. He's an Ole Miss Rebel!" Jordan doesn't judge people by the camo they wear, as competition is just a reality in the business world. As others I visited with have acknowledged, camaraderie in the hunting world transcends brands. He said, "I like people for the people, and I like what PRIMOS® did for the industry." Looking back, he agreed that the timing of what he, Will, and other entrepreneurs did was a fortunate combination of timing and initiative. "Back in the day when I started Realtree and others were starting their companies, we were all pulling for each other. We've all got older; some of us don't get along as well physically as we used to, but we've always just been a phone call away."

A way that PRIMOS® differentiated itself from others in its production call company genre was by embracing the digital platform. Although the company maintains a television show, they have a sustained presence on YouTube and social media. Others dabbled, some avoided it altogether, but the marketing team at PRIMOS® has demonstrated through every media channel how they are tuned in to where potential customers get their information. That approach is hard-wired into the company goals provided at the end of this chapter.

Among the many who uniquely contributed to the success of PRIMOS® is Jeff "El Diablo" D'Agostino. That nickname was jokingly coined by Jimmy, who initially struggled to pronounce Jeff's last name. Jimmy told me, "Jeff was one of our original ProStaff, and as we grew, we couldn't be everywhere. There are too many Cabelas, Bass Pro locations, and seminars, so we developed ProStaffers to help us. We didn't just give 'em a hat and send 'em out. We had to meet and interview each one, and we checked their references. We wanted to be sure they would represent us in a positive way. At one time, there were over fifty guys across the country, and they had to meet points (an activity-based points system) every year to stay on. We had one employee whose entire job was to manage the ProStaff. It was very organized, the envy of the industry. We had a manual that Jeff helped write and organize, and that manual got them on autopilot."

D'Agostino told me, "As a part of his strategic vision and intent to be number one in each call category, Will knew that he needed outreach across the country, coupled with reliable distribution and strong brand recognition. That's where the ProStaff fits in. When I started, it was a couple dozen fellows across the country. Working Joe's like me that had a passion for the outdoors. Will knew that the ProStaff was mostly an untapped resource. He asked me if I would help organize and structure the ProStaff to enhance PRIMOS® marketing and brand. I eagerly accepted and drafted the first ProStaff manual. It outlined expectations, a points-based rewards and incentives system, and established how ProStaffers would serve as volunteer goodwill ambassadors. Responsibilities included doing in-store promotions, working sports shows, conducting seminars in their respective parts of the country, and working with manufacturer's reps and distributors to enhance brand awareness. While I was there, we doubled in size to fifty ProStaff!"

D'Agostino is a human Swiss Army knife, full of talents. PRIMOS® would tap him to update the artwork for calls and packaging. D'Agostino recalled, "As Will and I spent more time together doing seminars, trade shows, and hunting, he realized my passion and God-given gift of drawing wildlife. He approached me about doing a series of what we ultimately called "action animals." I drew twenty-eight different sketches of animals in action, ranging from a gray squirrel to a bull moose and everything in between." Jimmy shared, "He was very artistic; he helped to grow us." If you have seen the gobbling turkey, bugling elk, howling coyote, and other such PRIMOS® wildlife art featured on their calls and show, you are admiring D'Agostino's handiwork. An award-winning NWTF callmaker, D'Agostino once gifted Will a wingbone call. Given that Native Americans once used such calls, it awakened the history and innovation interest in Will, given his fondness for such things. "Little did I know that that wingbone call I made for him would be used as a template for an injection molded production trumpet yelper," said D'Agostino. That would be the PRIMOS® Wingbone Yelper, featuring the wild turkey art from the original call D'Agostino gifted to Will.

Jeff D'Agostino art used by PRIMOS®

Every employee and ProStaffer at PRIMOS® contributed to the company's growth. The drumbeat to maintain quality was one that Will and Jimmy started but was picked up by everyone who joined the tribe. Jimmy shared, "Our employees share our passion for what we are doing, and that is reflected in product quality. At one time, we had 160 employees. The forklift driver and the lady making mouth calls, they all would get frustrated if they couldn't get orders out. When we got bought out in December 2006, the new owners wanted to farm out customer service, but Will and I fought that tooth and nail. Our families have been a big part of our success, supporting what we did. We were away from home a lot; there was sacrifice. So many people cheered us on in the early days, and we met a lot of great people along the way. The hunting industry is just not that big, and relationships are important."

In that sense, any award for someone at PRIMOS® can be shared and celebrated by all who have ties to the company. A tribute that especially touched Will Primos was given in 2017 when he was inducted into the Mississippi Outdoor Hall of Fame. Billy Johnson, the executive director of the Mississippi Wildlife Heritage Foundation, said about Primos, "He is one of the most humble, modest, generous ambassadors that the state of Mississippi has ever produced. Long after all of us are gone, Will Primos' footprint will be here."

Mary and Will Primos at Primos' 2017 Mississippi Outdoor Hall of Fame Induction

While reluctantly talking about the honors he has received, Will shared, "Cuz, he called me a year and a half ago and said the National Hunting Hall of Fame at Bass Pro in Springfield, Missouri, wanted to induct me. They had reached out to me, but I didn't want to do it." Cuz informed him, "They don't understand why you won't become part of this," to which Primos gave his patent answer, "It's not about me." Through Cuz's encouragement, Primos agreed to the induction the following year. Primos may be realizing that the recognition extended to him validates the people around him who helped him do what he did. It also includes the staunch supporters and admirers who have been part of the company's journey. I liken it to rooting for a sports team: we love the brand and what it stands for and want to be part of a winning team.

The moment Jimmy considers his most significant honor was, "After the 9-11 attack in 2001, Will and I saw an interview with one of the few survivors that had been trapped in the rubble of the World Trade Center. Will Jimeno was a Port Authority Police Officer whose squad had gone in to help when the towers collapsed on top of them. So, all the politicians and media came in to pay respects and told him he'd become a celebrity. They attempted to cheer him up by telling him the New York Yankees team would like to come meet him and asked who else he'd like to meet." To Will's and Jimmy's enduring shock and surprise, he said, "I'd really like to meet those PRIMOS® guys and Mossy Oak guys!" We are good friends to this day," said Jimmy.

PRIMOS® fans were in abundance and growing and in 2000 construction of a 54,000-square-foot building in Flora, MS; before it was completed in 2005 it expanded to 110,000 square feet to keep up with the company's rapid growth. Then, in 2005, they had to expand again to about 110,000 square feet to keep up with the company's rapid growth. In many industries, the price of success is consolidation and buyouts. The game call industry is no exception. PRIMOS® is just one of the game call companies that grew so big and fast it caught investors' eye. Jimmy said, "To grow a company is like gas to an auto, the more gas you give it the faster it goes. We got to a point where to grow was going take a lot of gas." Primos added, "We were debt-free in 2002; we didn't want to go back into debt. We had reached a plateau in what we were doing and were gonna have'ta expand into other categories of hunting products. Will adds, "We had a guy reach out to me, a mergers and acquisitions guy. He turned out to be very honest, but it took four years to get everything aligned to sell in 2006."

A private equity group out of Chicago bought PRIMOS® for millions of dollars. It's remarkable for a company that started with one man sledgehammering out one aluminum diaphragm frame at a time on his garage floor. Jimmy said, "The private equity model worked for us because they provided financial backing for a few years to help us grow but left us in place as management." Will added, "I still worked for the company for another few years as President. Jimmy stayed in his role as Chief Operating Officer, and we had a little stock from that going forward until we were later sold a second time."

Jimmy Primos socializing and playing an old PRIMOS® YAWK BOX at the 2020 NWTF Convention

With PRIMOS® continued growth after their purchase, the private equity group cashed in on their investment in 2011 by selling PRIMOS® to Bushnell. Primos had taken the operation from his garage to a business with 140 employees and revenues of nearly $60 million. In turn, Bushnell got bought out by ATK, the company that owned Federal Ammunition, amongst other brands. Jimmy told me, "ATK had started to expand their market share in the outdoor industry and wanted to be the biggest player. They were a large company already; part of their company even made aerospace rockets! To meet their goals, they spun off the aerospace and defense businesses and then reformed as Vista Outdoors about 2015. They had the biggest footprint at the SHOT Show. PRIMOS® is actually still part of the Bushnell group within Vista Outdoors." That second sale officially ended Will and Jimmy's ownership; however, they remain outstanding brand ambassadors.

Don't kid yourselves; Will and Jimmy may be successful businessmen, but they are still hunters before that. I asked Jimmy what he loves and fears about turkey hunting today. "I love hunting turkeys," he quickly responded. "I am 76 years old and don't get around like I used to. It is not as much about killing for me now; I just love being there when someone gets one. What I don't like is someone that takes more than the limit; there are some who make it about how many. That's not me."

Will, too, is quick to identify himself as a turkey hunter, though he is grateful for his additional time with family these days. Primos is grateful for the course of his life and conceded to me that he is one of a few 'outliers' in the game call world. That refers to Malcolm Gladwell's book, *Outliers*; Primos is a perfect example of an outlier. As defined in the book, such individuals accomplish things that go beyond the realm of the ordinary. In Primos' case, he told me he was enabled to achieve what he did based on "God's timing. If I had done what I did twenty years earlier or later, I couldn't have done it! Like Bill Gates couldn't have done what he did if a computer house wouldn't have let him come to program computers at night, which became the story of Microsoft. There was a tremendous amount of luck in our timeline and the technology available to us."

Primos also recognized that "The return of the wild turkey captured the imagination and spirit of the public. The NWTF and Tom Kelly's book *Tenth Legion*, both in 1973, helped get the word out." He pointed out the perfect timing of the audiocassette as a technology for him to instruct others. Then, the videocassette brings actual footage into people's homes, helping him create interest in his products. "We benefited from technologies coming from auto parts molding and improvements to production equipment for mass production that were incredibly precise. That technology became available to the public at the right time for us."

What should we expect in the future from PRIMOS®? Some classic best-selling calls like The Heart Breaker, Lil' Heartbreaker, The Freak Crystal, and The Jackpot Slate are now being resurrected under the PRIMOS® Select line of calls. I would ask you, the reader, to ponder a question: What if there were no PRIMOS®? I, for one, can't imagine it. It would have altered how I learned through their video and audiotapes and my success early on in the woods with a PRIMOS® Power Crystal and Lil' Heart Breaker box call. It would take back moments of anticipation as I waited for the next year of "The Truth" to come out, and the handshakes with all the PRIMOS® HUNTING crew at conventions and being part of a crowd of fans waiting to have things signed. It would steal so many smiles and memories, not to mention the countless people supported by that company, the many innovations brought to game call manufacturing, and the benefits to the wild turkey and our hunting culture made by the generosity of Primos and his company. A world, especially a turkey-hunting world, without PRIMOS® is sobering to consider!

Thanks to Will Primos, I am including the PRIMOS® Mission Statement at the end of the chapter. Note commitments numbers four through six in support of the mission he put forth, as I think you will recognize the essence of Will Primos in those: **A commitment to listen. A commitment to do our part. A commitment to do what is right.**

Here, it is also important to revisit Primos' affection for the movie and message of *Jeremiah Johnson*, which go well beyond one of mere pop culture interest. In a sense, Will Primos is in that story. "It is the story of mankind, the story of all of us," he had told me. "Things don't go well, and we struggle. It is about the ultimate sacrifice and forgiveness." Primos' life is a study of those principles, as he has pushed through challenges in life and business but kept his true north fixed on living as a Christian in all aspects of his life, which he admits has been blessed. To Will and Team PRIMOS®, I would like to say, "Mission Accomplished!"

YELP & GOBBLE, INC.

PRIMOS® HUNTING TIMELINE

(* = approximate date)

1929 – Angelo "Pop" Primos, Will and Jimmy's grandfather, a Greek immigrant, opens a restaurant in Jackson, MS. Pop would grow the business to multiple restaurants run by his family.

1947 – Jimmy Primos is born March 13 in Jackson, MS to Aleck and Billie Claude Primos.

1952 – Will Primos is born March 2 to Kenneth and Mary Ann Primos.

1959 – 12-year-old Jimmy Primos takes 7-year-old Will Primos on a blackbird hunt. The hunt creates in Will a love for the hunt and an appreciation for the food at his table.

1963 – A duck hunt with his Uncle Gus leads a young Will Primos to investigate how game calls work and make his first game call. "It all started with duck calls in 1963," Will has since said of the significance of this event.

1969 – Jimmy graduates from the University of Mississippi.

1969-1972 – Jimmy Primos enters the Marine Corps and serves as an officer (2nd Lt.) in Vietnam in 1970 to 1971. He then becomes a broker with Merril Lynch, later getting into real estate.

1970 – 18-year-old Will Primos joins the Air Force. After taking his aptitude test he becomes a Marksmanship Instructor.

1972 – The movie *Jeremiah Johnson* is released, which Will Primos has since watched thousands of times.

1973 – Jimmy Primos kills his first wild turkey in Pike County, MS. Tom Kelly releases his book Tenth Legion, which inspires Will Primos, and many since.

1974 – Eleanor Roessler shows Will Primos the triple-stacked framed mouth calls she makes for hunters; that and a double-stacked framed call by Brossie Dantone get him interested in mouth call design. He begins experimenting with making mouth calls on his garage floor, just selling to friends. Will Primos graduates with a business degree from Belhaven University in Jackson, MS.

1974-988 – Will Primos works at the family restaurant while starting his game call business, but he doesn't take money out of the game call business; he lets it continue to grow.

1975* – Will Primos calls up his first wild turkey by himself. He also first sells the mouth calls he is making to a dealer.

1976 – While continuing to work at the family restaurant, Will Primos starts his game call company.

1976-1984 – PRIMOS YELPERS becomes the first name of the company.

1976-2001 – Jackson, MS, is the company location.

PRIMOS® HUNTING

1977-1984 – The YAWK BOX is made for PRIMOS YELPERS by Rev. Wiley Reid; this and other calls (like the Forney Bros. Dual Reflector pot call and Kenny Morgan's tube call) are resold by the game call company to expand their revenue and consumer base. Those same years, Will Primos had a hen and gobbler that he raised, Conway and Loretta. He studied them to have a deeper understanding of their language.

1981 – Miss Vivian Latta gifts Will Primos a Gibson box (it was the first box call patented, in 1898) that belonged to her father. He promises to share it with others, which he will do in 2018 (see that entry).

1985-1986 – PRIMOS YELPERS name evolves within this period as follows: PRIMOS YELPERS, INC., PRIMOS, INC., PRIMOS & COMPANY, PRIMOS GAME CALLS, PRIMOS GAME CALLS AND ACCESSORIES.

1986 – PRIMOS® endorses Mossy Oak and in 1987 Will Primos and Toxey Haas would be featured in an ad together. An incredible era of partnership and growth is started that continues today.

1986-1987 – PRIMOS gets a video camera in 1986; with the help of Boyd Burrow, they release and instructional video, "Spring Turkey Hunting with Primos: A Video Textbook" in 1987. The first deer call was also released as the company expanded.

1987-1993 – PRIMOS WILD GAME CALLS is now the company's name as the business grows.

1988-2017 – The first hunting video in what would become a PRIMOS® series phenomenon, "The Truth About Spring Turkey Hunting," launches. The series runs 28 seasons on VHS and (later) DVD. Boyd Burrow, Ronnie "Cuz" Strickland, Chuck Jones, Ron Jolly, Jeff Sherwood, and many others would gather footage and lead the Video Division at the company.

1990-2012 – Brad Farris starts working part-time as a videographer in 1990, then comes to PRIMOS® full-time in 1997 to continue "The Truth" video series and launch *PRIMOS® TRUTH About Hunting* on the Outdoor Channel in 1999; even now he is one of the pillars of the show and is a fan favorite. He is one of Will Primos' closest friends.

1994-1995 – PRIMOS WILD GAME CALLS name changes to PRIMOS, INC.

1995 – The PRIMOS® Battey World Class premieres; that call design by Mike Battey continues to be sold as the Ol' Betsy.

1996-1998 – PRIMOS, INC. and PRIMOS HUNTING CALLS AND ACCESSORIES appear as the company name.

1997-1999 – *For the Woods!* ™ is the game call company's slogan.

1999-current – PRIMOS® TRUTH About Hunting premieres on Outdoor Channel and is still in production. PRIMOS® launches another pot call designed by Mike Battey; the PRIMOS® Power Crystal, which is still in production. The PRIMOS® Heart Breaker, designed by Anthony Foster, is introduced; that call has recently been brought back under the PRIMOS® Select line. A strong year!

1999-2010 – PRIMOS® HUNTING CALLS is now the name of the game call company.

2000-current – *Speak the Language*™ is now the company slogan.

2000-2021 – The Flora, MS facility is built, which started at 54,000 square feet and, during construction, expanded to 110,000 square feet to keep up with the company's rapid growth.

2002 – Anthony Foster's White Feather callmaking business in Flora, MS, is purchased from Foster and is brought in-house as part of PRIMOS®.

2003 – Will Primos commemorates the 200th anniversary of the Lewis and Clark expedition and takes a bull elk using a reproduction of the .54 caliber flintlock carbine designed for Lewis & Clark. That hunt is featured on the DVD by PRIMOS®, "Big Bulls 6."

2006 – A private equity group out of Chicago bought PRIMOS® for millions of dollars. Will Primos stays on as President, and Jimmy stays on as Chief Operating Officer. Both keep some equity interest going forward.

2007 – Mossy Oak releases the Dixon vest honoring the late Bob Dixon. He was beloved at PRIMOS®; PRIMOS® makes a Limited Edition of 100 Battleship box calls for the first 100 vests.

2011 – With PRIMOS® doubling their sales after their purchase, the private equity group cashed in on their investment in 2011 by selling PRIMOS® to Bushnell. Shortly thereafter, Bushnell gets bought out by ATK for 1 billion dollars. That sale officially ended Will and Jimmy's ownership; however, they remain outstanding brand ambassadors for PRIMOS®.

PRIMOS® HUNTING

2011-current – PRIMOS® HUNTING is now the company's official name as the extensive product line has grown to include hundreds of products for hunters.

2014-2017 – The limited edition Grand Slam box and pot call series is sold, a different sub-species of wild turkey each year for four years. This would lead to the PRIMOS® Custom Mill Shop.

2015 – ATK spins off its space-based rocket technology and emerges with all outdoor products under the Vista Outdoors brand.

2017 – Will Primos is inducted into the Mississippi Outdoor Hall of Fame.

2018 – Anthony Foster and Will Primos make replicas of the Henry Gibson box call that Will had been gifted to help the National Wild Turkey Federation raise money for conservation.

2022-current – Brookhaven, MS, is now where game calls are produced; the company offices are now in Madison, MS.

2023 – Mossy Oak releases the Mr. Fox vest in honor of Fox Haas; PRIMOS® makes a limited number of Fox Haas 1944 box calls for the launch of the vest. Now with 41 brands, Vista Outdoors splits; PRIMOS® becomes part of their new outdoor products collective, Revelyst, Inc.

PRIMOS® MISSION STATEMENT

Primos® mission and goal is to make each and every customer successful at selling Primos® Products.

The following three circles and where they intersect define and clarify our focus in order to complete our mission.

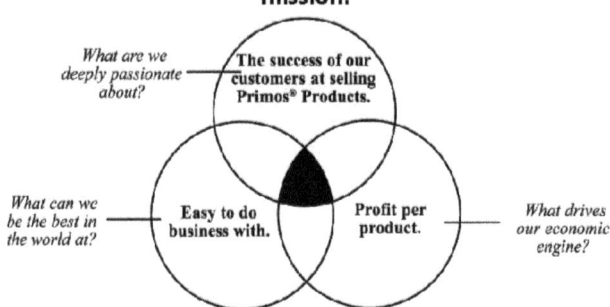

GOALS

What are our goals at Primos® Hunting Calls™ that allow us to accomplish our mission?

We design, build, package and inventory solid hunting products that are shipped on time. These products are then backed by intensive marketing that brands not only the mind, but the heart as well. The final goal in our mission is to provide support and service to all of our customers.

COMPANY PRINCIPLES THAT KEEP US ON AUTO PILOT

Our foundation is based on two principles that ensure we are headed toward fulfilling our mission and goals on a minute-by-minute basis:

FIRST: Primos® recognizes the value of all employees. Without employees, there would be no company.
We strive to provide safe working conditions, as well as competitive salaries and benefits.
Employees include all Primos® staff, Prostaff and manufacturer's representatives.

SECOND: Primos® recognizes the important role our vendors play in supplying raw materials and parts to build our products.
We strive to provide an efficient, timely service and payment to each of our vendors.

These two principles create a full-circle effect where each employee and vendor involved with Primos® is on auto pilot to achieve our goals and accomplish our mission. If Primos® takes care of its employees and vendors, they will in return, take care of our customers on a daily basis.

COMPANY PRIORITIES THAT DEFINE OUR CULTURE

Every business has a culture. That culture is defined by the leadership and management of the company.
If we truly care about our customers and their success, our attitude will reflect that and will be defined by the priorities we set for our daily work. Below is a list of company priorities that define Primos® culture.

1. A commitment to a sense of urgency to take care of our business no matter what our individual job may be.
2. A commitment to say yes or no on a timely basis.

3. A commitment to answer emails promptly, to return phone calls and to communicate in general.
4. A commitment to listen.
5. A commitment to do our part.
6. A commitment to do what is right.
7. A commitment to look for opportunity, especially in the face of obstacles.
8. A commitment of understanding that things are going to change.
   We must change, adjust, keep up and keep on growing. We must be a part of the solution and not the problem.
9. A commitment to build and package each and every product like it is the one WE would buy.
10. A commitment to provide inventory year-round, which enables us to ship 100% complete 12 months a year.
11. A commitment to plan for tomorrow so that our company may grow profitably and in turn, provide more opportunity for our employees and vendors.
12. A commitment to keep our business fun and rewarding; and to change things if it stops being fun and rewarding.
13. A commitment to always remember that:
    IT'S NOT ABOUT PRIMOS®; IT'S ABOUT THE CUSTOMER!!!

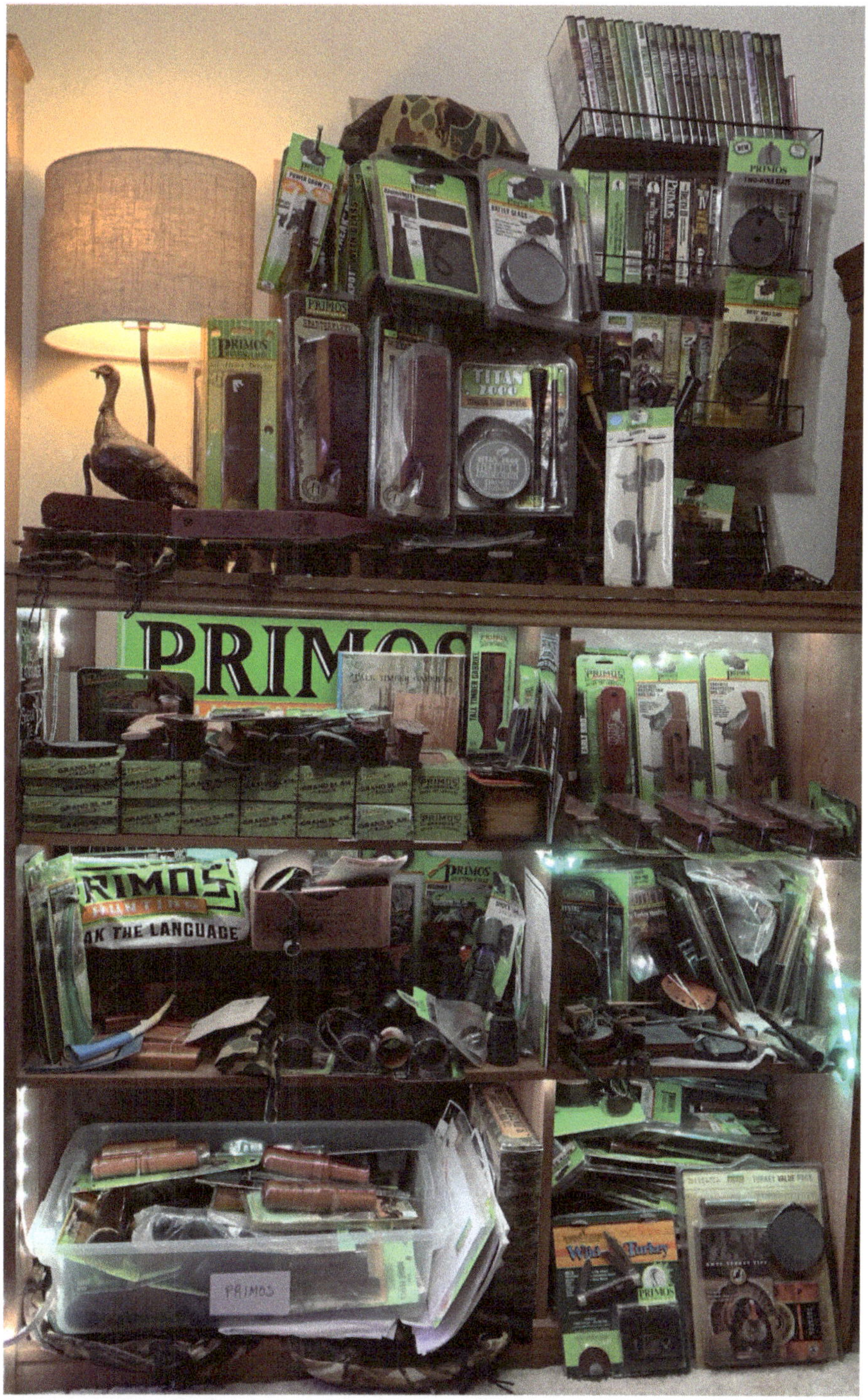

The author's collection of PRIMOS® game calls and products

Photo by Brent Rogers

YELP & GOBBLE, INC.

Chapter 3

QUAKER BOY®

The young hunter shivered, and not just due to the spring dawn's chill. The tremors were first triggered by the guttural snarling of coyotes at a nearby deer carcass. After a brief and welcome silence, a wild turkey cock's boisterous gobble shattered the stillness. In his excitement, he was shivering again.

He had watched the videos, read the books, and peppered the older turkey hunters he knew with questions in preparation for this moment. Nothing he had learned had prepared him for the smallness he felt now when he might soon be under the wary bird's scrutinous gaze. He had observed the gobbler from a distance when scouting before the season opened. The strutting bird's feathers had shimmered in the sunlight as it pirouetted in the field. Roosted in the dark forest canopy above him, it seemed a more intimidating presence now. He shifted the diaphragm call in his mouth, re-positioning it from the inside of his cheek to the roof of the mouth.

The gobbling continued intermittently, causing his pulse to quicken even more until the young man heard wings flapping. He was pretty sure this was the turkey flying down. His mouth went dry, and the eagerness to use the call faltered. He overcame his apprehension by focusing on

The late Dick Kirby, founder of QUAKER BOY®

the cadence of the hen yelps he wanted to make. He had practiced and practiced with the QUAKER BOY® diaphragm, to the chagrin of his family. As he called now, his last yelp was cut off by a thundering gobble, causing the youth to recoil with surprise and euphoria. A turkey hunter was made for life.

After being introduced to a gobbling turkey, many hunters have just such a first-encounter experience to covet. I didn't kill that particular bird, but it didn't matter. The details are forever etched into my gray matter; it changed my identity going forward. "Turkey hunter" moved alongside other ways people would know and refer to me. I took great pride in being referred to in that manner, and still do. Part of that experience will forever include the tools I used, like that QUAKER BOY® mouth call. Years later, when I would meet Dick Kirby at the National Wild Turkey Federation's (NWTF) National Convention, it was like meeting a celebrity. Here was the man whose company produced that very call, and the personalized boat paddle I got from him at the Convention served me well in the woods for years.

Richard "Dick" Kirby died tragically in 2010 from unexpected complications and a weeks-long coma resulting from surgery. His wife, Beverly "Bev" Kirby, would head the family business until their son, Christian "Chris" Kirby, and his wife Michelle bought QUAKER BOY® from Bev when she retired in 2020. Chris had been doing much to help run the company for years and proudly told me, "We are the last original owned and operated major game call company with calls made in the U.S. We are still the American Dream."

Like others of his peer group highlighted in this book, native New Yorker Dick Kirby's life was inextricably changed by an encounter with the wild turkey. Kirby was fortuitously born on November 28, 1942, which would position him perfectly in time and place for his future. Had he been born even a couple of decades earlier or later, he may not have had the same opportunity to become a leader in wild turkey game calls.

In 1708, just eighty-two years after the Dutch established New Amsterdam (now part of Manhattan), the colony of New York had to issue protection orders for their once-abundant wild turkeys, ruffed grouse, and heath hens. The heath hen is now extinct, and the state's last remaining native wild turkeys were extirpated by the mid-1840s. Over-hunting and heavy deforestation, a problem for tree-roosting species like wild turkeys, resulted in a New York that did not have the habitat to support wild turkeys. Only after some farms were abandoned as people moved to urban centers did enough trees, shrubs, and grasses again grow to support wild turkeys' life cycle.

According to New York's Department of Environmental Conservation, it was around 1948 when wild turkeys from a small remnant population in northern Pennsylvania crossed the border into their state, the first after an absence of one hundred years! In 1959, the New York State Conservation Department, led by the late biologist Fred Evans, began a trap and transfer program for wild turkeys to grow and expand the flock. A limited fall season in New York was established in 1959. Fall was accepted as the traditional time to hunt turkeys, but

NY Wildlife biologist Fred Evans with a wild turkey to transplant

Plaque commemorating the first turkey transfer in NY at Allegany State Park

spring turkey hunting had roots in the deep south. In 1898, of the twenty-eight states that had defined wild turkey seasons, eleven southern states had seasons that stretched into March, April, or May. Chris pointed out, "Turkey season is the ONLY spring hunting season! People are ready to get out of the house and get out in the woods." New York's first spring season would finally be set in 1968. This local restoration of the wild turkey would lead a barber and a beautician to follow their hearts and wade into the unfamiliar territory of game call production.

Kirby was one of four children born to Clarence and Hazel Kirby, who raised their family south of Buffalo, NY. Kirby was taught to appreciate the outdoors by a father who enjoyed hunting and fishing. Later, he would pass that love of hunting and the outdoors on to his children, Scott, Chris, and Rebecca. One of the things now most recollected about Kirby was his passion for educating and helping beginning hunters, including sportsmanship. A profoundly spiritual man, he wore his devotion to his Savior on his sleeve; he was known to wear a "He's First" patch in the form of a cross amongst the various outdoor patches on his clothing.

He nurtured a musical gift through his singing and used that within his church, where he would meet his future wife while singing in the choir. Kirby's musical ear continued to be an asset that would serve him well in turkey calling competitions and callmaking. Like many of his Vietnam-era countrymen, he enlisted in the National Guard and served as a barber. With his marriage to Bev on April 24, 1965, Kirby's foundational values of faith, family, service, and love of the outdoors would continue and support his future endeavors. Incidentally, had he had the opportunity for turkey hunting before that time, I suspect his wedding may not have fallen during the spring turkey season in much of the country! Dick and Bev Kirby would raise their family in Orchard Park, NY, where their future business would be based.

Dick Kirby as a young outdoorsman

As a youth, I felt a kinship with the QUAKER BOY® brand and imagery, as I was raised attending a Society of Friends (Quaker) church, albeit in rural Iowa. Though the Kirby's were dedicated Wesleyans, the town of Orchard Park was founded by Quakers seeking an agricultural and quiet community life. They began settling there in the first decade of the 1800s. "Our school mascot is a Quaker," Chris Kirby told me. "When Mom and Dad formed their business as a barber and a beautician, Dad framed up and closed in the front porch of our house on W. Quaker Street, and they hung out the shingles for the Quaker Boy Barber Shop and Quaker Girl Beauty Shop." Little did Dick Kirby know then that he and a fellow barber featured in this book, Harold Knight of Kentucky, would soon retire their scissors as the wild turkey would redirect their lives.

A passionate outdoorsman, Dick Kirby pursued just about everything locally with fins, feathers, and fur that he could fish, hunt, or trap. The opportunity to hunt wild turkeys locally wasn't yet possible while he was growing up. But the story of how he started QUAKER BOY® can't be told without explaining his initiation into the sport of turkey hunting. Chris told me who broke that ice; "Bob Wozniak took Dad on his first turkey hunt in 1971, and Dad heard one gobble. That got him!"

Bob further explained, "I worked for the New York State Environmental Department. We had some wild turkeys migrate up from Pennsylvania into the Allegany State Park area, and then wildlife biologist Fred Evans set up a trap and transfer program. We started moving them around the state. Helping with that, I got very interested in turkeys, and in hunting them. I knew a guy who had been stationed in Alabama for military service, and he learned to hunt turkeys there. So, I learned from him and read everything I could get my hands on. I have the unique position of taking Dick Kirby out and helping him kill his first turkey."

Wozniak told me the details about his and Kirby's turkey hunting "origin stories," which would intertwine. Wozniak had called in his first turkey in Pennsylvania's inaugural spring season in 1967. "My brother-in-law Bob Mazuca had a cousin that flew helicopters to check gas lines for leaks; while visiting this friend the evening before the season opened, he informed me he'd seen a small flock of turkeys on a bench just below the top of a big hill near Galeton, (north and central) Pennsylvania. Also at his house was a Deputy Game Warden, and when I decided that's where I'd go, the warden asked if he could come."

Having a Deputy Game Warden along for a first turkey hunt might be disconcerting for some, but given Bob's vocation, he was glad to have the company. "We met early the next morning, where the gas line crossed the road, and headed up," Bob recalled. "We set up at the base of a hemlock tree, which made it darker than the open gas line. The gobbler ended up being roosted right above us. He flew down into the cut, and it was still early. The warden was watching his watch as it wasn't legal shooting hours. When he said, "Now," I shot, and it was still dark enough that flames leaped out of the muzzle!"

Dick Kirby in 1971, admiring the first of many wild turkeys he would harvest

New York had their first season in 1968, and Wozniak would be among those who took a bird in that hunt. Kirby entered the picture after Wozniak's third successful New York spring turkey season in 1970. Wozniak said, "Dick was my barber. We always talked about fishing and hunting when I was getting my hair cut. He said my enthusiasm about wild turkeys was so infectious that he wanted to go with me. It was a two-week season then, and you could only hunt 'til noon. Dick was off on Wednesdays from the Barbershop, so we went out that first Wednesday of 1971. The first place we went, I called in a hen. We then went to another place, and there I called up a gobbler. The turkey was just standing there looking at him twenty-five yards away, and he missed it! It flew, and he downed it with his second shot. The following two years, I called a bird in for him again; then I told Dick it was time for him to call in his bird, which he told me he was intending to do."

But Wozniak's part in the story is far from over. "The first calls I bought and used, including those I used when I took Dick out, were Penn's Woods diaphragms. I had to buy a dozen calls to get two good ones; they were inconsistent." Dick had told him, "We can do better than that," and encouraged Wozniak to make some calls with him. Wozniak had recently got cedar siding put on his house, and they used the discarded aluminum siding to fashion the frames of the first calls, along with latex cut from gloves for the reed."

Kirby was relentless in his obsession to master the mouth call. I could hear the amusement in his voice when Wozniak told me, "When we went trout fishing together, I had to take aspirin

Bob Wozniak and Dick Kirby proudly display wild turkeys in 1970s

along, as Dick would be blowing those calls all the time, enough to give me a headache!" The men were genuine students in their approach, as through his job, Wozniak had a lot of recordings of wild turkeys. They used a tape recorder to record their calling and judged it against the voices of those wild turkeys.

Those first hand-made calls in 1975 would begin to attract attention. Kirby's first sale of calls was to a trapping supply store. Wozniak told me, "We made the owner up a couple dozen calls and he wrote a check out to Dick for $100. Dick couldn't wait to get home and show Bev, as that was a lot of money to us then." She had understandably found his excitement for this new hobby amusing at first. Wozniak continued, "When we walked in, he showed the check to Bev and said, "Look at this, you can't laugh at us now." Bev gladly grabbed the check and said, "Great, I'm going grocery shopping!"

Putting food on the family table turned this hobby into a noble pursuit. "It became his passion," Wozniak said, "His farsightedness was tremendous in what making turkey calls could become. Dick talked about making it into a business. I told him, "It is a pain in the butt when guys come over late in the evening wanting a call." But Kirby's response to him was prophetic, "There are a lot more than just the guys around here that want to buy turkey calls!" Kirby doubled his efforts, but the process was painstakingly slow. It involved cutting horseshoe-shaped frames out of that aluminum siding with tin snips. He then inserted pieces of a pink balloon between the upper and lower frames to serve as the reed and secured it with duct tape around the frame's outer edges. Chris recalled, "Through his connections in the barbershop, he started making more for other people. This is when the NWTF was starting, and he began attending a few local sports shows. Dad's big breakthrough came by leveraging better technology for the rate-limiting part of the process of cutting out the frames."

Acquiring a punch press through friend Doug Oak allowed Kirby to make calls significantly faster while increasing the consistency of quality. He now had the means to make enough calls available to market them. "There are business owners that plan and do the numbers. Others are artists with a vision, and that was Dad," Chris told me. "There wasn't a business plan, but there was a passion that was aggressively pursued once he started down that road. The demand for his calls created the business opportunity that led Dad and Mom to start QUAKER BOY® Game Calls as a side business."

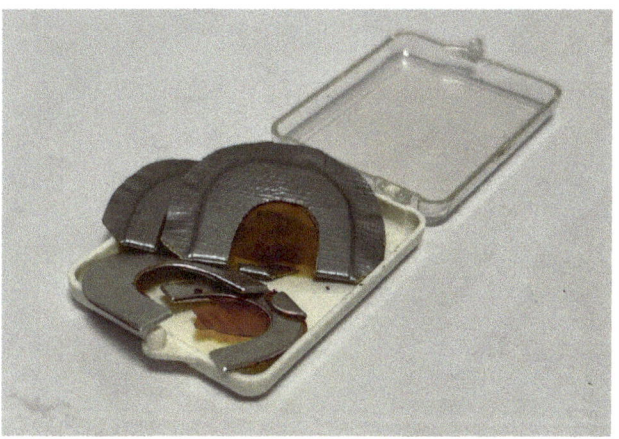

Some of the first diaphragm calls that Dick Kirby made at his kitchen table

Make no mistake, while Dick's face would be most visible, the business was a joint effort between him and Bev. Chris emphasized, "The most important person at QUAKER BOY® was, and is, my Mom. She kept products getting built and managed the hiring and firing, all while keeping up a house with three kids. This allowed Dad to be out promoting, teaching seminars, and selling. Bev is the glue holding it all together. She is still doing great in retirement and stays busy with grandkids." Paul Butski, who competed against Dick in calling competitions, and who would be a significant part of the future business, saw firsthand how vital Bev and Dick's partnership was to their success. Paul said, "Bev was Dick's right-hand man, in a sense. She pushed him. She went to a lot of calling competitions with him and the boys. In 1981, we all went to

The industrious Bev Kirby helped raise a family and a business

Dick and Bev Kirby

Chris Kirby as an aspiring turkey hunter

the SHOT Show in New Orleans, pulling a trailer of mouth calls to sell at our booth. It was Dick, Bev, Chris, myself, and my wife Halina all together. My wife babysat Chris. He was so little; she took him all around New Orleans!"

Chris Kirby was pretty much reared in the culture of turkey hunting. He was only 5 or 6 years old when his Dad took him on his first trip to the woods in pursuit of wild turkeys. Chris recollected, "That was in the 1970s, before the availability of the video camera, and that day, we were going to shoot turkeys with a camera instead of a gun." Chris was already showing signs of an intense interest in the outdoors and was eager to do something his Dad was passionate about. "When we heard a gobble some distance away, I looked at Dad, thinking this was pretty cool! He hurriedly threw a camo tarp over me, all the while the turkey is getting closer, until the woods seemed like they were exploding with gobbles. I was getting nervous, and when this big, black-bodied, red-headed creature emerged, I could have crawled into the tree-I would have done it! I was terrified! I guess I have gotten over my fear of the wild turkey and gotten even with a lot of them!" Chris chuckled.

Not that Chris, or Dick for that matter, ever had a grudge against wild turkeys. Although Dick Kirby was fiercely competitive and reveled in the joy of a successful hunt, the Kirby family has a deep appreciation for the wild turkey. "That gobble is infectious," Chris relayed to me. "Pressing the trigger is part of it, but conservation is part of hunting, and no true hunter wants all the animals

*Scott and Chris Kirby with their father, Dick Kirby.
The wild turkey would infuse pleasure and work into the family's lives.*

dead." That may seem paradoxical to those whose roots aren't established in the tradition of hunting as part of a healthy lifestyle. Driving to the store to pick up groceries someone else grew or killed and then packaged so that the consumer is presented with a nice, clean product is a detachment from reality. Hunters learn the value of life through understanding the cost of taking one to preserve their own. And it is well documented that hunters played a crucial role in funding and working to restore the wild turkey.

Dick Kirby would build a reputation as a master turkey hunter. He traveled the United States for the rest of his life, hunting all four primary subspecies of wild turkeys (Eastern, Osceola, Rio Grande, and Merriam's) in their native haunts. He would establish an unprecedented feat for the time, achieving twenty-seven straight annual "Grand Slams," where he harvested all four subspecies yearly. Competitive in all he did, Kirby would complete Slams exclusively using a ten gauge shotgun, twelve gauge shotgun, a muzzleloader, a .44 Magnum handgun, and archery equipment. In some years, he would achieve double, triple, and quadruple Slams. Helping to drive Kirby's early success was his affinity for competitive turkey calling. He had jumped in with both feet after he had experienced the gobble of a wild turkey, attending

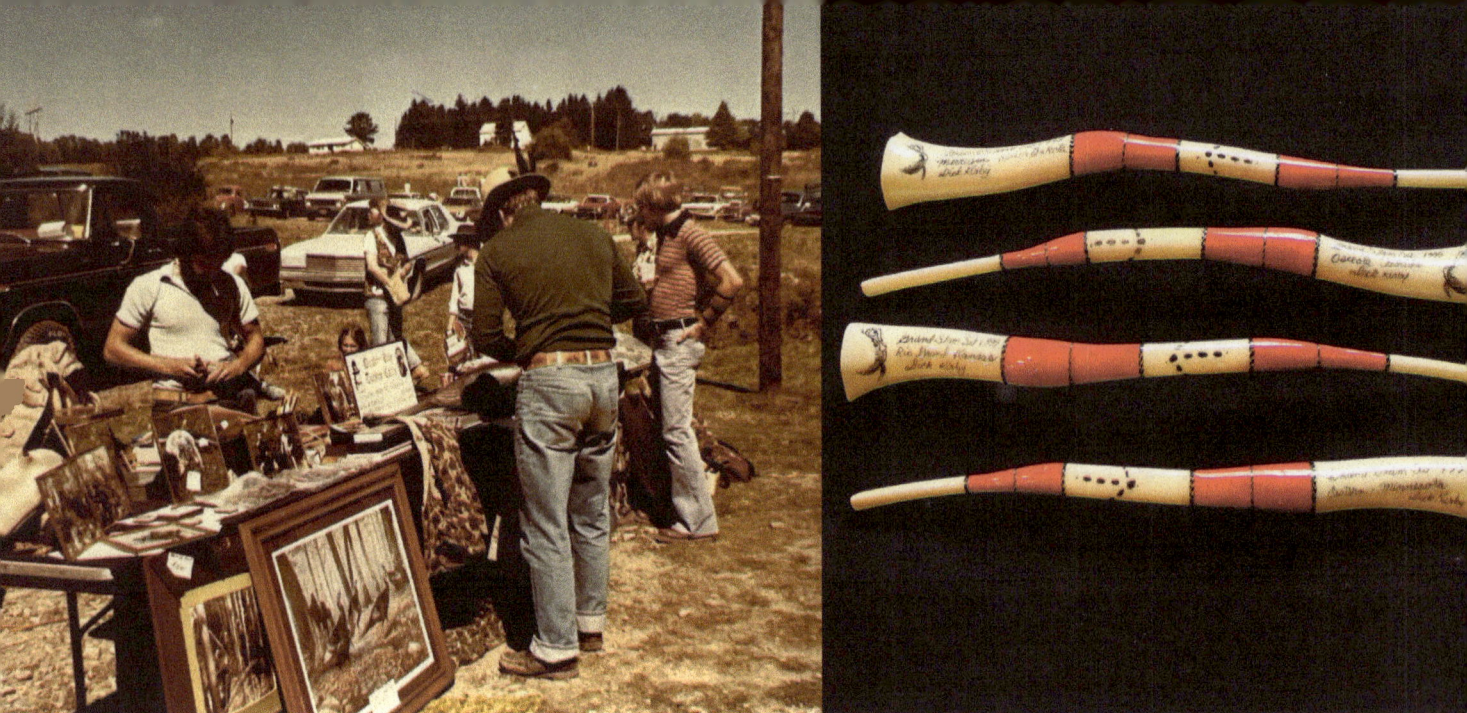

The Kirby family traveled to sell turkey hunting products to the rapidly growing number of turkey hunters following the restoration of the wild turkey

Dick Kirby made and sold many Grand Slam call se including wingbone calls such as these

The traveling turkey hunter: Dick Kirby sold calls and hunted gobblers from coast to coast

every venue he could that hosted a calling competition. Chris recalled attending a turkey call competition in Blaine, Pennsylvania, early on as a family. "The stage was a hay wagon, and they would pack cannons full of straw and shoot them off for fun. It was great! Local NWTF Chapters would host them; they didn't have to be fancy. If there was a competition, we loaded up the station wagon, camped in a campground, called in the contest, and then sold calls out of the back of the car."

The calling competitions were a turkey hunting hub. Chris acknowledged, "Rob Keck, who became CEO at the NWTF, as well as others, recognized the importance of calling to the turkey and the turkey hunter. A turkey calling contest at its root is a teaching tool," he shared. Far from being only about the money or the status, Chris said, "Although it is fun to compete and to win, it is not to glorify the competitor or their calling." Such competitions had been around for decades, but before the restoration of the wild turkey, such competitions were smaller and localized to a few areas. Chris continued, "In the early 1970s, we were in an era where there were yet few books and magazine articles on turkeys and no shows about them. People would attend the events because they began seeing turkeys and heard about turkey hunting." This interested hunting public would gather at calling competitions to learn the basic language of wild turkeys and to connect and learn from other hunters. Chris said, "They were inspired to learn new types of calls, like mouth calls. I get a kick out of people that think there is no way they can do it, but you give 'em a diaphragm, and next thing you know, they are making sounds and start to gain confidence."

In addition to places in the southern U.S. like Mobile, Alabama, and Yellville, Arkansas, there was a strong wild turkey calling culture in Perry County, Pennsylvania. Turkeys there had never been extirpated, and one of that county's native sons, Rob Keck, recalls when he first encountered an eager Dick Kirby. "I did a radio show, WBEN Buffalo, right after I won the World Championship. The first half hour, we talked about turkey hunting, and the second half of the show was a call-in. Most were pranksters, but a barber from Orchard Park called in and was interested in learning more about calling." Keck and Kirby would meet, and Keck recalled, "Dick stayed at my home (in Pennsylvania). I introduced him to a lot of the Perry County callers. There, he and others learned not only turkey calling but how to improve mouth calls. For instance, Chester "Chet" Lesh could show them how to get the mouth call frames to clamp the rubber reed properly."

Hunters today may not appreciate how everything was a mystery at that time with turkey hunting. There had been no turkeys for most to hunt for a couple of generations. Paul Butski, who would have a future with QUAKER BOY®, recalled, "Back then, we mostly used box calls, like the Roger Latham box from Penn's Woods, and there was only a fall season." Chris emphasized, "There were no true turkey vests or guns back in that day. Dad would hunt with a ten-gauge mag shotgun. Mark Banser, who was a gunsmith out of Pennsylvania would cut down barrels and put a choke in 'em, helping to develop a more specialized gun. We, as hunters and the hunting industry, created the need for a turkey section of the store. We all had a finger in it: Penn's Woods, Perfection, Scotch, and others. We went from teaching end users how to use the call to helping store owners and buyers learn so they knew how to operate and sell a call."

Calandrelli fondly recalls those first days and said, "When I started turkey hunting and calling, Dick was one of the first individuals I met. He was very outgoing and personable; he'd go out of his way to make you feel comfortable. I met him at Owego, New York, at the first competition I ever went to. It was at a sports show, and the competition was great at the time, with lots of guys from Pennsylvania and all over. Ben Lee, Jim Clay, Kelly Cooper, and the

Rohm brothers were all there. It was pretty exciting! Until then, I had no idea that Dick and I lived just forty-five minutes apart. I'd never heard of him. He was so generous. Right off, he gave me a call to use." As Calandrelli would learn, that was a good sales tactic, and it worked! He got to work practicing with the call immediately and, later that day, placed second in the competition's amateur division! "After that, he'd call me to go to competitions with him," Calandrelli happily recalled. "We'd take his vehicle, and he'd buy the food, pay for the hotel, and keep giving me calls. In return, I'd help him sell his calls."

Butski became part of the QUAKER BOY® family through his friendship with Calandrelli. "Ernie and I went to school together. I met him in seventh grade, and we've been lifelong friends," Butski told me. "We are both Niagara Falls boys. We became so passionate about turkey calling that we'd be going somewhere every weekend. Pennsylvania was really big in competitions in those days, especially with those Perry County boys like the Rohm brothers. We were all like family; we all stayed at each other's houses. Ernie introduced me to Dick in 1978 in Owego, NY, at a calling competition."

Kirby, Calandrelli, and Butski would form a bond that would transcend competitive calling.

The three amigos, Kirby, Calandrelli and Butski

The fact that they all excelled at turkey calling only drove them farther and faster. Butski said, "When we were getting involved in turkey calling competitions, I good-naturedly told Dick he was the showboat of the bunch. He was passionate, a great Christian guy, and a great friend. He was innovative, and when it came to competition, it was balls to the wall! He would put everything else on the back burner. We got good at the same time. We fed off of and helped each other."

Friendship did not set aside the reality of competition. "Dick was very competitive," laughed Ernie. "And it wasn't just with turkey calling. Anywhere we went, and whatever we did, Dick and I would make friendly side bets with sports. And he loved playing basketball. If there was a hoop somewhere we'd stay, he would play against the kids in camp and he wanted to win! In calling competitions, Dick and I went back and forth. The first one he took me to, I won. The other guys said to Dick, "Who is this guy, and why did you bring him?" Then he emphasized, "But pretty much everyone back then was friends, you looked forward to spending time together." Dick Kirby would win over 100 calling contest championships, including being a two-time Grand National Senior Division champion and a two-time Champion of Champions title-holder. He also won both the Masters' Invitational and the U.S. Open.

Though an individual sport, calling contests forged a tight bond between Kirby, Calandrelli, and Butski, leading to Kirby hiring both other men to help him part-time. Both Dick and Bev were still cutting hair and began to find that they couldn't keep up with the demand of their "hobby." Ernie said, "They first would hire me to do shows and to sell calls." Paul recalled, "I was a machinist, and the union went on strike in seventy-seven. So, after meeting Dick in 1978, I started to make calls in his basement while he was upstairs cutting hair. It was about 1980 when I went full-time." They would start to share the woods as well, letting their passion continue to lead them down the path of their destinies in the wild turkey world.

Although he was a young boy then, Chris recalls, with amazing clarity, his folks' decision when they knew they were at a crossroads. He said, "I was only 7 years old, and I know now it was a leap of faith." A revelation had come to Kirby after setting up a booth at the Harrisburg, PA, sports show in 1980. It is a huge regional show

The Kirby family displays turkey calling contest awards: Front, L to R: Rebecca, Chris, Scott. Back, L to R: Bev, Dick

The Kirby home in 1980; The Quaker Boy Barbershop sign is yet hanging above the Quaker Boy Turkey Calls sign, indicating Dick was still cutting hair at the time

that continues to this day, and the interest in turkey calls was compelling enough that Kirby would publish his first company catalog that year to reach more customers. The Kirby family had gone to one income after Bev had to close her beauty shop to raise three small children and help with her husband's turkey callmaking pet project. Dick had traditionally taken Wednesdays off from the barbershop to do other business, and now that time was spent making calls, as was every evening and spare moment.

When Dick suggested to Bev that they go into the game call business full-time, they didn't have the capital. Bev gave me a firsthand account and said, "One of the hardest things we encountered with QUAKER BOY® was getting the funds to get it started. We were young; we didn't come from money. Dick thought we could make a go of it, but we needed a loan of $2000 to start the business. It was the hardest thing to convince a bank that a turkey call company was a good idea. We talked to several before finally establishing a relationship with one." Like the other successful game call companies from the time, healthy strategic relationships were strong enablers. The one they had with Marine Midland Bank would be one such. In 1990, Dick Kirby would be honored by the bank and the U.S. Small Business Administration as the upstate New York's "Small Business Person of the Year" for his accomplishments.

So, in 1981, Dick and Bev decided that he would shut down his barber shop, and they would

The Kirby home in 1985: Dick ceased cutting hair in 1981 and the sole sign is now that of Quaker Boy, Inc; Dick originally designed the QUAKER BOY® logo for his barbershop and continued it with his hunting products business.

go into making hunting calls full-time. Kirby officially transferred the Quaker Boy name to his callmaking venture, and they worked out of their own house, as well as those of employees. By 1987, the Kirby home had been transformed into a business, and although Bev laughs about it now, she realized they needed some personal space. She said, "We had boxes and boxes of turkey supplies and turkey calls in nearly every room of our house; then it expanded up to our bedrooms." She remembers telling Dick, "Enough is enough, we have to move this out of here." In November 1988, QUAKER BOY® built a 13,400 square-foot facility at 5455 Webster Rd. in Orchard Park, NY.

It took a superhuman effort to start, maintain, and grow their fledgling company. "We just worked all the time, and we all worked," said Bev. "The first thing I had our kids do was help us fold the little instruction papers. To sell products, we had to make a name for ourselves, so we went to conventions and events everywhere. I put the kids in the old car and prayed we'd get there. We'd set up a table and sell turkey calls together. The first ten years moved so quickly, and we had to raise our kids and business at the same time. We had challenges just like everybody else." One significant hardship came when 18-year-old Scott Kirby was diagnosed with cancer. Bev said, "We weren't sure he was going to make it for several years. We had to go to Minnesota for him to have a bone marrow transplant. It took a lot of faith, prayers, and support. Everyone in QUAKER BOY® supported us; all the people who worked for QUAKER BOY® contributed. Scott survived it; it changed his life, but he enjoys hunting all the time. And some of our employees, too many to thank, have continued to work here; some have retired after thirty-year careers."

They were all wading into unknown territory. Fortunately, the Kirby family made good decisions about the people they would surround themselves with to help build their business. Dave Streb was an avid outdoorsman and a U.S. Post Master before working as the Vice President of Sales and Marketing for QUAKER BOY® in 1982. He would remain until his retirement in 2015. Calandrelli would continue to work there through his retirement, moving from part-time to full-time in 1985. Ernie said, "I was a welder, and when I got laid off at work, Dick and Dave got together and talked about it. Dave called and offered me a job. I took a huge pay cut but thought, "The Lord hates a coward," so I went for it!"

His courage was rewarded, as Ernie told me, "I got paid to do what I love for thirty-five years, full-time. I liked it so well that sometimes it seemed like what other people do on vacation." Calandrelli chuckled, "I walked in the door, and Dave handed me a yellow pad and said, "You are Production Manager!" Though he got flung into it, he would quickly sort things out. "We were making few of our own parts then, so I had to make sure parts were purchased- and at a good price by working with vendors. I would line up the kids making the calls by puttin' together a schedule. I did shows and seminars and ran the video camera...I did whatever needed to be done."

Agility was necessary for the young company to navigate the unknown, and as time passed, titles and responsibilities changed. Calandrelli told me, "Once I went to the SHOT Show, and

Calling Contests: It Ain't Just for Bragging Rights

Turkey calling competitions quickly grew in popularity as benefits increased. Chris Kirby explained, "When we first started, you'd get a trophy and a title if you won. As events got Sponsors to provide money and prizes, a winner could receive a knife, clothing, or even a gun. When we first started attending competitions, there would only be five competitors. Then there were ten, then twenty, and the next thing you know we had to have two rooms at the NWTF Grand Nationals because there were sixty finalists. By the 1990s we started to get some cash. I got $4,000 when I won the World Championship in 1995 and $5000 for the Grand Nationals in 1998."

Even QUAKER BOY® would reward successful callers, in the form of incentives for their ProStaff that placed in competitions.

QUAKER BOY®

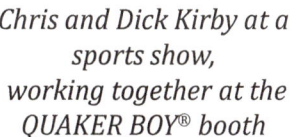

A young Chris Kirby winning at a calling competition

A young Chris Kirby winning in the turkey woods

Chris and Dick Kirby at a sports show, working together at the QUAKER BOY® booth

Photos: Chris Kirby

at that time, they made me Publications Director. I later ended up being the Public Relations and Advertising guy. I set up a lot of hunts, and brought in the outdoor writers, and they told me I was the easiest guy to work with. Even if you didn't kill nothin,' we still had a helluva time. It was built on relationships, and if you had that, you'd go far." As the industry grew, so did opportunity. Butski said, "There was a point where Ernie and I were doing a lot of seminars, and we were winning a lot of competitions. I was the first full-time employee, but then went with Ben Lee from 1982 to 1983." The industry was expanding fast, and there was a constant drip of job possibilities. Butski then said, "But Dick wanted me back, so I came back." Butski helped design and sell calls, and Chris said, "Paul Butski is a tremendous salesman. He was then with us for twenty years before he did his own thing."

Being a Kirby kid meant being surrounded by the best turkey callers in the nation. It is no surprise that the two Kirby boys would eventually take the stage. Chris and his brother, Scott, would make the family proud as they became nationally known as calling personalities. Butski admires both boys and says, "Great kids, like father-like sons. They became passionate about turkeys, and they were calling at the Senior level. I have nothing but good things to say about all the Kirby's." Ernie praised them and said, "When Chris was coming up, you could see he had something. Scott was good, too. What Chris did with mouth calls seemed effortless. I used to crush him at golf, but then, with golf and turkey calling, he started thrashing me! He was a "pretty" turkey caller, meaning it sounded really good and really flowed well. His kee-kee runs were fluid. He didn't win all the time, but he won all the majors and then hung it up; I always respected that."

Chris recollected, "In 1980, I won my first Grand Nationals as a Junior, and in 1981, the U.S. Open. There, I met guys like Stevie Stoltz and Ray Eye. There was no animosity amongst the callers; it was a unique time. It was in Pennsylvania where I qualified for the Senior division and beat Paul Butski in that competition. It is one thing to practice and be good, but when you are on stage, and the Emcee is asking you to call, it gets real!"

Moving to the Senior level in calling competitions was an eye-opener. Chris emphasized, "Now, all of a sudden, I am calling against Dick Kirby, Ernie Calandrelli, Paul Butski, and Walter Parrott. I would wonder why I thought I could ever beat them. Then, I remember winning the Georgia State Convention. It was my first Senior division win, and I thought, "I could do something here." Chris recalls being shocked after that first win, realizing, "I beat my Dad! I called for eleven years in the Grand Nationals. I never missed a cut, but I didn't win until my tenth try. You lose a lot more than you win!"

As competitive callers, chasing a better call would drive innovation for Dick Kirby and his inner circle. The first revolutionary call he designed was dubbed the Old Turk, the first raspy-style mouth call. That would be his predominant caller until 1979. At that time, the double-reed QUAKER BOY® Special was added. These early calls were made to be raspy, simulating an older hen, and Chris shared, "The corner of a reed on a call tore, and it was laying on top of the trash. I picked it up on a whim and ran it, and that would lead to our corner-cut raspy calls." In 1985, Paul Butski would design the Cutter, a call with a notch in the middle of the reed. He had won his first U.S. Open with it, and Chris recalled, "Dad wanted to see the call he was using; finally, Paul showed him." Kirby would pay Butski royalties on it, and Butski said, "That call is the one I use to this day!"

In starting his game call business, Kirby had the prudence to grasp that a more diverse offering could mean more purchases per customer and increase the consumer base. Similar to what Penn's Woods had done decades prior and Will Primos did when formally launching his company, QUAKER BOY® came out of the gate with several products that appealed to the turkey hunter. The second catalog Kirby put out in 1981 demonstrates that he was already innovating and expanding on existing call lines. The mouth call offerings had grown to seven (each offered in a Standard or Small Frame). The Grand Old Master box call, which has become one of their standard-bearing calls, was offered to meet varying consumer preferences. The three models included the #1 Presentation Model "made of the highest quality American Walnut;" #2 Supreme Grade "made of the highest quality American Walnut, Poplar, and Cherry woods," and the #3 Field Grade "made of unfinished Walnut, Poplar and Cherry."

Similar to the approach used by other game-call production companies, Kirby would also offer calls for resale that were sourced from other makers. This helped him keep the cost of his assets down and increased the speed to launch new products. The first pot call that the company offered was the "Quaker Boy Turkey Taker – "Stowe Away." The catalog from 1981 shows a square call, but the following year, it was the more familiar stop sign-shaped single slate call. The Stowe-Away was made by its namesake, Lewis Stowe of North Carolina, whom Kirby befriended on the calling contest circuit. The second pot call that QUAKER BOY® would offer came in 1982: the D.D. Adams Double Slate. A testimonial in the 1982 catalog read, "Dick Kirby used it during the Spring of 1981 to call 14 gobblers to the gun."

At the home of D.D. Adams who became well-known for his pot calls

D.D. Adams and Dick Kirby bring home wild turkey for the table in 1982

D.D.'s pot calls had been showing up in call competitions, and Butski told me, "Dick and I went to D.D. Adam's house; we stayed with him and watched him make calls." Kirby quickly worked out the rights to make and sell the first in a line of D.D. Adams inspired pot calls. Chris also remembers those days and said, "I can picture D.D.'s house and pond. And I remember he had a bald eagle mounted in his house that predated the federal ban; I thought that was something! He had a turkey skull in a drawer with what I know was a number six BB in it, as he was an old-school guy that would only shoot two or four shot to break bones. So, he was testing turkey heads before almost anybody to determine the lethality of a load. Back then, turkey shooting was a wing sport to many. But it was learned over time you didn't have to body shoot them, especially after you went from a single bead sight on a shotgun with a six-foot pattern to having better guns, loads, and sights."

Chris recalled, "The base of those original brown D.D. pot style calls were made from molded brown plastic flower pot "rain catchers." Flower pots had this rain catcher underneath, and we would buy thousands of those water catchers and drill them out. And we cut the slate ourselves; I don't know how many we did. I have the calls numbered one, two, and three of about everything that D.D. made." In 2002, the NWTF would name an annual Grand National Callmaking Competition award after D.D. Adams and present it to innovators with the best-sounding friction call and striker combination. QUAKER BOY® would, over time, launch over two dozen different pot calls, including four more inspired by D.D. Adams.

I have calls in my collection that provide testimony as to the number of calls Dick Kirby was already selling shortly after the debut of his business in 1981. I have a 1982 QUAKER BOY® catalog, which provides call prices by model. The Grand Old Master #1 Presentation Model box call had serial numbers and were dated as Kirby tuned them. At $39.95, it was a premium-priced call, which limited interest to a select clientele, likely those such as me, who are fanatic turkey call collectors. Mine bears the inscription, "#191 – 1983." He was selling only a few dozen of the more expensive models a year. The #2 Supreme Grade, priced at $24.95, was

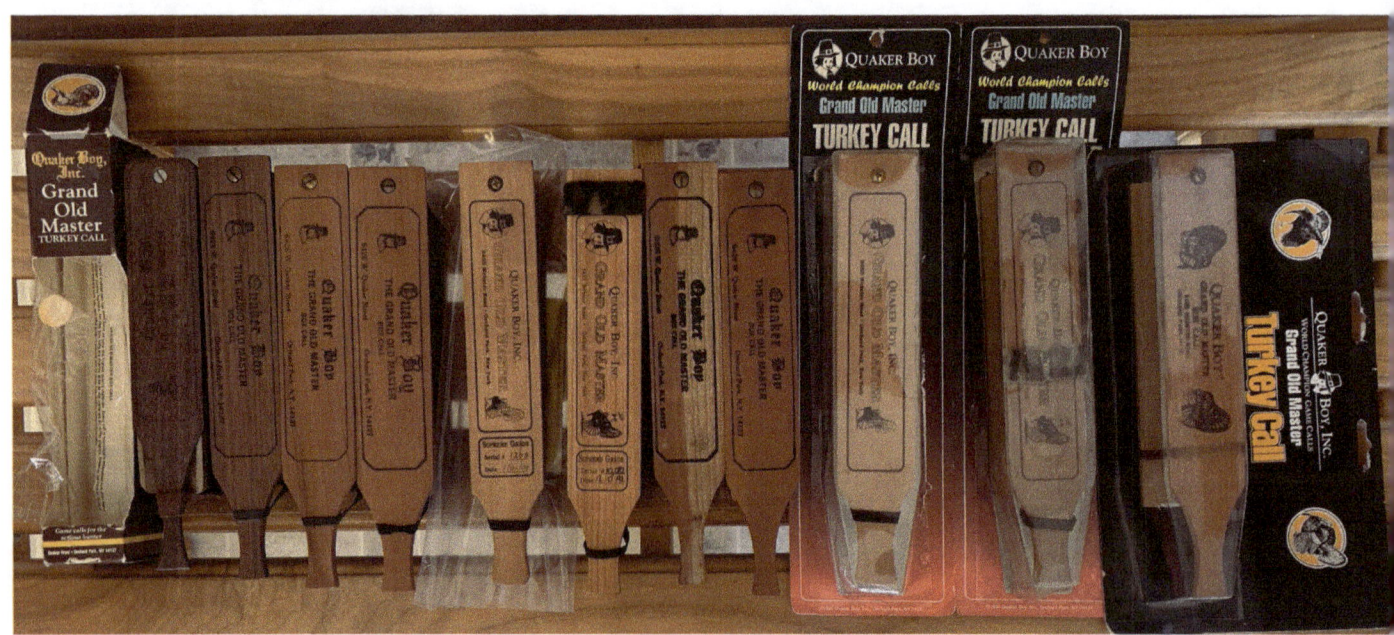

Some Grand Old Master box calls over time: Top of paddle view

Some Grand Old Master box calls over time: Bottom of base view

also numbered and dated; The earliest one I have is labeled "#1252 12/1/82." A respectable pace at several hundred per year; one can speculate that the economically priced #3 Field Grade for $17.95 sold at a much higher volume; indeed, the number of them circulating for resale now would attest to that.

All manner of calls and accessories were presented for sale in the early 1980s company catalogs. Calls listed by other makers in those first few years of QUAKER BOY® included the juice-can style owl hooters made by George Wasinsky, the 'Eight-Hooter" made by Niles Oesterle, and a Turkey Gobble call made by Scotch Game Calls. There was a Snuff Can call, coming on the heels of the success of KNIGHT & HALE's tube calls. Most people don't associate a scratch box with QUAKER BOY®; to my knowledge, they only offered one for a short time in the first years. "The new Mini Box Turkey Call…can be used with most any slate call," the description reads; it was essentially a typical scratch box without the "scratcher" and was intended to perform more as the striker itself when stroked along a slate pot call. Pot call strikers and a box call holster were advertised.

Including accessories like box call chalk and glass defogger (important to spectacled hunters) was brilliant, as some of those were consumable products that would bear the need for occasional, if not yearly, replacement. The camouflage clothing articles spoke to the desire of the turkey hunter to be shielded from the distrustful eye of the wild turkey: hat, gloves, and face mask. Even with his descriptions of products, Kirby was teaching even as he was

One of the first Quaker Boy catalogs (1980s). Dick Kirby did this cover sketch

selling. In his lengthy paragraph about the face mask, he writes, "Perhaps the one single cause of most unsuccessful turkey hunts is the lack of proper concealment from the eyes of an oncoming wild turkey. Every bit of exposed skin reflects light and is picked up immediately by his keen eyesight...this is the most important item any turkey hunters should consider, next to his gun and shells." Finally, decorative items were also available for purchase, which speaks to the emotional need Kirby recognized in turkey hunters to showcase their love of turkeys and turkey hunting. Hunters could wear their hearts on their sleeves by purchasing clothing patches or display them in their homes with the art prints he resold by other artists.

By this time, Kirby had perceived his potential customers' need concerning learning how to hunt turkeys. Education was a sales opportunity, but more importantly, it would sustain and grow his consumer base by creating more successful hunters who would want more "stuff." He was among the very first to leverage a relatively new automation, where people could learn without leaving their own homes to travel to call competitions or seminars. The Compact Cassette (also commonly called the cassette tape or audio cassette) had begun to dominate the recorded audio world by the 1970s when cassette players became available for in-home use (and were installed in vehicles). By 1982, Ben Lee and Kirby had been early adopters and recorded tapes. In the 1982 QUAKER BOY® catalog were three instructional audiocassette tapes: *Talkin' Turkey, Talkin' To Spring Gobblers*, and *Talkin' To Fall Turkeys*.

When business is good, it is good, and Chris illustrated, "We were doubling the revenue every year at first, but when you start at zero, it takes a while to gain traction." Kirby had the foresight not to limit his thinking to callmaking and recognized a new technology that could help the business. Video cameras were first purchased by some in the hunting industry in 1984 when they became available. Mike Battey had a front-row seat and told me, "Dick was helping me as a competition caller somewhere in the mid-1980s when I was on the QUAKER BOY® calling team. It was like thirty to fifty guys at that time; I wish I still had that nice satin ProStaff jacket!" Mike had just started to do some video work, and Dick mentioned that he wanted to capture a turkey gobbling on the limb. Mike said he could do it and recalled, "I had to rent a professional camera and equipment; it was $750 for three days! I actually ordered the first video camera for Dick. It came to my house, then we met in Selma, Alabama to film a hunt, and I taught he and Ernie Calandrelli how to run it."

The first video cameras were expensive, heavy, had short battery life, and a tape would only hold twenty minutes of footage; they are not today's handheld Go-Pros and phones. QUAKER BOY® was one of the first out of the starting gate and shot footage in 1985, if not in 1984, that would lead to their first hunting video, "In Quest of the Grand Slam." The first wild turkey hunting VHS tapes I am aware of were released by five companies in 1985, followed by another five in 1986, of which this QUAKER BOY® tape was one. Scott Kirby had an extensive role in capturing and editing many of the videos that the company would release.

"We got in on the infancy of VHS tapes," said Chris proudly. "We sold them then for $49.99, just like others were doing. When that era came about, the videos became a

The first QUAKER BOY® video release was in 1986: "In Quest of the Grand Slam"

teaching tool, and that is our mantra: to be teaching. Videos showed all the new hunters at the time how to hunt from start to finish." With thousands upon thousands of new hunters having the opportunity for the first time in decades to put a wild turkey on the table for Thanksgiving, the VHS became a marketing home run. It provided a platform for potential customers to get to know the people behind the product and see it in action. This would lead to QUAKER BOY® ultimately releasing nineteen different VHS tapes, three DVDs, and three TV shows. They helped drive sales, which increased to over 2 million dollars a year by the early 1990s.

Although some may think it naïve, Chris admitted, "Our focus was never really about the bottom line. The biggest measure of success is smiling hunters! Sure, the balance sheet has to be good, or we couldn't stay in business and have stability for our family and employees. But we have kept things practical for the hunter." In the 1970s, QUAKER BOY® mouth calls sold for $5; they now sell them for $9.99, a modest price. Chris explained, "People may think they are getting a better mouth call if it is more expensive, but we have been building our mouth calls by hand since the beginning and still do."

When asked how the company differentiates itself, he said, "Something we do as well or better is the consistency of our manufacturing process. You can go anywhere and buy our products, and they will perform the same. We'd had some better raw material suppliers. We don't make changes to products to save money. The biggest such change was when Johnson

& Johnson stopped making the tape we used for mouth calls, and we had to change it then. It wasn't a choice. We weren't out looking for the cheapest tape. We strive to make a high-quality product and service it well."

Another ingredient to the company's success was the reputation and impact made by the ProStaff the company has maintained. "The ProStaff was, and is, an extension of QUAKER BOY®," Chris stated. "We had over one hundred guys at one time. Joe Judd, Bill Epeards, Adrian Hare, and Randy Opferbaeck have over thirty years with us." Here, Chris grew contemplative in considering the number and quality of those people who were their ambassadors as QUAKER BOY® grew. He recalled, "There was Mark Scroggins, Jeff Probst, Tad Brown, Arnie Jonathan, and Wayne Gendron. Wayne was a taxidermist. He and his wife, Janice, were out of Missouri. Wayne was a ProStaff elite, running the country for us; we sent him all around the country. He was in all of our camps, and he could call with anything! Wayne was a tremendous asset, and Janice helped as well. There were others, too many to name!" Chris viewed all those representing QUAKER BOY® as influence and information centers. He said, "They are grassroots human beings that we want to just be themselves, be a part of their community, be a participant, and be more of a giver than a taker."

Managed by the capable Calandrelli, ProStaffers would host seminars, put on hunting clinics, and train store owners and salespeople to operate the calls sold in their stores. ProStaffers nationwide were encouraged to attend and volunteer in local conservation groups and events. "We told them they were leaders of the turkey call world in the community they lived in." ProStaff was a growth agent for the company through direct efforts to distribute information and increased exposure in outdoor media. The 1980s and 1990s had brought an explosion of magazines and magazine articles on the popular new sport of turkey hunting, and the many ProStaff offered writers a chance to get the material they needed. "The writers were a huge part of our success," confirmed Chris.

As QUAKER BOY® matured and others like the ProStaff shouldered the load, more of Dick Kirby's time was spent traveling, promoting, and selling; he had understandably not been making many calls himself. But his passion for creativity and connecting with turkey hunters never went away. As Chris got more active in running the business, Kirby started making more personally-built calls, both with the Neil Cost Reproduction Call line and his Dick Kirby Originals.

"Dad never stopped piddling," Chris said. "He was always making and trying something. He got a lot of interest and sold a lot of the limited edition series he made with Wally Turner's art back in the 1980s. That stemmed into the Dick Kirby Collectibles. He loved to design calls, build calls, and play calls. He also loved to tell and listen to stories. He would be on the phone with one person for one box call numerous times, designing and building it to their specifications; he just loved talking to turkey hunters. To make these, he turned his garage back into a shop where he could do his own thing. He would take these calls to the NWTF show, whose Board of Directors he was on then. People would line up at his booth to buy calls or bring calls to have him do art on them. He liked controlling what he did with the originals he made from start to finish." This would be one way Kirby would be unique from others of his production company peer group, in that he got back to his roots and started a custom call type of side business.

Visiting Quaker Boy's current website reveals a section called "Dick Kirby's Personal Collection." Chris explained, "He loved all things collectible. At the NWTF Grand National Callmaking Competition, he used the money he made selling his calls at his booth to buy calls from the callmaking awards auction. He probably had well over 1,000 collectible calls, his and other callmakers calls, when he passed away. It was the result of a lifetime of trading and bartering." Chris and Bev share a belief that a turkey call doesn't belong in a warehouse, so instead of packing them up, they have slowly been selling some so others can enjoy such historical items. I have been fortunate to purchase some of those in the past few years, calls by Dick Kirby, as well as some like a fine Frank Hegler Pine Needle trumpet and some decorative wingbones by Dave Greer in wood cases with hand-painted turkeys.

Dick Kirby visits with Neil Cost at Cost's home in Greenwood, SC

Chris remembered when he first met another iconic callmaker that Kirby would work with, similarly to D.D. Adams, "We would travel near and far to win a trophy and sell calls. I can remember going to a show at Hershey, PA. There in one tiny room was Neil Cost, Harold Knight, and Jim Clay." Along with the Kirby crew, that is an impressive gathering of callmakers! Chris added, "The longest relationship Dad had in the industry was with Neil Cost. Neil was on the custom side, not a direct competitor, but they hit it off."

Chris recalled, "My personal interactions with Neil was when I was younger; I mostly knew him from the NWTF Convention. Dad and Neil had a great relationship through my eyes. Neil never wanted to be a big company; he made and sold his calls when and where he could. Dad went down to Greenwood, South Carolina, several times to spend time with him." This would result in Kirby commissioning some calls to be sold through his company. From 1990 through 1993 (according to the book *The Last Hurrah*, although some calls may have also been done in 1994), Cost made twenty-five calls numbered and signed each year that he sold to QUAKER BOY®. They were labeled "Neil Cost Original Boat Paddle Reproduction Call." Besides the interest and collectability of Kirby's handmade originals, these calls made by Cost are valuable and highly desired by collectors.

The first calls reproduced by Kirby himself were labeled "Neil Cost I give it my personal signature Reproduction Call," and Cost personally tuned and signed the calls. Chris told me, "Dad had a vision of Neil Cost and what he meant to the industry. Any time Dad made a reproduction, he called that out." In 2002, Kirby put out a supplement to the QUAKER BOY® catalog, Dick Kirby Collectibles. Inside the front cover is a short bio on him and then one on Neil Cost. In Cost's biography, it is divulged that "In 2001, Neil and Dick Kirby, a long-time friend and admirer of Neil's, came to an agreement. In permitting Dick to trade mark his signature Neil gave Dick the exclusive rights to use that signature in the crafting and selling of Neil's reproduction turkey calls."

Through this agreement, QUAKER BOY® would reproduce several of Cost's calls. Following what he had done with the Grand Old Master box call line, Kirby offered Cost's Boat Paddle call in a Presentation Grade (checkering on both sides was done by Marlin Watkins) with an Indian Head penny embedded in the paddle, a Signature Grade that sported an Indian Head penny in the paddle, and a Field Grade model.

Dick Kirby also advertised other "Reproductions of Neil D. Cost Box Calls" in his 2002 Collectibles catalog, including Standard Box Calls in an "Old Hen" Grade (the sides had a single row of checkering done by Marlin Watkins) and "Signature Grade" (double rows of checkering done by Watkins). He also offered Cost Reproductions in both the Old Hen Signature Grade (checking all done by Watkins) in a "Shorty" that was a more diminutive six and a half inches, a One-Sided Box Including a "Lefty" model, and a "Do Dat" Short Boat Paddle. Other Cost Reproduction calls he sold were Hen Tricks (a "peg-box" style call) and a Spring Hen Scratch Box.

Later, additional Cost Reproduction calls featured Greg Turner or Kirby's art; those calls were labeled "Neil D. Cost™ Reproduction Boat Paddle ™". All of the calls made by Kirby as Reproductions had a trademarked signature of Cost's either written or (later) stamped on the call.

I was curious about the checkering, as, to my knowledge, Neil Cost never checkered his boat paddles, save for a pair owned by Rob Keck. Don "Marlin" Watkins is a friend, so I called him to learn the details. Watkins told me, "I had been checkering some boat paddles; that is probably where Dick got the idea to do it and then called me. Dick didn't know how to do the checkering and asked me to help." Watkins agreed, and Kirby would send him around ten calls at a time. Watkins said, "I'd do the checkering and send them back; he would always write something like "checkered by Don Watkins" on the call. Then, it got to be too much to keep up with. I had a friend, Harry Hancock, that I trained to do it; Dick would send Harry the calls, and he checkered them after that for several years." Incidentally, the calls done by

Hancock didn't identify who did the checkering, so it is easy to discern which man's hands the calls passed through.

The relationships Kirby made weren't limited to competition callers and callmakers. Over time, he, and later Chris, worked in some capacity with all of the significant outdoor clothing and camouflage companies. Chris explained, "Dad helped Duxbax design a turkey huntin' vest. It had a specific box call pouch and a better seat." Later, the Kirby family would build relationships with the first well-recognized camouflage company, Trebark. Chris said, "Jim and Sherry Crumley, who had Trebark, I love them as if they were my own mom and dad. We also worked closely with Bill Jordan and the Realtree® team. And we work closely with Toxey Haas and Mossy Oak now."

Bill Jordan, founder of Realtree® shared that he has a property in Alabama with a field named after Dick Kirby. He said, "When Dick came down to hunt, and we'd ask him where he wanted to go hunting some morning, he'd always want to go to this particular field. Turkeys would love hanging around that area in the spring; now that is Kirby Field." Jordan told me that Kirby was "one of that particular group that came through a period when I didn't know where Realtree was going, or he didn't know where Quaker Boy was going. We were all just trying to make a living and help each other. As I saw the success of turkey hunting, other companies, and the NWTF getting started, I know there couldn't have been a better era to be a part of."

Mossy Oak was launched by Haas in 1986, and they have worked with all of the major game call companies over time. Mossy Oak's Ronnie "Cuz" Strickland told me, "I was a big fan of the turkey calling circuit. Mossy Oak promoted calling contests; we

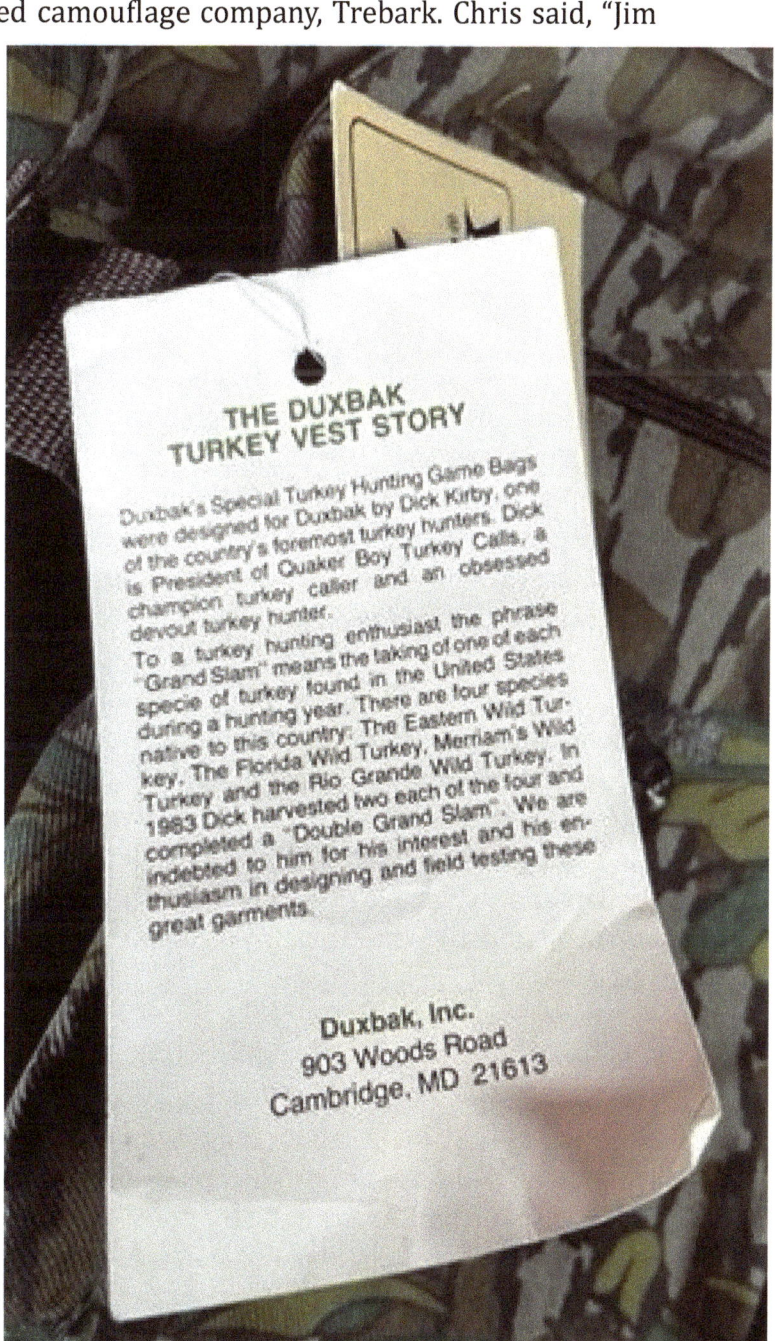

The Duxbax Turkey Hunting Vest that Dick Kirby helped design

sponsored them. There was a lot of rivalry between the northern and southern groups, both full of talent. That northern bunch was so good, guys like Dick Kirby, Paul Butski, and Denny Gulvas." Strickland didn't have a close relationship with Kirby until later in life but had admired him from afar. He said, "We took Dick hunting in New York in the late nineties, and I remember he was carrying a big ole Ithaca ten gauge. We filmed the hunt and put it on our *Hunting the Country* TV show; I personally was thrilled when we did some work with QUAKER BOY®."

The third, and to date, the last TV show QUAKER BOY® was involved in was initiated after Chris received a call from Strickland. Chris said, "It was around 2009 or 2010, and Cuz presented the concept of a show called *Turkey THUGS*. That call would lead to their partnership on the show, which launched in 2011. The word "thug" may seem off-putting to some, but for those who tuned in, the real meaning was revealed. THUGS was an acronym for "Turkey Hunters United for Good." Strickland told me, "That was a unique opportunity that people enjoyed; they got what was behind it, and we were glad to partner with Chris and QUAKER BOY®.

QUAKER BOY® made a line of calls bearing the show's name, and Mossy Oak did the same in their clothing line. Part of the proceeds went to help veterans coming back from overseas duty. Chris told me, "We were all about it! We had a highly successful line of themed calls placed at Walmart for three or four years. I was the "turkey call information guy" featured on the program." Paul Butski was one of the featured hunters on the show, which spanned a few seasons. In the end, "It got expensive doing TV," said Chris. "The internet and digital content became the way many people started to learn or find entertainment."

Television played a role in all of the game call companies featured in this book. It is just one way QUAKER BOY® and their contemporaries had to modify their marketing and selling approach as the industry grew. As turkey hunting went nationwide, they had to conform to new sales channels that had become part of the game call supply chain. Like others, Dick Kirby had started his company by making calls in his house and selling them to friends. Attending sports shows was a logical next step, where calls were still sold directly to customers. Selling through (mostly) local sporting goods stores was next, along with doing mail-order by putting together flyers and catalogs.

However, that was not enough to reach enough potential consumers to capture the existing demand, especially with the name recognition that video and television brought to the hunting public. Tapping into bigger point-of-sales would require going through a "middleman" who had access to product placements not typically available to a manufacturer. Chris explained further, "As the industry grew, we partnered with distributors and began attending distributor shows where people were buying a few hundred calls to stock at sporting goods stores. Dealers wanted calls quicker and faster, so we got distributors that could warehouse large numbers of calls." Distributors tend to form close relationships with manufacturers like QUAKER BOY®. They become representatives of the company and, in turn, sell to all sizes of dealers or retailers. Chris told me, "We had to train the distributor's salespeople." In time,

The Mossy Oak Turkey THUGS television show was a collaboration between Mossy Oak and QUAKER BOY® to raise money for U.S. military veterans returning from overseas duty

QUAKER BOY® would also sell directly to the distributors who were intermediary buyers for the retail stores. These distributors would buy products from several companies to stock at warehouses.

Buying behaviors had changed, driving the need to supplement direct and mail-order sales. Big-box retail stores like Walmart or sporting outfitters like Cabela's and Bass Pro Shops had become shopping destinations for sportsmen. With the popularity of turkey hunting, such retailers were hungry to keep calls on shelves; only production call companies could meet that demand. The volume required, along with the need to streamline the process, led them to sell directly to big retailers. Chris said, "We were one of the last companies to sell to Walmart in the mid to late 1990s due to the loyalty of our distributors."

Hunters at such stores were not just buying turkey calls. For instance, there are over three times as many deer hunters as turkey hunters. Success for a company can come through diversification, and Dick Kirby ensured the growth of QUAKER BOY® by expanding into hunting accessories and other types of game calls. While the wild turkey has remained central to the culture and brand of the company and its employees, Kirby had begun expanding almost from the beginning, with duck, goose, and elk calls offered in the 1980s. It wasn't a stretch for him; he enjoyed calling and hunting almost everything.

Mike Battey said, "Dick Kirby was a good caller. He could take to any type of call, even other game species: elk, duck, goose, similar to me. People knew us because we were all-around Dr. Doolittle's. We could run the snot out of anything. Brad Harris, Dick Kirby, and I were recognized then as the best all-around game callers." Kirby would win an all-around World

Game Calling Champion title in 2000. Dick Kirby's achievements in calling competitions, enhanced through familiarity provided to customers through multimedia channels, lent credibility to his complete line of calls. A visit to the company website shows a thriving family of calls is still available.

The apple didn't fall far from the tree with Chris. He is a highly decorated caller, an accomplished hunter, and shares his late father's values. Most importantly, just as Dick Kirby picked a superstar spouse that would be an ideal partner in life and business, so too did Chris. He recently told me, "Michelle didn't hunt or fish when we met, but she quickly picked it up and dove in. She is getting in a tree stand tonight! My wife is a sweetheart to put up with all she has over the years." Their marriage on June 4, 1994, ushered in a new generation of Kirby's, and, with Bev's retirement, Chris and Michelle now own and run the company. In 2018, they purchased a 10,000-square-foot building about twenty minutes south of Orchard Park in Springville, NY. They moved operations to Springville In 2020 and sold the original building to fund Bev's retirement.

The passage of time offers the chance to reflect on the significance of how challenges and change shape who we ultimately are. Bev told me, "When Dick and I were married, I was a little city girl and knew nothing about hunting. I learned to turkey hunt from seminars, as we were always at them with Dick as an instructor and for us to sell calls. At first, turkey hunting was very frustrating for me, but Dick was patient enough to stick it out with me. I grew to enjoy turkey hunting and the outdoors. Back then, women just didn't do that; I always tell men and women to give it a chance. Give yourself a break, and get out there and hunt. I did a lot of hunting over the years with our family. That is what we did together."

Chris recalled the early days of QUAKER BOY® and recalled, "I had a humble upbringing; if we had to go to Goodwill to get school clothes, we did. The family car was never a new one.

(Left) QUAKER BOY® has had three President and Chief Operating Officers over time; Dick Kirby was succeeded in that role by his wife, Bev Kirby

(right) Chris Kirby, one of Dick and Bev's children, is now the third President and Chief Operating Officer of the family business

Summer Bible School, Christian Camps, and church are where Mom and Dad gave us a great foundation. They didn't just teach it; they lived it. We weren't ever in poverty, but things got better as things took off. But the humble roots were never lost. Mom still lives in the same house they bought nearly sixty years ago. It was always more about giving back than always taking. Dad gave thousands of calls to kids. We are an NWTF Double-Diamond Sponsor, and without them and the Trap & Transfer program, there would have been a barrier for all the companies in this book."

The NWTF would later honor Dick Kirby by creating an award in his name and qualifying "The award is named for turkey hunting legend Dick Kirby, who was the brains and heart behind Quaker Boy Calls. He also was one of the original members of the NWTF, serving nine years on the NWTF National Board of Directors in the 1990s. The Dick Kirby Award is given to a callmaker or company that has made significant contributions to the NWTF and shown dedication to the Save the Habitat. Save the Hunt. initiative."

The quality of people in the wild turkey world is reinforced through the mutual respect shown amongst those men who represent the major game call manufacturers. Chris assured me, "Although we were fighting for every bit of peg space, we were all supporting the cause. I have a tremendous amount of respect for the guys of my Dad's generation: Harold Knight, David Hale, and Will Primos. They built it, I'm working it. Yes, we were competitors. Yes, there would be mistakes. Calls get copied, and there are patent infringements, but those of us who care work it out. Once, I called Will and said, "I made a mistake," and they worked with us. We have several patented products and trademarks as well. We kept each other on our toes and, in doing so, upped each other's game. If you weren't innovating, you were going to lose, and that drove us all to build it better and make it easier to use."

The competition was good and required constant vigilance in every aspect of their business. Chris said, "I don't know if any of us was better than the next. We had similar principles, and we were all good for each other. We had to be on our toes, and as a result, our calls got better." Between his musical ear and his understanding of the turkey vocabulary, Dick Kirby had a keen eye for recognizing a call that would appeal to hunters, visually and functionally.

Chris's appreciation for others in the turkey hunting industry is vast, too much to try and capture it all without risk of offense. He acknowledged that "I hunted with many others in industry" and got to know them off the show floor or calling stage. He specifically mentioned, "Matt Morrett, who was ProStaff for H.S. Strut, and I butted head on the calling competition stage; he kept me on my toes, and we love hunting together now. There is not a name you could bring up we don't have a history with."

While names like Streb, Butski, and Calandrelli might be familiar to many in the hunting world, there have been many other key people whose talents and contributions are part of the QUAKER BOY® success story. As Chris reflected on where the company is now, he shared who some of those "unsung heroes" were along the way. "Bob Wozniak was there from the beginning. He came on full-time for ten years," Chris said. "Mark Schiralli also built mouth calls for the first ten years when we were making calls and packaging them out of people's homes. And, behind the scenes, there is one significant family in particular, the Couell family." The family's backyards touched, and three different generations have done work for QUAKER BOY®. Chris revealed, "Rick Couell started as a production worker and has now been our Production Manager for thirty-five years; he's still with us. Rick's Dad, Bill, originally cut the slate for our D.D. Adams Double Slate and his Mom, Connie, ran our shipping department for a number of years. Rick's older sister, Mary, worked for us, and his kids, Megan and Ryan, have both worked part and full-time here at QUAKER BOY®."

As they needed more manufacturing capabilities to keep up with demand, one of the first people tapped was Dick's brother, Ken Kirby. Chris shared, "My Uncle Ken was the first one to build the box calls that Dad designed. He was a pastor by trade as well as a woodworker. Uncle Ken made all the Grand Old Master box calls that were numbered and the first Easy Yelper pushpins; they were all built by him in his garage." The operation eventually outgrew Ken Kirby's garage, so the Kirby family drove out to Long Island, where Ken resided, and brought everything back to start a full-time woodworking plant. This second facility was a 13,000 sq. ft. woodworking shop. It was located in Bradford, PA, and would initially be run as a full-time facility by John Kelley. Chris told me, "Kelley Isadore was one of our early hires in the production arena in January of 2000 and now oversees the Bradford plant. Rex Farr and Bill Parslow have been turning raw lumber into finely tuned turkey calls together since 1996. Kelley's Mom, Renee has been sewing our Bandit and Bandito headnets since 1997."

QUAKER BOY® now has forty-six seasons under its belt. Bev reinforced that Kirby "was not your average Joe! Dick was his own person, and this was his passion. He had a drive to succeed and a willingness to make it happen. I didn't have it; I had the ability to support him." Chris said, "I'm proud of the company's strong consistency. Mom and Dad built the company as big as they could without any third party's help. We have been approached multiple times but haven't sold. We have a commitment that is shared by our employees. Our first tagline was "The Choice of Champions" because Dad was winning call competitions and helping others do it. Then it went to "Champions Choice," and finally to "Hunter's First Choice," because hunters are the ones using the products."

The wild turkey's gobble is infectious, and its grip on Chris is as firm as ever. "I love the gobble!" Chris said enthusiastically. "I love to hear and see them all year long. It is not just business-oriented; it's knowing we were a small part of getting the wild turkey re-established in this country. I know when I go out hunting now, I have a chance, at least, to kill one; it wasn't always like that." Chris' biggest concern is not that wild turkeys will go extinct, even with a downward slide of populations in some areas. "It is the safety aspect of our sport. We have to keep grounded on the fundamentals and even more so with experience. We can get complacent. Friends of mine have survived hunting accidents. It is heart-wrenching, especially knowing that accidents are preventable. We gotta slow down and put the puzzle together. Pressing the trigger on a misidentified target is never worth it. Turkey hunting is incredibly safe, and we need to keep it that way!"

The premature loss of the spirited Dick Kirby on September 30, 2010, stunned the turkey world. I can remember the flood of laments and tributes on outdoor forums. I was hesitant to ask Bev about losing her life and business partner, but she volunteered, "It was such a sad series of events. But it happened, so you deal with it. I had to get more involved, but that is when Chris really took hold. He came from the bottom of the company to the top. Thank God he was willing to step in and eventually take over." Chris shared, "My Dad was with me for my first breath, and I was at his bedside for his last breath, along with Mom, Michelle, and our Doctor. I thank God daily for blessing me with such an inspirational, loving Dad!"

Dick Kirby's death shook the QUAKER BOY® inner circle to its core. Bob Wozniak said, "I was with him in the hospital the day before he

Successful Game Call companies like QUAKER BOY® went beyond turkey calls. Pictured are some of the first duck calls they made

died when he was in a coma. The next day, Bev called me and told me he passed away; it was just so shocking. I am glad for all the fun we had together; through Dick, I met a lot of great and interesting people." Ernie Calandrelli remembered, "I had that same surgery prior to Dick. As a guy that knew and loved him, I understood he was going through a lot of pain. We talked about it. It was a routine surgery, but any surgery is bad. It was devastating when it happened." Butski recalled soberly, "Those days with Dick were a special time. Even after I left QUAKER BOY® to start my own business, we remained great friends. I miss him. I miss him!"

A memorial left by a friend on the funeral home's webpage captured succinctly what impact Dick's life, and his death, meant to many; "Dick was a great barber, then champion game caller, but best of all a caller of men to know the Lord." Through his speaking at Christian sportsman's dinners, it was shared on the same web page that Dick's testimonies had led to hundreds of people coming to know their Savior. The family graciously asked for any memorial funds to be directed towards two causes that Dick was so dedicated to a Wesleyan church camp and the NWTF's J.A.K.E.S. (youth hunter) program.

The Kirby family legacy is alive and well. Significantly, the founder's vision has not been lost with his company's growth; it has been amplified through those who became a part of it. Dick Kirby was initiated into the NWTF Grand National Calling Championship (GNCC) Hall of Fame in 2020 (see photo in Chapter 1 of presenters and inductors), the same year as his dear friend, Paul Butski. In 2024, Chris Kirby will be inducted. His impressive pedigree includes four U.S. Opens, two Masters Invitationals, a World Championship, and the Grand Nationals. Winning those four venues completed his "Majors Grand Slam." Chris believes, "I am one of only a few people that have won all of those: I know Walter Parrott did." Chris would win seventy-five contests across the country before retiring from the calling circuit. "You have to be good at something in your life!" he said, chuckling. "It was a fun phone call to receive; it is truly an honor."

Undoubtedly, Chris' induction will be a deeply touching moment for the entire family. We are instructed in the *Bible* that there will be no more death, mourning, crying, or pain for those in Heaven. When Chris accepts his award, I will listen intently for a "Hallelujah"- and perhaps a fly-down cackle made on an Old Turk diaphragm from the Pearly Gates!

Dick Kirby's dream and passion live on, as QUAKER BOY® still thrives after 46 years

YELP & GOBBLE, INC.

QUAKER BOY® TIMELINE

(* = approximate date)

1942 – Dick Kirby is born November 28 in New York.

1946 – Beverly "Bev" Bautz, future wife of Dick Kirby, is born February 23.

1958 – Dick Kirby Graduates from West Seneca West High School.

1959 – The New York State Conservation Department begins a wild turkey trap and transfer program.

1964 – Dick Kirby joins the National Guard and is later Honorably Discharged.

1965 – On April 24, Dick and Bev Kirby are married.

1966 – Dick & Bev Kirby open the Quaker Boy Barber Shop and Quaker Girl Beauty Shop.

1968 – The first modern-day spring turkey season is established in New York.

1970 – Christian "Chris" Kirby is born on May 15 to Dick and Bev; he is one of three children the Kirby's will raise and who will help in the family business.

1971 – Bob Wozniak takes Dick Kirby on his first turkey hunt. Dick gets his first wild turkey, but it is hearing one gobble that gets him hooked.

1973 – The National Wild Turkey Federation (NWTF) is formed, helping to drive calling competitions, turkey trap and transfer, and education as the population of turkey hunters grows alongside that of the wild turkey.

1974 – Using aluminum siding, Kirby and Wozniak cut diaphragm frames and build their first mouth calls. Dick continues to make mouth calls at his kitchen table.

1975 – Dick Kirby sells some mouth calls he built to a trapping supply store for $100 and this new hobby becomes his passion. The Old Turk raspy-style call is his signature call.

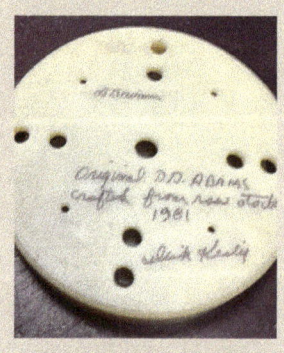

1976* – Chris goes on his first turkey "hunt" with Dick, using a 35 mm camera, at age 5 or 6. Acquiring a punch press through friend Doug Oak helps ramp up production and consistency of mouth calls.

1977 – Dick Kirby competes in his first turkey calling contest; it might have been at a fairground in New York: He meets Ben Rodgers Lee there.

1978 – Ernie Calandrelli meets Dick Kirby at a calling contest in Owego, NY. Ernie introduces Paul Butski Kirby; the three will form a close bond as they begin building calls in Dick's basement and hunting together.

1979 – QUAKER BOY® introduces a double-reed raspy mouth call: The QUAKER BOY® Special. Chris Kirby competes at the Blaine Sportsman's Club in his first turkey calling contest (as memory serves).

1980 – Dick Kirby has a revelation at his booth during the Harrisburg, PA sports show; he believes his calling is to make turkey calls. He puts out the first QUAKER BOY® catalog. Chris Kirby wins his first Grand National Calling Competition as a Junior.

1980-1986 – Paul Butski goes full-time at QUAKER BOY®, with a brief period in 1983 and 1984 where he worked for Ben Lee.

1981 – Dick Kirby closes his barbershop to focus on the callmaking business; The

QUAKER BOY®

Kirby family and Paul and Halina Butski attend the SHOT Show in New Orleans, where they set up a booth and sell calls. Chris Kirby wins the U.S. Open calling competition as a Junior. Dick Kirby uses a D.D. Adams Double Slate to call 14 gobblers to the gun.

1982 – QUAKER BOY® launches the D.D. Adams Double Slate. Quaker Boy becomes incorporated. Chris kills his first wild turkey in Pennsylvania when he was 12 years old; at the time youth couldn't hunt in New York until age 14.

1982-2015 – Dave Streb is hired as the Sales and Marketing Vice President.

1983-2010 – Dick Kirby takes all four subspecies (Eastern, Merriam's, Osceola, and Rio Grande), a "Grand Slam" in the U.S. for 27 straight years and registers a total of 67 Grand Slams. He completes individual Slams with a ten gauge shotgun, twelve gauge shotgun, a muzzleloader, a .44 Magnum handgun, and archery equipment. He would achieve double, triple, and quadruple Slams in some years.

1984* – QUAKER BOY® obtains a video camera through Mike Battey; Dick Kirby and Ernie Calandrelli begin to record footage.

1985 – Dick Kirby wins the Grand National Calling Championship for the first time. Paul Butski designs The Cutter mouth call, with which he won his first U.S. Open.

1985-2020 – Ernie Calandrelli goes from part-time to full-time at QUAKER BOY®.

1986 – The first of 19 VHS and DVD releases by QUAKER BOY® over time is "In Quest of the Grand Slam."

1987 – QUAKER BOY® introduces the first full wire frame headnet, which is awarded a patent: The Bandit.

1988 – Scott Kirby is diagnosed with cancer and courageously battles through it. Post-cancer, Scott would enter into and excel in the videography and editing of many QUAKER BOY® VHS tapes.

1988-2018 – QUAKER BOY® builds a 13,400-square-foot facility at 5455 Orchard Park, NY.

1990 – Dick Kirby is honored by Midland Marine Bank and the U.S. Small Business Administration as upstate New York's "Small Business Person of the Year." Dick Kirby's friendship with Neil Cost leads to commissioning and selling a few of Cost's calls through QUAKER BOY® through 1993.

1990s – Dick Kirby serves nine years on the NWTF National Board of Directors; The Dick Kirby Award was named in his honor and is given annually to a callmaker or company that has made significant contributions to the NWTF.

1992-current – A 13,000-square-foot woodworking plant is established in Bradford, PA, to accommodate QUAKER BOY®'s growing business.

1993 – Dick Kirby wins the Grand National Calling Championship for the second time.

1994 – Chris and Michelle Kirby are married on June 4th.

1995 – Chris Kirby wins the turkey calling World Championship.

1998 – Chris Kirby wins the Grand National Calling Competition; this is the first time (and as of yet the only) a father and son have won.

1999-2009* – QUAKER BOY® ran their first two TV shows in this timeframe. *Gobblin' Fever* TV was a collaboration with Dick Kirby and Mark Scroggins (Cross Timbers Ent. Inc.) and ran from 1999 through 2007. *QUAKER BOY®'s Born to Hunt* TV, edited by Mark Scroggins and hosted by Chris Kirby, aired on the Men's Channel through 2009.

1999-current – Chris Kirby is named President of Quaker Boy.

2000 – Dick Kirby wins an all-around World Game Calling Champion title.

2002 – Dick Kirby Collectibles is initiated; for several years, QUAKER BOY® will reproduce Neil Cost's calls.

2010 – On September 30, Dick Kirby unexpectedly passes after complications during post-surgery care.

2010-2013 – Tac Robinson and Ronnie "Cuz" Strickland approach Chris Kirby with the idea of a show called *Mossy Oak Turkey THUGS* to raise money for returning U.S. military veterans. The show runs three seasons and the themed calls from QUAKER BOY® and clothing from Mossy Oak raise money for a good cause.

2010-2020 – Bev Kirby serves as QUAKER BOY®'s second Chief Operating Officer.

2011 –The NWTF's highest honor for a volunteer, the C.B. McLoud Award, is awarded posthumously to Dick Kirby. The award is received by: Bev, Scott, Chris, Michelle, and Rebecca Kirby.

2018 – Chris and Michelle Kirby purchase a 10,000-square-foot building in Springville, NY and rent it exclusively to Quaker Boy.

2020 – After helping found QUAKER BOY® and build it into the success story it is, Bev Kirby retires. She has served in many roles: Owner, CFO, COO, advisor, shipper, and accounting; Bev did it all.

2020-current – Chris & Michelle Kirby purchase QUAKER BOY® Inc. from Bev Kirby and the Estate of Richard C. Kirby. Chris remains President, adding Chief Operating Officer/ Owner to his title.

2024 – Chris Kirby will join his father by being inducted into the NWTF GNCC Hall of Fame.

Thanks to QUAKER BOY® for providing the following Innovation Milestones timeline.
Timeline of Innovation Milestones

1974	Dick makes his first aluminum mouth call with a pair of tin snips, aluminum siding, a piece of balloon and duct tape
1975	Quaker Boy introduces the first-ever Raspy Style Mouth call-The Old Turk
1979	Quaker Boy introduces the first ever Double Reed Raspy Mouth Call-The Quaker Boy Special
1982	Quaker Boy introduces the first Pot Style Slate call to the industry-The Double Slate
1985	Quaker Boy introduces the first-ever Notch style call to the industry-The Cutter
1986	Quaker Boy introduces the first-ever Aluminum surface Pot Style Call-The Aluminator
1987	Quaker Boy introduces the first full wireframe headnet-The Bandit. Followed by the first ever ¾ headnet-The Bandito. Both were patented
1988	Quaker Boy introduces In Quest of the Grand Slam VHS
1991	Quaker Boy introduces the first-ever double sided pot style call-The Double Face
1991	Quaker Boy introduces the first-ever turn over style bleat call-The Bleat in Heat
1999	Quaker Boy introduces the first-ever adjustable box call to the industry-The Clover Leaf 10 Sider
2000	Quaker Boy introduces the first-ever three-surface pot style call-The Triple Threat
2001	Quaker Boy introduces a four-surface pot call-Quad Threat
2002	Quaker Boy introduces the first-ever Freeze Proof grunt call-The Ridgerunner
2005	Quaker Boy introduces the first-ever Curved Lid Box calls-The Curve and The Boat Paddle
2006	Quaker Boy introduces the first-ever squeeze style bleat call-The Squeezin' Bleat
2008	Quaker Boy introduces the first-ever silent adjust tube system for a grunt call-The Brawler
2010	Quaker Boy introduces the first-ever Turkey Vest / Blind combo-The Vestablind

Thanks to QUAKER BOY® for providing the following Industry Leading timeline.
Industry Leader From the Start

1976	First "Raspy" Mouth call invented and introduced (Old Turk)
1979	First Multi reed Raspy mouth call invented and introduced (QB Special)
1982	First Pot Style call introduced (DD Adams Double Slate)
1985	First Cutter style mouth call invented and introduced
1986	First Aluminum Pot Call invented and introduced (Illuminator)
1986	First Wild Turkey Specific VHS Video released (In Quest of the Grand Slam)
1987	First Full Wire Frame Head-net invented and introduced (Pat# 5,025,507 #5,091,996)
1991	First Multi Surface Pot call invented and introduced (Double Face)
1991	First Ever Flip over Bleat Call introduced (Bleat-in-Heat)
1999	First Adjustable box call invented and introduced (Pat# 6,168,493)
2000	First Triple surface pot call invented and introduced (Triple Threat)
2001	First Quad surface pot call invented and introduced (Quad Threat)
2002	First Freeze proof grunt call invented and introduced (Ridgerunner)
2002	First Directional pot call (Sidewinder)
2005	First Curved lid box call invented and introduced (Pat# 6,942,539)
2006	First Squeeze style bleat call (Pat#7,785,166)
2008	First Silent adjustable grunt call invented and introduced (The Brawler)
2010	First Vest/Blind combo invented and introduced (Pat# 8,042,196 #8,402,563)
2015	First Seal Rite mouth call invented and introduced (Pat# 8,016,638)
2015	First Open Lid Box call introduced (The Odyssey, 8-Ball)
2015	First Internal push pin call invented and introduced (Trigger Finger, Slider)

The author's collection of QUAKER BOY® game calls and products

QUAKER BOY®

Photos by
Brent Rogers

YELP & GOBBLE, INC.

Chapter 4

MIKE BATTEY: THE CALL DR.

Mike Battey, The Call Dr.

"I am in the sound business, not the game call business," Mike Battey told me of his work with turkey calls. Like many others who pursue that trade, Mike had roots in competitive turkey calling. However, some might not fully appreciate his impact, as the majority of calls that he designed were sold through other companies. Mike's inclusion in this book is essential to telling the story of overcoming challenges in making mass-produced game calls of good quality. Many turkey hunters, including the author, have Mike to thank for their success; he is behind some of the bestselling production friction calls ever made.

Mike is an Edison-like figure in the game call world. Howard Harlan, in his historic book, *Turkey Calls: An Enduring American Folk Art*, describes him as an "inventor, innovator, expert and callmaker extraordinaire." Mike has spent decades researching, developing, and testing innovative new products for an eager game call industry. He quickly acknowledges that much of his success can be attributed to the opportunities that PRIMOS® HUNTING, KNIGHT & HALE, M.A.D. CALLS and others gave him.

If "genius" isn't the right word for Mike Battey (who prefers to be referred to as just "Mike" in this chapter), "The Mad Scientist" is appropriate. That is the nickname that Mossy Oak's Toxey

Haas gave him in 1988, just as Mike started his career. Mike was appreciative of that alias, and it captured him well. Mad Scientist usually conjures up images of equal parts brilliance and eccentricity, with Mike being no exception. I recall our first phone call a few years ago when he eagerly dove into running one of his pot calls. "Listen!" he said as he demonstrated various aspects of calling to me; I loved it! If you are passionate about wild turkeys, I challenge you to match his enthusiasm! He is proud of what he has accomplished, and learning his story will tell you why; his goal was to provide the public with the same call he carried in his hunting vest.

The DNA of an inventor is in Mike's genetics, as he is a direct descendant of Eli Whitney. Regardless, he has earned what he has done through strenuously applying himself to study and experimentation with any task he takes on. He advised me, "If you are not a student of something, your creation is limited." Mike's story isn't that of a classically educated college graduate applying information learned in a classroom. Mike is an applied learner, digging deep into a subject that interests him. He also has a creative gene through his mother. Mike explained, "My mother was a portrait artist, and my attention to detail was learned from her. That helped me, as later, I recognized that visual recognition and eye appeal are important to those who buy turkey calls. I make sure people can recognize my pots, trumpets, or other callers." Some of the physical features of his pots would help buyers connect to his work.

Mike Battey grew up in North Carolina, and that state still owns his heart. Unlike much of the country, North Carolina's turkeys were not completely extirpated in the 1800s and early 1900s. Remnant populations were to be found in less accessible areas that were swampy or more heavily wooded. Although fall hunting was the predominant time to hunt turkeys then, the season extended as late as May 9th in some counties, well into "the gobbling season." The presence of turkeys allowed for a culture of turkey hunting to be passed along through generations in that part of the southeast. Despite that, Mike wouldn't have the opportunity to hunt turkeys as a youth.

He explained, "We didn't have deer or turkeys locally then. We had to drive forty-five miles to go deer hunting." In any case, Mike is certifiably 'batty' about all things wild turkey now. He comes by it honestly, as he is from a family with a strong hunting heritage. "I grew up with a shotgun in one hand and a fishing rod in the other," he said. "That was a critical thing that led to what I did; I was raised hunting and fishing with my Dad, Robert, and Grandad, Ed," Mike told me.

That foundation established a lifelong enthusiasm for hunting. Mike has consistently been connected by his vocations to the outdoors in his adult life. The time he would spend in a gun store started by his uncle in the 1950s would prove to be his gateway to first discovering wild turkeys. "Hardware stores are where people commonly went to buy guns in the old days," Mike shared. "My uncle owned the Ace Hardware and Guns store; it was half hardware and half gun shop. I always had a technical brain and became a gunsmith in the 1980s." Mike would eventually buy and own the gun shop, putting him on a collision course with turkey hunting.

Mike's grandfather, Ed Battey (on left) with an eight-point buck strapped to the running board of a Model 8 Ford

In addition to gunsmithing, Mike told me, "We had three counters of game calls at the gun store, all types of game calls. People would come from fifty miles to come to my store, as no other gun stores were carrying them. One local gun store owner skeptically asked me why I had the displays of game calls." The skeptic argued, "You can't make much money selling a ten-dollar game to pay an employee's salary." Mike justified his savvy business decision by saying, "Yeah, but when he is in my store, a guy looking for a call doesn't just buy a ten-dollar call. He buys clothes, ammo, and a gun!"

Some of those customers were turkey hunters. Mike said, "I had a customer with a Model 12 Winchester that he wanted to be restored. I got to talkin' to him, and we became friends. He had health problems so that he couldn't drive; he invited me in 1983 to go deer huntin' near the Roanoke River above Raleigh. His name was Ray Sutphin, and he became my turkey huntin' mentor."

You might only fully appreciate who Ray Sutphin is if you are a rabid collector of wild turkey calls, like the author. Turkey call collectors will recognize him as being included in Earl Mickel's first book about those turkey calling instruments and those who made them: *Turkey Callmakers Past and Present*. Sutphin started making turkey calls for his own use in 1974, thereby becoming known to other sportsmen. There was an informative chapter about him in another book, *Good Friends Fashioned From Feathers*, by John Good. Good was another that shuttled Sutphin and then shared the turkey woods with him. Mike said, "Ray had a mounted turkey gobbler in his den, and I was captivated by it. He was a dyed-in-the-wool turkey hunter."

Mike's turkey hunting mentor was old-school hunter Ray Sutphin

Mike told me, "My formative years were influenced by the diehards, the pioneers of turkey hunting, and later competition callers. Ray was hunting turkeys back when there weren't many killed in North Carolina. When I first went deer hunting with him, I got to his place, and he was playing turkey calls, and it got me hooked! That fall, he killed a hen in Virginia and made me a three-piece wingbone call out of it, and he also made me a scratch box. He showed me how to make my own mouth call from a piece of dogwood with a penny balloon; basically, a two-reed call, although I never liked or played that well." They would begin hunting turkeys together in South Carolina because it was the closest place that held a good population of turkeys. Mike said, "Ray was the one that taught me calls and calling. I learned the fundamentals of hunting turkeys from Ray, though when we hunted, he would go one direction, and I'd go the other. That's the way the old timers did it. I had to put together what I could by gleaning it from him and others."

One of the hunts with Sutphin introduced Mike to a hunting method and some turkey vocabulary he later realized was ahead of its time. "I was hunting with Ray one time, and we were 500 yards apart, and Ray killed a gobbler. He told me the turkey came 300 yards across a field but then hung up," Mike recalled. Ray told him, "Then I decided to do the old "scold" call. I hit 'em with that, and that gobbler came out of strut, and he came running. I had two choices: drop my drawers or shoot in self-defense!" Mike laughed at the memory but then said respectfully, "I heard my first known example of a turkey's excited cutting call from Ray Sutphin. He called it the "scold call" and demonstrated it to me on a mouth call, years before I heard it anywhere else, or in competition. There was no cutting in calling competitions when I started."

Turkey hunting rearranged Mike Battey's priorities. "I became obsessed," he admitted. "Every morning, I would go out for three hours in the morning before I went to work. The first one

I killed was in the spring of 1984. The funny thing is that I had already joined the National Wild Turkey Federation (NWTF) before I killed a turkey. I already knew Rob Keck and Carl Brown, who helped run it." I guess you could say that the rookie turkey hunter entered the organization with a bang. Mike thought his first turkey was good enough to enter into their records. He said, "My first longbeard weighed twenty-one pounds and two ounces, had one inch and an eighth spurs, and a nine-and-a-half inch beard. It ended up being a North Carolina state record for weight at the time. It was number four overall, behind turkeys taken by Dick Kirby, Neil Cost, and Richard Grubb."

With the hook set, Mike used what he knew with vim and vigor. He said, "At first, I went out and was killing turkeys with a wingbone and scratch box because it is all I had. I tried and couldn't play a mouth call." Those first calls he used, the wingbone and scratch box, would become less popular over time. That may be attributed to new types of calls that sought to be user-friendly first…even if there was a tradeoff in sound. But he told me a story about how effective those old-school, oft-overlooked calls can be. He said, "I was down at Bill Jones' one year, and there were some other serious turkey hunters there too." One of them was Craig "Cornbread" Corbett, a very talented maker and user of air-operated calls. Mike continued, "I was callin' on the scratch box, and I called up Cornbread!" I got the rest of the story from Cornbread himself. He said, "I was fishing off of a dock when Mike started running that caller around 200 yards away. I would never walk haphazardly towards a hen's call," but knowing it was Mike, he went to investigate. "The calling was the purist turkey I'd heard in some time," Corbett said. "Mike had been using a scratch box by the master call maker Lamar Williams."

Mike's first wild turkey gobbler was taken using a scratch box call in 1984

Like many turkey hunters, Mike would test other types of turkey calls, searching for that perfect turkey-killing sound. Something that would propel him on his future course even faster was his introduction to turkey calling competitions. He recounted, "When I entered my first turkey calling contest in 1985, I ended up fifth. I wasn't that good, but the calling took me from local to state to national exposure. I got connected in the network of other turkey hunters all across the country. The form of communication was connecting at shows and talking on the phone." In addition to honing his calling skills, he increased the tools in his turkey hunting arsenal by getting and mastering new types of calls. "My first trumpet was a Penn's Woods," he said, "and then in 1985, I got a Billy Buice trumpet from Lewis Stowe for $25. I knew the virtue of a suction call from using a wingbone." The trumpet call would become a go-to call and an obsession for him.

Though much of this story is about the work Mike did on production pot calls, for which he is best known, people may be surprised at his interest and success with other types of calls. "It was about 1986 when I saw a Southland tube call in a gun store, so I pulled it off the shelf and figured it out. I started killing turkeys with a tube call," he said. He has also used boat paddles (commonly called longboxes or paddle calls) with great success. He said, "When I got my first boat paddle from Lamar Williams and started killing turkeys with it, I was sold! It was over thirty years ago. Back then, you couldn't give a boat paddle away. Guys didn't want to have to carry such a big call. But how did locating a turkey start? It was the boat paddle! That was before most guys were usin' crow calls and owl calls."

The only box calls Mike designed were plastic boxes manufactured by PRIMOS® (The Graphite Prospector, and then The Prospector) and M.A.D. Calls (the Carbonator call series). The plastic box calls he had designed didn't have staying power. However, in 2006, he contracted at least eighty-eight snakewood and holly boxes from the notable callmaker Albert Paul to resell under his personal WildTalker brand. Paul informed me, "The first twenty-three WildTalker Series calls were made and shipped to Mike, and he distributed those. The other numbered calls were shipped from me. The total number of calls made as of today was eighty-eight. Mike got that last one." They originally sold for $250. "That was a lot of money back then," Mike stressed. "I gifted one to my competition calling buddy, Paul Butski, and he man-hugged me!" That would have been appropriate then, and even more so now, as some calls have resold for over $400.

Mike was divorced in 1988 and looking for a fresh start. He rented a 10' x 40' trailer on Long Cove Marina outside of Charlotte, North Carolina, and lived alone. He had set his sights on winning the state's turkey calling contest, which he would do twice! He would also win the Owling competition in 1989, and that trophy is the only one he has kept from all his years of competition calling. "I saved that one because it is a decorative piece of artwork, not just a trophy," Mike divulged. He has never leaned towards surrounding himself with tokens of past achievements. "I measure my success by how many of the calls I design are in hunters' vests," he said matter-of-factly. "More than anything, I want to make a call that the everyday, common person could afford and go out and kill a turkey with."

Competitive calling is why he would make his first slate call and dip his toe into the pool of game callmaking. Whereas most competitive callers used mouth diaphragm calls, Mike wanted a call he could get to "roll over" for his clucks and purrs, which he could not do on a mouth call. He had trouble with mouth calls getting soggy after being in his mouth awhile,

North Carolina State Turkey and Owl Hooting Champion Mike Battey, pictured at his gun store

Mike's best friend for the last 48 years, Fred Tornow (on left). The pair are pictured with a turkey called up using Mike's WildTalker Alpha Trumpet

therefore losing their "tune." He had no choice but to try something different.

Fred Tornow became Mike's best friend for forty-eight years and counting after they met at Fred's wedding. Mike was using a slate call made by Lewis Stowe in competitions at the time, and one day, while at Fred's house, they were discussing Mike's plans. Feeling his unexpected but newly found freedom, he proclaimed, "I can do anything I want; I think I'll make turkey calls." Fred had a drafting board, and Mike got to work, even though he didn't know a thing about game call design.

This is not a fairy-tale story where an inspired moment led to a vision that translated quickly into a perfect product. Mike's path was unclear, but his tenacity led to learning through what worked and what didn't. Mike began working on two different projects. One was to design a better material for a mouth call reed (which will be covered in more detail later in the chapter, but keep in mind this was all happening simultaneously) and the other was to develop a pot call that he liked the sound of. He drew his first pot call out on a pure guess. After many attempts, he accepted that it was a failure. So, out of what some would call desperation, at the heels of $2,000 spent on making a plastic pot mold, he took a different path. Knowing what worked, he tried a single slate and drilled two holes in the surface of his pot, like Stowe's call. It worked!

Mike went to Stowe with his design, as given the similarities, he would not sell it without Stowe's permission. Stowe's

The first (failed) pot Mike made sits on top of the piece of slate that he cut the surface of the call from

The first successful pot Mike made after drilling two holes in the slate; Haydel's Game Calls was one of Mike's first clients

pot measured three and three-eighths inches in diameter, while Mike's was three and a half. Stowe looked at it and told him, "That is your call, not mine," that blessing opened the door for the aspiring callmaker. Stowe was a champion turkey caller and a rising callmaker, selling his designs to P.S. OLT Co., Barney Larue (B&R Turkey Calls), and some to the well-known Ben Lee. Mike told me, "Lewis Stowe was the first one to use an acoustical grade pot. He gave me one of his pots and told me about the materials he used and helped me understand the principles of how it worked. If it hadn't been for Ray Sutphin and Lewis Stowe, I wouldn't have been where I am today. I was a product of the turkey hunting explosion and had the best mentors of that time."

Pot calls at the time were gaining popularity with hunters, given the control the user could exert when calling. Pot calls can mimic a wide range of turkey vocalizations, and volume control is easy, which is helpful in various hunting situations, such as long-distance "locating" or close in "finishing." Mike said, "At that time, there was a two-hole slate made by Lewis Stowe, the D.D. Adams pots and some guys in Pennsylvania making what were called flower pot callers. There weren't that many pot calls out there. I understood how changes I made were affecting the sound but had to figure it out from just hard work. It was plain old R&D. Like Neil Cost said when asked what he did to make box calls work, "I took away everything that doesn't sound like a turkey."

With his musical ability, he had several guitars. Mike realized that his Ovation guitar was the only one he owned that had a plastic back, so he knew plastic could work for a musical instrument. He called that company's research and development leader, as he wanted to "talk to someone there about acoustical grade plastic." He said, "I learned graphite is the highest conductor of musical vibration, more than any other composite. They (manufacturers) were adding powdered glass to make their plastic sturdier. "Think of adding something to Jell-O to give it strength," he had told me, helping me to visualize it.

Mike said, "I found a molding company thirty miles from my house. I lucked out, as during that time period, they ran two shifts, so I could go in at night and have someone put my mold up on the machine. Then, I could do cause and effect testing. It would be hard to find someone to let me do that now!" In 1988, Mike helped make his own acoustical-grade reinforced plastic by working with a third party to incorporate graphite. It wasn't as simple as just sprinkling some in. Mike explained, "I would hand-make each blend using different ratios of the graphite. I would make the test pots, take them home, and do a "tap test" to determine whether it had the sound or musical quality I was looking for."

A young Mike Battey had a passion for wild turkey hunting and calling

Mike claimed, "I killed the flower pot style call with my plastic molded design." With his and others' new ideas, pot calls would boom in popularity. Every game call company wanted new pot models to launch every year. In the world of pot calls, there are highly variable opinions and preferences amongst turkey hunters and callmakers as to what's "best." In the custom (handmade) call world, one honor sought by many is the NWTF's D.D. Adams Award for the best-sounding friction call and striker combination. Bill Zearing of Pennsylvania would form Cody Calls and win the first D.D. Adams award in 2002 with a wood pot, for which he set a standard. Mike would become the premiere plastic pot guy. His innovative designs would be imitated by many others, used in calling competitions, and become best-selling calls of major game call companies.

There were multiple variables to investigate related to the quality of a production pot. "What I did was look at how softness or hardness would affect vibration with incorporated graphite," Mike said. "By adding it or taking it away, I could see what was actually influencing sound. I also started changing soundboard supports to understand cause and effect. I would glue up two pots with just one different characteristic." Even a different glue created different results. Other surfaces to produce the sound would be something he would tackle later, but when he started, he went with a classic: slate.

Making a good call isn't just slapping together random parts that make turkey-like sounds. "You have to pay attention to the sound, not just sell calls," Mike instructed me. Being a guitar player, he credits his musical ability with giving him an ear to understand sound and a familiarity with musical instruments that contributed to his call-building endeavors. Even at the gun store, customers had noted this skill. He had told me, "A guy brought a slate call in, told me there was something wrong with it, and wanted me to look at it. I can make calls work and get the best out of 'em. When I started making them, designing them to be easier to run for the average guy was important to me, where even playing it wrong could still produce good enough sound. I did have to shave a little bit off a call's performance in order to do that," he said.

At that time, no round slate discs were cut to fit a turkey pot call and available for purchase. Callmakers then had to buy sheets of slate, and chalkboards were commonly used. He knew Stowe was using a drill press to cut his discs out, but the upstart Mike didn't have a drill press; he had a compass and a sander. With painstaking labor and care, the slate for every call he prototyped had to be manually cut out. Each one took an hour, and then he had to set and glue it into one of his pots. "The experimental process was excruciatingly slow," he admitted. To make things even more complicated, the rise in turkey callmaking was causing a supply shortage of slate boards, so in Mike Battey fashion, he busted through that problem by contacting a quarry to get round discs directly.

It is hard to appreciate the perseverance it took for Mike to succeed in his endeavor. It took six months for him to make that first pot call mold. He told me, "After I got it made, I only had 200 calls sold, and I had to move back in with my parents. I was broke. My parents and best friend were all encouraging me to just get a job. They were worried about me. I was living on beanie-weenies on a shoestring budget." But he knew he was standing at the right place and time in history. "Call it a spiritual thing. If you believe in something enough, you will do what it takes to make it a reality. Like Calvin Coolidge said, "There is nothing more powerful than persistence." That is quintessential Mike Battey persistence. He said, "I drove to the NWTF National Convention in Nashville with only $500 in the bank and didn't have enough to buy a tablecloth to put on my booth table." Yet, being there was an intelligent move by Mike, as it would put him directly in front of consumers and customers. But it was now a game of playing for keeps; he was all in.

Jami Linder was one of the few ladies competing in the call competition in 1989, and she came to his table, picked up one of his pots, and made some calls. She was astonished at how good it was; she liked it so much that she played his call in the finals. That was unheard of, as Mike said, "This was a different call than she qualified for the finals with, and one typically doesn't switch calls. Linder ended up being the only woman to place in the top five of the

Mike with Jami Linder at the 1989 NWTF Convention. Note Mike's Hunter Game Calls shirt insignia; his first business venture

Jami Linder won fifth place in the friction division at the 1989 NWTF Grand National Calling Championship using one of Mike's pot calls

Grand National calling competition that year! The top five were Paul Butski, Walter Parrott, Skeet Thomas, Mark Drury, and Jami. She is still the only woman to place in the top 5." Ladies, here is your call to action! Mike sold $3,500 worth of slate calls at the show. It seemed like his gamble was paying off. "Von Eubanks was running a mouth call with my RX-1 latex. With Jami and Von running my callers in the finals, it created quite the buzz. Thirty days later, he got a call from Allen Jenkins at M.L. Lynch, and the fuse was lit for the future explosion of calls he would design.

Many hunters are familiar with M.L. Lynch as a game call company, as that company started in 1940 and had a wide range of calls over time. Lynch was an innovator and, along with Tom Turpin, one of Mike's heroes. The book *The Most Perfect* by Raymond M. Masciarella II is a comprehensive look at the history and chronology of his calls. Allen Jenkins bought the company in 1969, and Mike worked there for a time. He recalls how innovative Lynch himself was, seeing some of the prototypes Lynch had made. Jenkins had taken note of Mike's work and hired him to make calls that would launch in 1989. The contract was for $50,000 a year and Mike had a clause included so he could make a pot call model at the same time for friend and fellow calling competition personality Paul Butski. That call was already in the works, and his loyalty to a customer would pay off, as Butski commissioned several more pots from him. Butski told me, "Mike is a great guy, an innovator who had a passion for designing pot calls. I sold them under my name. I had him design a couple, and he put his tweaks on them."

The magnitude of what was happening wasn't lost on Mike. He relayed incredulously, "I went from having $500 to my name to making $50,000 a year!" His pot design was revolutionary at the time for a production game call. Its design allowed it to be mass-produced, and the

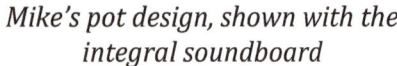

Mike's pot design, shown with the integral soundboard

The M.L. Lynch Pro-Mini Slate; The one on the left is the original release

technology available with injection molding and materials allowed for tolerances that produced reproducible sound quality. The pot he did for Jenkins for the M.L. Lynch brand was called the Pro-Mini Slate. It was small, three inches in diameter, but mighty. There are people today who still seek it out.

The M.L. Lynch Pro-Mini Slate was unique, Mike told me. He said, "That was the first friction call ever designed that used the same plastic for the sounding board as was used in the pot. The soundboard was designed to be integral in that it was mounted to the inside of the call. Soundboards are located underneath the calling surface and are typically smaller in diameter. They are usually affixed onto a pedestal inside the bottom of the pot. Mike used solvent glue to mount his on the pedestal. He said, "There are a lot of variables involved, so not all pots made are equal. The soundboard, surface, and pot materials and more all have effects on dynamics like pitch, rollover, and break."

When production turkey call companies were looking for the best guy at going from concept to the shelf, Mike Battey was on the lips of many. He said, "Part of the story is companies wanting to add pot calls to their lineups." The biggest obstacle in front of most inventors is fear: among them, a fear of failure, fear of insecurity, and fear of the unknown. Mike has that right combination of indifference and cockiness that it takes for creativity and risk-taking to survive the judgment of others. In the 1980s and 1990s, turkey hunting was growing fast, as the resurgence of the wild turkey through conservation work produced millions of turkeys. Many turkey hunters followed, and garage operations that turned out a few calls blew up into nationally known brands. Amazingly, while Mike had his pot call in development, he somehow found the time and energy to work hard on another technical challenge related to mouth calls simultaneously.

New product development should solve consumer problems; Mike had identified one from personal experience. Mouth calls often would only last for a while because the latex used for the reed would get soggy. He is an assertive guy once he gets an idea and tracked down the R&D director for Hygenics. For years, they had been making dental dams. Mike explained, "The latex gets too soggy after being in my mouth for 45 min." The advantage of a mouth call is not just good sound but also freeing a hunter's hands. Therefore, a hunter pops in a mouth call and may leave it in his or her mouth for hours while hunting. "We went back and forth," he said. Persistence would pay, and he had it to give.

"I was getting hand-poured samples from them, where they were changing the molecular structure to get latex that would repel water, repel moisture," Mike said. He would mail the samples to the three-time World Turkey Calling Champion Paul Butski of New York. He knew Butski from the competitive calling circuit, and Mike was running Butski's diaphragms in competition. "The green stuff, I called it," Butski laughed. "I would make Cutter-style calls with it; I had a Cuttin' Light series I used it in."

Butski would make mouth calls using Mike's Hygenics latex samples to determine what worked and didn't. All this required Mike to enter into a contract with Hygenics. He took a leap of faith. "I had to buy one hundred pounds of experimental latex every time," he said wistfully. "That was a whole machine run." He recalls that they wouldn't admit they made the material for him as they didn't want to carry it in their inventory. But this also gave him some exclusivity, of a sort.

Preston Pittman's Game Calls Black Diamond call with green RX-11 latex (Mike Battey called it RX-1)

Mike would call the result "RX1." The "RX" was about medical vocabulary (like, this material is just what the Dr. ordered), and "1" signified his first new latex. With this new material, he had fulfilled a consumer need for a mouth call that field testing showed held up longer. He wanted the latex made in a distinct color so it was immediately recognizable by turkey hunters when used on a call by one of his game call clients; he chose green. He sent some of it to the game callmakers Kelly Cooper and Preston Pittman.

Pittman seized the opportunity, launching The Black Diamond diaphragm with Mike's signature green latex. That became Pittman's premier diaphragm and was

181

very successful. Pittman told me, "Mike Battey was the composite man, the Mad Scientist and inventor that helped just about every-damn-body out there. He had more knowledge about the different materials than just 'bout anyone. I paid him thousands of dollars for the formula to RX-1 latex. That was a lotta money back then! Unfortunately, I can't get that latex anymore, as the minimum order is too big. That formula will go to the grave with me."

The 1993 Paul Butski Game Calls catalog included several Battey-designed pots; The "2 'N 1 Call glass/slate flipover," at top left was the first in 1990

In 1989, Mike ramped up his pot call making efforts. Working with an injection mold company, his first order was for 1,000 pots. Rod Haydel, of Haydel's Game Calls, was an early adopter. Others on board early were those he had bonded with through calling competitions and who lived for turkey hunting. He refers to this group he was a part of as "The Young Guns." Several would become customers, such as Paul Butski in 1990. Preston Pittman utilized Mike's pots as well as mouth calls. Eddie Salter, Mark Drury, and others were to follow.

Hunters tend to be innovative in their methods and tools. Native North Americans faced the challenge of feeding larger numbers of people as they formed family units and social structures. Harvesting bigger and more elusive game species meant creating spears, then atlatls, and eventually, bows and arrows. Hunters continue to drive innovation to improve their success and experience. Many who stepped up to the challenge to make improved turkey calls were those in turkey calling competition circles. Mike was one of many who tried to improve on available calls to gain a competitive advantage.

Another competitive caller who expanded from calling to callmaking was Mike's friend Mark Drury. Drury is a six-time World Champion turkey caller, and like many others doing competitive calling, he leveraged his notoriety by beginning to sell game calls. Drury and his brother Terry were preparing for the launch of M.A.D. Calls (M.A.D. is for Mark A. Drury) in 1993. Though they could make diaphragms, they wanted other calls to sell. This led to Mike's first significantly sized order, which came from Drury in 1992—eleven different M.A.D. Calls models would eventually be Battey-designed pots. One of the later M.A.D. Calls with a Battey pot was the popular Super Aluminator. The 1993 order from Drury was the crest of a wave of work for clients that validated his plans to do this work full-time. Meanwhile, Mike's relationship with another game call company, PRIMOS®, started in 1991 and would take his success to another level.

The first calls he designed for PRIMOS® in 1991 were the Two-Hole Slate and the Two-Hole Glass. Those were done in four and an eighth-inch pot diameter and are easily recognizable by the larger lanyard tab than on his later designs. This opened the door to some legacy-creating calls between the two parties, which is a great story. In one conversation, Mike asked me quizzically, "Do you know how Ronnie "Cuz" Strickland helped change the history of PRIMOS® pot calls?" He had this to say about it; "When I started making pot calls, I still had to work at Sports Authority for the income. That was back when Cuz was involved in helping PRIMOS® shoot videos for *The Truth* video series, and I had given Cuz one of my early "competition cup" pots." Cuz liked the pot and showed it to Will and Jimmy. Subsequently, Will asked Jimmy to contact Mike to have a call made from PRIMOS®. Jimmy did just that in 1994, and it would lead to the longest ongoing relationship Mike has had in the industry.

This was a tipping point for Mike, as he could no longer work at the Sports Authority and continue his side business of designing calls in every spare moment he could squeeze out. Until this time Mike had kept this other job, but now he saw the pool of opportunity filling up and he decided to take the plunge. To meet this new obligation with PRIMOS®, he told me, "I asked my boss for six weeks off to design another call for PRIMOS®. My boss said, "Well, Mike, it looks like you need to make a decision. Do you want to work for the Sports Authority, or do you want to work for PRIMOS®?" Mike replied curtly, "Well, let me do the math in my head. Let me see, I will make $10,000 in six weeks with PRIMOS®; how long would I have to work here to make that?" He answered his own question, punched out on the time clock, and the only time he went back was to get his last paycheck.

In 1995, PRIMOS® would come out with his namesake call, the Battey World Class, in both slate and glass models and with another recognizable pot-back pattern. At least eighteen models of PRIMOS® calls would be launched using Mike's designs, more than any other person or production call manufacturer he worked with. They include the Two Hole Glass and Two Hole Slate (1991), Battey World Class Slate and Battey World Class Glass (1995), AlumiMite, AlumiSlate, MiniMite, and Power Crystal (1999), Ol' Glory, Power Slate, and Titan 2000 (2000), Wicked Hen Slate (2001), Ol' Betsy (2003), The Freak Frictionite (2003), The Freak Crystal (2004), Purple Haze (2016), Foggy Bottom Ceramic and the Foggy Bottom Glass in (2019).

Remarkably, the Power Crystal has been in continuous production since it launched. Several other models have been promoted and re-launched with changes; perhaps only crusty collectors of a perfectionist nature such as I record these "variants" of call models. Regardless, if you are fortunate to get one of the Battey World Class calls that includes the word "Graphite" on the back of the pot, you have a rare bird; there aren't many from that original mold in circulation.

Prototypes of the first calls Mike did for PRIMOS®, including the molded striker head

PRIMOS® Two-Hole Slate and Glass models. The calls that started a continuing relationship between the parties

Mike's namesake pot done by PRIMOS®, the Battey World Class

Battey World Class; a view of the bottom of the pot

After PRADCO purchased KNIGHT & HALE, they hired Mike in 1998 to design calls, which he did for them through 2004. Harold Knight and David Hale would tag him with the handle "The Call Dr." in recognition of what he was doing by applying new ideas and materials to the old-school business of game calling. He didn't just focus on turkey calls. Mike told me, "I developed the rattle bag (2 Bucks in a Bag system). It was a six-inch bag that was 20% louder than a conventional eight-inch bag through the harmonics of different rods. No two antlers are the same." Turkey calls were his primary focus, and during his time there, at least a dozen different ones using his pots were launched. Many of those would be with a pot design that set a new standard for a plastic pot: his injection-molded graphite "competition cup" with an integrated soundboard. The three evenly spaced rows of five sound holes around the outer edge of the pot's back made it instantly recognizable.

KNIGHT & HALE launched one of Mike's bestselling production pots in 1999. The KNIGHT & HALE Ol' Yeller featured his competition cup pot and a unique yellow ceramic material he

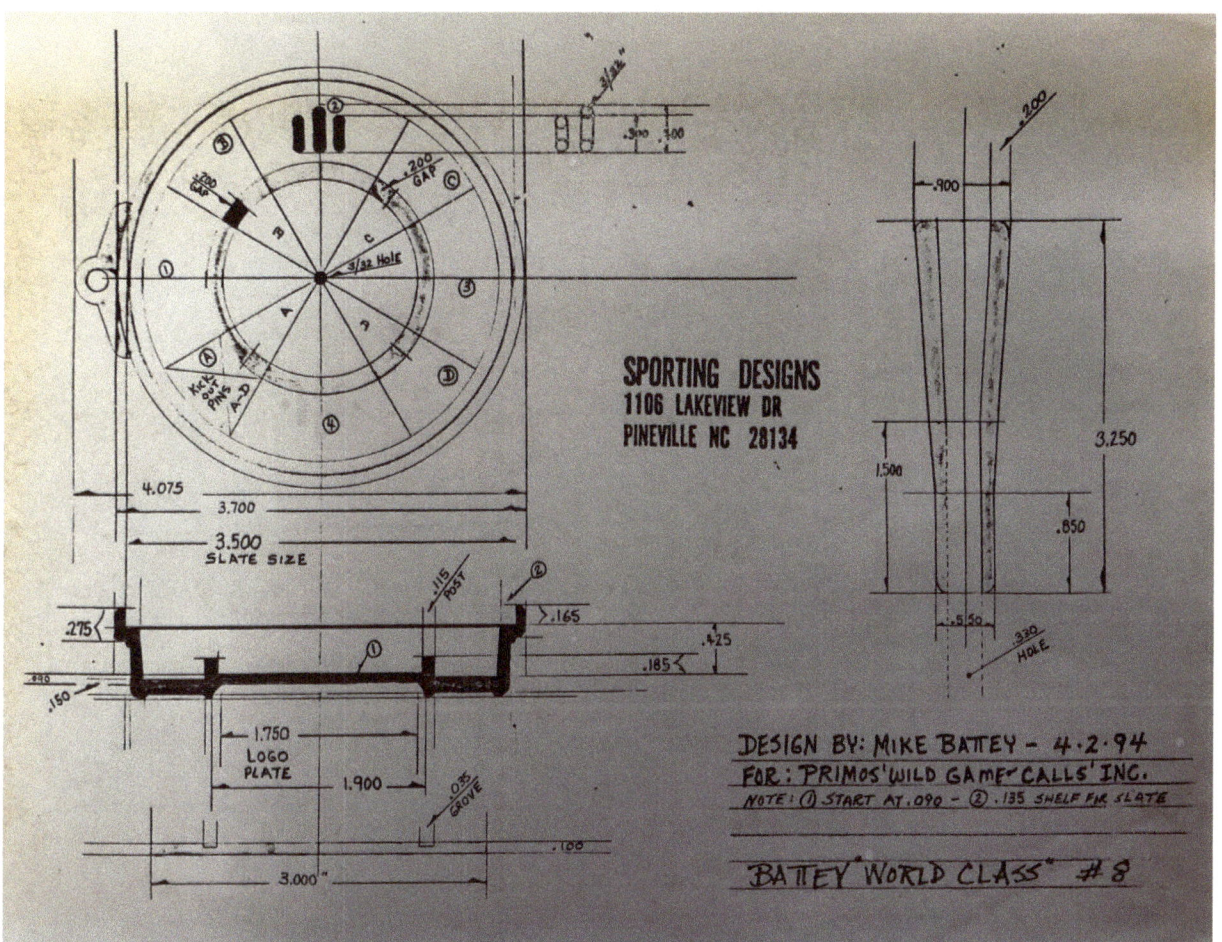

Original design drawing for the Battey World Class call

formulated and molded into a disc. Mike said, "David Hale was the first one to recognize the potential and say, "Winner, winner, chicken dinner!" It is still popular today, as bidding wars on e-commerce sites will attest to.

Mike had been trying to mold a disc for a calling surface with a composite moldable plastic. The results were not what he was looking for. He said, "Then I found out through my research that ceramic was moldable and tunable," compared to other substances he had worked with. The Sla-Tek ceramic disc that is the calling surface of the Ol' Yeller pot was thus created. The formulation is proprietary, although others would begin working to make their own ceramic surfaces. Not all are created equal in quality, and Mike acknowledged, "There are variables they don't know how to get right, like the thickness of the disc. The formulation is also important; you can add material in different proportions to make it harder and softer, but it affects sound. This was the pinnacle of what I innovated in the friction-calling world. Everything that I did with friction calls was all in tuning the plastic to make it conducive to sounding like a turkey; that still required me at the machine to do it right."

Of note with the Ol' Yeller call, its popularity ensured it was around for many years, although

A 1999 Ol' Yeller advertisement, the year that best-selling call was released by KNIGHT & HALE

it was re-launched several times as changes were made. The first three "variants" of the Ol' Yeller call all have the word "Sla-Tek" printed on the call's surface. Of those three calls, the first had a black pot, the second green, and the third yellow. None of the later models of Ol' Yeller had the word "Sla-Tek" on the label because that unique material was no longer being used to make the ceramic disc, nor was the pot one of Mike's. "Ol' Yeller wasn't as good of a call when we got away from the Battey pot," said Knight regretfully. "He was a genius with pot calls and crow calls. The Battey pot is as good as anything made."

Mike's impact on the industry was recognized in the Winter 1998 issue of *Turkey & Turkey Hunting* magazine. Roger. B Hook wrote the article "Unknown Legend: The Work of Mike Battey" about him. Hook wrote, "Battey, a call-innovator and self-described fanatic, is to friction calls what M.L. Lynch is to box calls." Mossy Oak's Toxey Haas is quoted as saying, "He's a true genius in the call business. He is a call-maker extraordinaire. This man has married history and high-tech information. He is steeped in the history of turkey hunting and is a leader of the industry of tomorrow."

The proof that his calls were getting the job done was evident in the exponential growth of the orders coming in. Mike told me, "M.A.D. first ordered 5,000 pots for The Super Aluminator, PRIMOS® ordered 10,000 for the Battey World Class, and they put in more orders afterward.

The first order for Ol' Yeller by KNIGHT & HALE was for 75,000 pots, then they put in another order for 90,000. This all happened in just one year!" Among the production pots designed by Mike are what he believes may be the top three all-time sellers for production pots: the KNIGHT & HALE Ol' Yeller, PRIMOS® Power Crystal, and PRIMOS® Battey World Class Slate (now with minor modifications, sold as the Ol' Betsy).

I have been collecting turkey calls for years now; As an R&D guy (I have a B.A. in Biology

Mike and Mossy Oak's founder, Toxey Haas, share the spring woods when Mike was a turkey hunting guide

and am an R&D Director in the food industry), how and what calls are made of interest me. That has given me an appreciation for the callmakers, the rich history of callmaking, and the innovations and art that are part of that story. My first awareness of Mike Battey came through books on callmaking, referenced earlier in this chapter by Howard Harlan and Earl Mickel. It was a matter of time before I began seeing commonality in the designs of calls I particularly liked. The trail led me to Mike. In my early call collecting notes, I recorded:

> Battey, Mike: inventor of acoustical graphite call; blends thermoplastics to specs. Designed pot calls, crow calls, and trumpets. WildTalker brand. Known as The Call Doctor. Behind the K&H Ol' Yeller and PRIMOS® Power Crystal I started with. Get his calls.

Mike would design fourteen different pot styles as he worked with other game call companies. That spanned from smaller one-man operations up to the industry's most prominent manufacturers. In catering to his client's specific ideas, he would customize all aspects of the call. This could include variations to any of the parts he used: calling surface materials, the pot itself, and the striker/s. Those individual parts might be able to be used across multiple game call companies. His various pot designs included a range of sizes and hole configurations in the back of the pot that contributed to the overall sound. In his designs, he understood "that

Brent Rogers

Mike has developed fourteen different pot molds; The "competition cup" is second from left in the bottom row. The call on the right of the bottom row is actually from the competition cup mold, however it is drilled with a different hole pattern

visual recognition and eye appeal are important to those who buy turkey calls. I make sure people can recognize my pots and my trumpets."

In my research and collecting over the years, I have earnestly sought out as many Mike Battey-designed calls as I could find. Those I am aware of so far include some pots sold by: Butski Game Calls (Paul Butski), Cane Creek Custom Calls (Doug Adkins), Cannon Country Game Calls, Inc. (Chris Parrish), Carlton's Calls (Wayne Carlton), Churchy's Turkey Calls (Doug Church), Eddie Salter Calls (Eddie Salter), H.S. Strut (Dave & Carmen Forbes), Haydel's Game Calls (Rodney Haydel), Hook's Custom Calls (Scott Hook), KNIGHT & HALE (Harold Knight & David Hale), M.A.D. Calls (Mark Drury), M.L. Lynch (Allen Jenkins), Peck's Custom Calls (Peck Martin), Pittman Game Calls (Preston Pittman), PRIMOS® (Will Primos), Rich-N-Tone (Buck Gardner), Springfield Game Calls (Barry Springfield), and Turkey Foot Game Calls (John Panepinto).

Callmaking legend Neil Cost sold a few of Mike's pots; Cost carried one of Mike's pots on his hunting belt

Mike with renowned callmaker Lamar Williams on a hunt in the mid-2000s. Williams sold some limited series of Mike's pot calls

Years ago, some of his pots were utilized by callmaking legends Neil Cost and Lamar Williams in numbered, limited edition runs they offered; these are arguably the most sought-after of all the pots Mike is associated with. More recently, a few of his original pot blanks (the pot with no surface glued in) have surfaced (pun intended!). These are popular with contemporary callmakers, who can take a piece of turkey call history and incorporate it into their craft. I have purchased a few that those callmakers have glued up recently, and they make as good of a call now as they did for the production call companies for whom they were first manufactured.

When asked about calls he designed that are difficult to find, Mike replied, "The Rich-N-Tone Slate Magic! That is the rarest friction call of mine to find. It was originally designed for Craig Schultz of Critter Getter Game calls in the early 1990's." Soon afterward, he said, "Craig sold the mold to Buck Gardner, the owner of Rich-N-Tone game calls. Although Buck agreed to pay $2,000 for the mold, he did not want to pay royalties to me. Instead, he put "Designed by Mike Battey" on the front of the call packaging. This is the only call so designated with my name, except for the Battey World Class by PRIMOS®. The call was soon discontinued by Buck and is rare."

The Carolina Classic gets the job done; It was a call Mike sold under his WildTalker brand for a brief time

Another rare call Mike made and sold himself under his own WildTalker brand is the Carolina Classic. It was made in a limited edition of twenty-five calls, though there may also be some non-limited ones. The call was paired with his Lightning Rod striker, which sported an aluminum peg. He would also commission Bill Zearing to make some calls for him. The calls featured walnut pots with a wood soundboard, a slate surface, and a two-piece Hickory striker. The back of the pot has his brand name, WildTalker, lasered in.

Success doesn't come without failure. Failure remains so only if it isn't learned from, and Mike was a good student. He was disappointed when the manufacturers of his ceramic Sla-Tek disk and his RX-1 latex either went out of business or could not make the product anymore. The blow that hit hardest was when his vendor of the graphite material for pots went out of business in 2002. "That, I could not reproduce," He lamented. "I miss that the most. Those pots had a unique sound and were my best callers."

Despite ups and downs, Mike hasn't held a "real" job except for the six years he led R&D for Kentucky-based KNIGHT & HALE. Primarily, what he did was freelance. This approach afforded him the time to pursue another interest that had been nagging at him since he had started hunting. "I knew that turkeys were always teaching me," Mike said. He believed more wild turkey audio was needed to educate people to be better callers or callmakers.

He explained, "If you are on stage winning turkey call contests, you want to sound like a real turkey. To do that, you want to have the best calls. I didn't encounter vocal hens in the springtime when I started hunting. You don't get a lot of one-on-one dialogue with 'em. That limits the amount of time you can hear and learn from 'em. Fall was when you could hear them calling more."

He had learned all he could, every way he could, with what was readily available. Mike said, "I had picked up the Penn's Woods Tom Turpin trumpet and read Turpin's book. I read Nunnery's *The Old Pro Turkey Hunter*, Tom Kelly's *Tenth Legion*, and *The Voice & Vocabulary of the Wild Turkey* by Lovett Williams, Jr. Of all those, Nunnery talked about a "hen mating call," as did Ben Lee on a cassette tape." Mike was baffled. "Over all the hours and days I hunted, I'd never encountered anything like that in the woods. I didn't think there was any such thing." As he always did, he sought out authority on the subject.

"I called up Lovett after getting his number from Lamar Williams. I said to him, "Dr. Williams, I have to talk to someone that is an expert. I have heard about a hen mating call, but I have never heard that myself. Does it exist?" Mike softly laughed, "He said, bleep no!" Mike continued, "Lovett had been recording since the 1950s. He was releasing his "Real Turkeys" audiotapes, and we just got along; we hit it off." He recalled, "At that time in calling contests, some callers were mimicking other hunters, not turkeys. Most of the records and tapes that had been made were demonstrating turkey calls instead of being recordings of wild turkeys. I started winning and getting better after listening to Lovett's tapes, which eventually led me to do my own recordings."

Mike killed "The Ghost Gobbler" at Cowden Plantation in South Carolina around the year 2000. Appropriately, he called it in with a white (ivory) trumpet. At twenty pounds, with one-and-one-quarter-inch spurs and four beards, it is a remarkable specimen. He knew the bird was not an albino as there was a streak of black on one feather, and it had dark eyes; a true albino has red eyes due to the lack of pigmentation. It was an all-white leucistic bird with a lack of pigmentation in the feathers due to a genetic condition

So, Mike again applied the lessons he learned from his calling competition days. That is to do whatever he did with determination and push to be the best at what he did. He told me, "No one remembers I was second place four times in a row in the North Carolina state turkey calling championship before I won first. And second place only puts your name at the top of the list of losers, which is what my mentor, Lewis Stowe, told me." No one who knows Mike can accuse him of taking the easy road in product development. He researched the available audio technology to do it right. "I found out a digital recorder had just become available and that I could be the first one to record a long segment of wild turkey calling in stereo versus analog." This was energizing to a guy who identified as "being in the sound business." He realized the potential of such audio for turkey hunters, callers, and callmakers alike.

It took six months for the equipment he ordered to arrive, but it was worth the wait. He taped turkeys at South Carolina's Oak Grove Plantation. He got thirty minutes of wild turkeys calling, which is still considered the gold standard. Matt Van Cise, who has won more Senior championships at the NWTF Grand National Calling Championship than anyone else (eight), said, "Spittin' Feathers" was a game changer for anyone wanting to sound more like a wild turkey. There were several short segments in the original production that I used for many years in my calling." Van Cise began calling competitively in 1996, and the release of "Spittin' Feathers" on Compact Disc (CD) in 1995 was perfectly timed for him.

The project is still one Mike is very fond of. He said, "It was the first Mike Battey project, the first product I made, marketed, and sold directly instead of through another company. It probably impacted turkey hunting more than anything else I did." He called Dick's Sporting Goods to see if they would stock it. That retailer knew who Mike was, as his pot call designs (through game call companies) at their stores were best sellers. His CD was included in their catalog, resulting in 200,000 copies being sold then; over 500,000 copies have been sold since that initial release.

Mike would earn praise from Lovett Williams, Jr. in his later book, *Wild Turkey Hunting & Management*, for his breakthrough audio work. Hunters and call competitors alike found listening to the sounds of real wild turkeys helpful. Mike had now come full circle in his dalliance with the wild turkey. He had hunted them, recorded their voices, developed calls to re-

Mike believes "Spittin' Feathers" is the project he did which made the most significant impact in the wild turkey world. Pictured are releases that Mike did of his real wild turkey audio recordings

create that voice, and used those calls in competitions. In every endeavor, he had sought out the best people and technology.

He developed a keen interest in the history of turkey hunting, started collecting calls, and became an authority on those subjects in his own right. Cuz Strickland told me, "Mike Battey, I know him well; he is the Mad Professor. When he did something, he would relentlessly work on it. The friction calls he made were legendary. Behind the scenes, quiet, but enthralled in turkey sounds deeper than anyone else. Mike probably never got the respect as a callmaker he deserved. He has a wealth of knowledge…he is the smartest turkey non-biologist out there."

In the 1980s, Mike had started his first business, Hunter Game Calls, before spending years doing work for game call companies. In 2005, he again started his own business, RealTone. He learned that the name was already in use and switched to WildTalker. He said, "I had always been a huge fan of trumpet calls, so I designed the Alpha as my first WildTalker caller. When I did the Alpha, it was to mass-produce a caller that was easy to play. I sold around 600 and quit making them. On the secondary market, they are fetching as much as $500 for the basic model and as much as $1,000 for the Limited Edition I did of 111 callers." He might claim to be the Alpha and Omega of turkey call trumpets. Mike has designed what he considers to be an even better trumpet than the Alpha and this new Omega Trumpet will be fully launched in 2024. He first made the Alpha trumpets with a synthetic called Nylatron and some with a

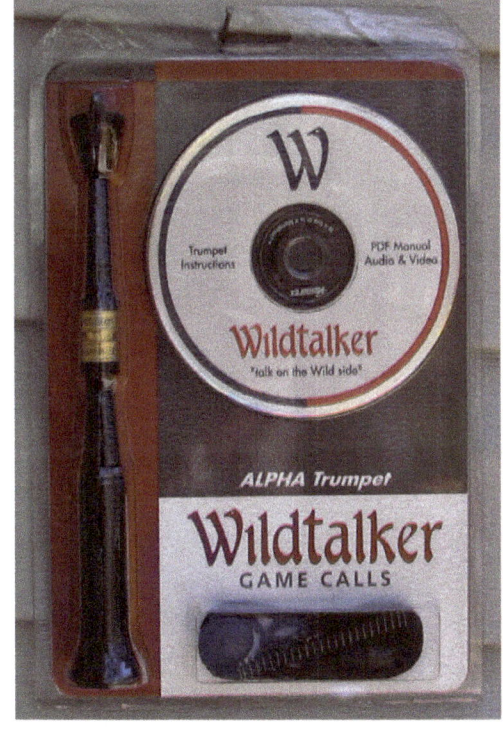

The Alpha Trumpet was released in 2005 under Mike's WildTalker brand; One new in the package would be very rare; he recalls selling less than five dozen like that

WildTalker crow calls; Mike is planning to make more after the 2024 launch of his new Omega trumpet

durable acrylic. As with pot calls, his construction materials were thoroughly researched and built to last.

Turkeys weren't the only species Mike designed calls around. After trumpets, his next release through WildTalker was a crow call. "In 2014, I launched the Champion Crow, which won the World and National championships two weeks after being introduced to the public. I also designed a goose call called Pegasus, which is still sold. Jeff Boyles bought the rights, and it is now called the High Plains Talker." He designed a mouth call carrying case made of plastic that didn't rattle when containing calls and had holes in it to allow the call to dry after use. Mike sold those cases to Preston Pittman Game Calls, Paul Butski Game Calls, Perfection, and others.

One simply needs to watch turkey call sales on eBay to see a steady upswing in the popularity of trumpet calls. Mike has followed such things closely. He told me, "Trumpets have kept getting more and more and more popular, and now they are one of the hottest things on the market." He pointed out that many of the early turkey calls were suction calls. From Native Americans with wingbones to Charles Jordan with Jordan-style cane calls, to Tom Turpin's trumpets, and the Roanoke River Basin yelpers. But Mike pointed out, "They were going out of style by the 1980s, and though custom callmakers made them, most people didn't have access to them. The mouth, box, and pot call dominated. If Ben Lee was playing trumpets way back, they would have stayed popular. But it got to a point where none of the influencers were playing a trumpet." He seems poised to take that on as his next challenge with the upcoming launch of his Omega trumpet.

Along the way, Mike has been adamant that the calls he designed for production game call companies should be as good as his personal calls. He said, "I wanted them to make the same sound as the calls I had in my vest." The hunting community seemed to approve of his designs, even though most may not have known the wizard behind the curtain. "At one point, one in six of the turkey calls being sold at Cabela's were my design," he said.

Looking back at what he has done, Mike acknowledges that the time he has lived through was unique. "I was in the right place at the right time. I couldn't start today, even with the skills I have now, and do the same thing." But he has not lost any of the drive to continue to innovate. Like anyone who celebrates enough birthdays, health challenges come and go. He has navigated such obstacles and kept his fire burning hot for wild turkey hunting.

In the past couple of years, Mike has become increasingly more visible in turkey circles. He has an eager following on his new WildTalker Facebook page. "I haven't lost my mojo," he said. It took him four generations of call designs to get his new Omega trumpet where he wanted it, even after others thought he had it perfected after Gen Two. And, after the Omega, he has already hinted at other projects in his future, including a WildTalker tube call. It's safe to say The Call Dr. is still on duty!

MIKE BATTEY: THE CALL DR.

Photos by Brent Rogers

The author's collection of Mike Battey-designed calls launched by other game call companies

The author's collection of Mike Battey WildTalker calls. Clockwise starting with box call: 1 Limited Edition box call made for Mike by Albert Paul. 2 pot calls: a pot call done for Mike by Cody calls and a 30th-anniversary Ol' Yeller call made by Mike. 4 assorted strikers, a crow call, and 6 trumpets: the 3 will mouthpieces facing down are 2005 Alpha trumpets and the 3 with mouthpieces facing up are 2023 Omega trumpets

MIKE BATTEY TIMELINE

(* = approximate date)

1950s* – Mike's uncle starts a gun store as part of an Ace Hardware business; the gun store is where Mike will later work and discover turkey hunting through a customer.

1953 – Mike Battey is born on April 1.

1975-current – Fred Tornow and Mike Battey become best friends after meeting at Fred's wedding.

1983 – Ray Sutphin brings a Model 12 Winchester into the gun store for restoration; he invites Mike to hunt deer. On the trip, Mike is introduced to turkey calls and is immediately fascinated by air-operated wingbone calls; the first call he makes is a suction call.

1984 – Mike takes his first wild turkey gobbler using a scratch box. At twenty-one pounds and two ounces, it was a North Carolina record for weight at the time.

1985 – Mike's first trumpet call is a Penn's Woods Roger Latham trumpet; then he buys a Billy Buice trumpet from Lewis Stowe for $25.

1986 – Mike serves as a turkey hunting guide in South Carolina for 15 years. He gets a Southland tube call; later he makes a tube prototype of his own with plans to eventually release a tube call.

1988 – Mike sets his sights on winning the North Carolina state turkey calling contest, leading him to experiment with making calls. He works on a latex product for diaphragm calls, and he makes his first successful pot mold and drills two holes in the slate surface, similar to Lewis Stowe; Stowe provides his blessing for Mike to sell the pot as his own, given the dimensional differences. Mossy Oak's Toxey Haas gives Mike the nickname "The Mad Scientist" for his experimentation with game calls.

1989 – Momentum builds for Mike as he wins the NC Owling Competition. He forms Hunter Game Calls and Haydel's buys 200 pots. He gambles, splurging for a booth at the NWTF National Convention in Nashville. Jami Linder uses his pot for a 5th place Grand National Senior Division finish; Von Eubanks runs his mouth call with the RX-1 latex. All of this puts Mike on the map as a call designer. He gets his first big break as Allen Jenkins of M.L. Lynch has him design the Lynch Pro-Mini Slate. Preston Pittman releases The Black Diamond diaphragm with RX-1 latex developed by Mike and it becomes a widely popular call.

1990 – Paul Butski launches the 2'N 1 Combo glass over slate call, which Mike Designed. Butski also uses Mike's RX-1 latex in diaphragms.

1991 – Mike's first collaboration with PRIMOS® results in the Two Hole Slate and Two Hole Glass calls. It would be the first of at least 18 call models Mike would do with the game call company.

1991-1994 – Mike works at the Sports Authority as he continues to reinvest in his callmaking ventures.

1992 – Mark A. Drury gives Mike his biggest order to date as he prepares to launch M.A.D. Calls with his brother Terry in 1993. Over time M.A.D. would launch 11 pots and 2 box calls with a Battey design.

1993-1994 – Mike wins the North Carolina turkey calling championship back to back.

1994 – Jimmy Primos calls Mike after Ronnie "Cuz" Strickland expresses his affinity for a pot call Mike made; this starts a chain reaction, leading Mike to quit his job at the Sports Authority and dive in full-time into game call design.

1995 – Mike competes on the NWTF GNCC stage for the final time. His namesake call, the Battey World Class, is launched by PRIMOS® in both slate and glass-surfaced models; that call is still in production and is now named the Ol' Betsy. Mike's audio recordings of wild turkeys in stereo are released as "Spittin' Feathers" on Compact Disc; over a half million copies have been sold to date.

1996 – M.A.D. Calls begins selling the Super Aluminator which the growing number of turkey hunters snaps up, leading to one of Mike's biggest orders to date.

1998 – *Turkey & Turkey Hunting* magazine's Winter issue contains the article "Unknown Legend: The Work of Mike Battey" by Roger B. Hook, which attests to the impact Mike is making in the game call world.

1998-2004 – After being purchased by PRADCO, KNIGHT & HALE hires Mike Battey to lead their R&D; David Hale tags him with the handle "The Call Dr." He contributes to a number of innovations there including the 2 Bucks in a Bag deer rattle bag, though turkey calls are his primary focus.

1999 – PRIMOS® launches four separate calls designed by Mike, one of which is the PRIMOS® Power Crystal, a best-seller with continuous production since. KNIGHT & HALE releases the Ol' Yeller in Mike's competition cup pot and a ceramic surface he formulated; it is an instant hit and best-seller.

2000 – Mike kills "The Ghost Gobbler" at Cowden Plantation in South Carolina using a white (ivory) trumpet. It is a remarkable specimen at twenty pounds, with one-and-one-quarter-inch spurs and four beards.

MIKE BATTEY: THE CALL DR.

2002 – The vendor of Mike's graphite material for pots goes out of business. This is a personal blow to Mike as that is something unique he cannot reproduce.
2005 – WildTalker becomes Mike's new business name, and he comes out with his first trumpet call: the Alpha trumpet.
2006 – Mike commissions Albert Paul to make 88 snakewood and holly box calls to sell under his WildTalker brand.
2014 – A crow call is offered in Mike's WildTalker line of calls; that call wins the World and National championships two weeks after being introduced.
2021 – Mike starts the WildTalker Facebook group as he begins designing calls again.
2023 – Mike completes the development of his new Omega trumpet call for a full launch in 2024.

YELP & GOBBLE, INC.

Chapter 5

ANTHONY FOSTER: THE MILLWORKER

Anthony Foster enjoying a rite of spring

"I was destined to do this, though I never set out to do it. No one knows God's plan," Anthony Foster said of his lifetime making turkey calls and running a call production facility. "When people would tell me something I always wanted to do was going to be hard, it only drove me harder." Anthony Foster is humble in his accomplishments but tenacious in his passion for making game calls. He is one of only two individuals getting their chapter in this book because he represents a critical piece of the production turkey call puzzle.

Starting as a custom callmaker, Foster has designed some of the most popular factory calls that have been sold while managing the production of a host of products for several different companies. An intensely personal man, he purposely avoids the spotlight and is content to be the working man behind the scenes. It is my pleasure to introduce him to you and to help establish how a multitude of successful hunters, in part, owe him thanks.

Foster grew up with a family tradition of hunting and regularly explored the woods by age 8. "I was always in the woods," he said, "There were few turkeys around in my early years, but I eagerly hunted deer and squirrel. Maybe because there were few turkeys then, my biggest enjoyment was just listening to them. Especially in the fall, the cackling and cutting fascinated me, and I first mimicked them with my voice and then with calls." Calling them in is what Foster loved. He would coax in several each year, some multiple times. It wouldn't be until five years after he built his first turkey call that he killed his first turkey at age 16. "It's funny, but it didn't even feel like it was my first turkey, as I'd called up so many before that," he told me.

A love of the outdoors took root during Anthony Foster's youth

While Foster enjoys slinging a turkey over his shoulder after a successful hunt, it is not the part of the hunt most vital to him. "Along the way, God gave me the gift of just enjoyin' the show. It's not all about the trigger pull," he said. "The thrill is still there, and I can just about pass out under the tree from the excitement! But when you come to my house, you will see a lot of photos and mementos instead of heads on the wall. I don't idolize the trophies; I treasure the memories."

Foster with son, Colton; Cultivating a new generation to appreciate the outdoors

Foster and his wife, Cindy, have two children: a son, Colton, and a daughter, Addyson. The time they share is most coveted; he has included them in his outdoor pursuits. Passing the hunting tradition to his family is now more important to Foster than hunting solo. "Now, killing a turkey just has to be the right time and place when it's just me, and for the last four or five years, I have limited myself to one gobbler, though I've helped dozens of others. My daughter is a super outdoorsman, turkey caller, and squirrel hunter. I have a rule that if you shoot 'em in the head, I clean 'em; I dress all of hers lately!"

In addition to inheriting the love of the outdoors from his Dad, Foster was inspired by his father's woodworking. His Dad had a woodshop behind their house in Brandon, Mississippi; Foster believes he may be a seventh-generation millworker. "Before I could walk and talk, I was sittin' in a wood shop," he told me. At a mere 11 years old, Foster got the itch to make his first call. That itch was relieved by making a scratch box type call, where one piece of wood is rubbed against another to emit a turkey sound.

Although his initial intent had been to make a personal call to hunt with, in true Anthony Foster fashion, he recognized there was room for improvement. He became engrossed in making a call that sounded more like the turkeys he enjoyed listening to. This mindset is a trait of the best callmakers who design calls to reproduce a wild turkey's voice instead

Foster's daughter, Addyson is a chip off the old block

Foster family woodworking tools that have bridged generations of Millworkers

of making calls that produce turkey-like sounds. If you don't understand the difference, spend time listening to wild turkeys, then run as many turkey calls as you can lay your hands on. You will soon note that there are winners and losers in quality.

In his quest to build a better turkey call, Foster made a few hundred scratch boxes, never quite nailing down what he was looking for. He soon began experimenting with every kind of call he could lay hands on. Over time, he developed a personal preference for a box call. He liked the resonating sound it produced, even though most people favored using the recently popularized diaphragm mouth calls. When he started working with his Dad in the woodshop, he learned to use a chain mortiser, which is like a small chainsaw on a drill press. This allowed Foster to take a block of wood and cut a square hole (mortise) in it, making the base of a box call (a hollowed-out rectangular block of wood).

At age 14, the ever inquisitive Foster said, "I had begun to play around with box calls, like an Ashby box I had, to learn how they worked." He even modified calls he purchased to get the sound he wanted. He was learning through observation and experimentation what worked and what didn't.

He was particularly fond of the one-sided Ashby Old Hen box. He also recalls a Birmingham-era Lynch box that may have been his grandfather's; "The glue was falling off...it sounded dead. But even after I re-glued the side back on,

ANTHONY FOSTER: THE MILLWORKER

If this box call belonging to Foster's grandad could talk it would have stories to tell. Note the hash marks on the paddle which may correspond to gobblers killed

it still didn't sound right to me," Foster said. "My Grandad, Joe Toler, also had a very old one-piece box, the interior of which had been excavated with a hand drill and chisel." Like the late 1800s and early 1900s-era Gibson box calls that were the first patented box calls, it had straight sides. To Foster, it just sounded "okay." The actual pedigree of the box is a mystery, though it was rumored to be one of the first boxes made by the iconic callmaker M.L. Lynch. Sadly, this has not been verified, but the many hash marks carved into the box testify to the number of turkeys it likely called to the gun.

All this exposure helped convince Foster of the merits of a Gibson-style call (a hollowed-out block of wood for the body, with a wooden paddle to scrape over it) versus those of the "sawn-and-glued" variety (several individual pieces of wood glued together to form the box body). He believed the solid one-piece wood body improved and preserved resonation. The trouble was the time it would take to hollow out a piece of wood by hand, even using the chain mortiser. Many modern custom callmakers also

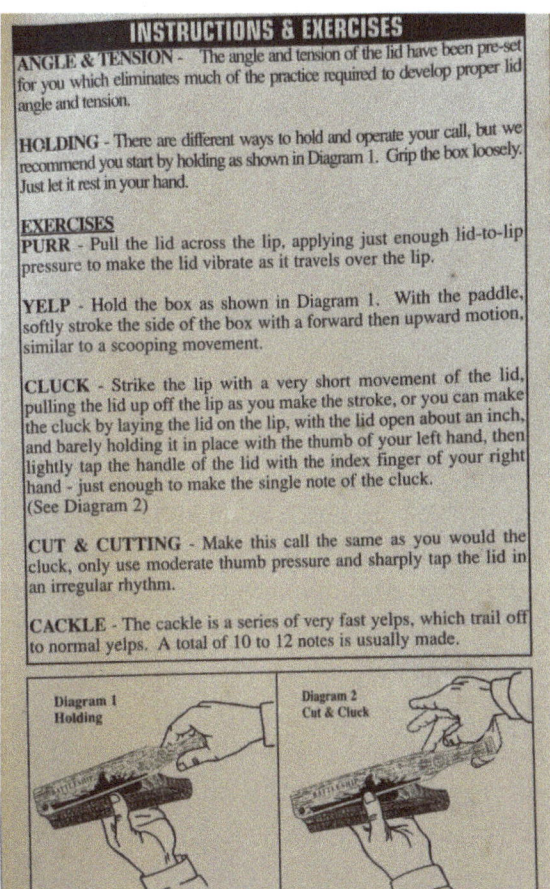

Basic box call operation

prefer a one-piece box call base, meticulously and skillfully using drills and chisels to hollow out their wood blanks. However, this method wouldn't work for the calls Foster would later make on a production line.

During High School, Foster attended Hinds Junior College, where he was introduced to their Computer Numerical Control (CNC) machine in their Diversified Technology class. Using preprogrammed computer software, a CNC automates milling method control, movement, and precision. CNC is commonly used in manufacturing for machining or milling all types of materials. He took a CNC class, providing a helpful technical foundation, later enabling him to be one of the first to usher in modern technology that is now an industry standard for game call companies.

Foster during his law enforcement days

Like many of us, Foster's path to his ultimate career was not straight. He set aside dreams of callmaking to attend college, launching a career in fire service and law enforcement. He continued to nurture his innovation skills there, developing several devices. These included a tactical law enforcement training device with a component that emitted a laser and then recorded a sound when a bullet fired by the shooter impacted a target. This helped inform the shooter of their aim, enhancing the user's muscle memory shooting. But the family trade was still calling him, and in 1989, he and his father, Jack Foster, established Foster Millworks, a cabinetry business focused on hotels.

Like everything Foster puts his mind to, Foster Millworks was a great success. They built an $18 million/year business based in Brookhaven, MS, focused on large-scale millwork for hotel chains. Thankfully, a healthy population of local turkeys reawakened his passion to build that better box call. In 1996, he picked up where he had left off and milled out his first one-piece box body using the CNC technology he learned about in High School. Despite Foster Millworks making good money, the allure of building game calls was too strong to ignore.

Foster believed a CNC machine would provide him with superior technology to achieve the curve he wanted in the sides of the box, just one of the many intricate details most users of turkey calls don't fully appreciate. He began to investigate different woods and to think of a box call as a musical instrument. "Resonation is key," Foster explained. "When a box call is in tune, it rings with a musical note. I played guitar and piano enough to know chords and notes and have a good ear. I even worked as a sound engineer in college. I set out to make the ultimate box call, not necessarily to sell, but for my personal use."

ANTHONY FOSTER: THE MILLWORKER

A friend, Donny Mullins, owned a local sporting goods store, and during a conversation there about turkey calls, Foster showed Mullins the box call he had just made. Mullins liked it; he liked it so much that he urged Foster to contact Preston Pittman. A nationally decorated calling competition champion who had started his own callmaking venture, Pittman always looked out for calls with "just that right sound."

Pittman is very complimentary of Foster and said, "Back before he was working with PRIMOS®, he helped bring CNC machines to life for making turkey calls. Anthony was about the only person down here that would do it. He had knowledge of what to do and how to do it. A lot of times, I would sit down and use a pocket knife and Dremel tool on a box call to get one I liked close to being finished, then take it to him," Pittman recalled. "He was much smarter at all this technical stuff, and he would look at the box and say, "How many thousands you want off?" Pittman laughed and remarked, "Thousands, what's that?" Pittman continued, "Anthony was just at a different level and could do things on the CNC that were hard to repeat by hand. Anthony could recreate anything or make it better."

Foster recalls that collaboration; "Preston was very interested in that box call I made when I played it for him. He asked me to make some he could sell under his brand." Pittman had a sawn-and-glued, double-sided call he had named the Gobble Box. Foster re-designed it in a one-piece body in 1997. Pittman loved it and honored Foster by signing the first completed and giving it to him. Foster recalled, "The first order was for 500 boxes, but they

Signed, #1 Gobble Box of Foster design for Pittman Game Calls

Top view of #1 Gobble Box of Foster design for Pittman Game Calls

Signed, #2 Boss Buster of Foster design for Pittman Game Calls

were well received. So, only a week later, Pittman called me and said in earnest, "I need 2,500 more!" Pittman would sell those at a National Wild Turkey Federation Convention.

This quickly led to a second collaboration with Pittman, a one-sider coined the Boss Buster. Foster still has the number two call of that run, signed by Pittman. Foster said that both boxes "had the combination of good resonance and rasp that I strive for. There is more to it than a box shape and a paddle. Everyone at that time knew the sound needed to roll over, and there is a transition over three-quarters of a paddle stroke for sound to travel, related to the various dimensions and other characteristics of the wood."

What he was learning, combined with this initial call designing success, was a confidence builder for the budding callmaker. In developing his early calls, Foster said, "From my millwork background, I knew I'd need to pick the right wood. The biggest thing that helped me is I knew wood forwards and backward. I learned about the different types of wood: How to select it, how to control moisture, knowing the softness or hardness, knowing the different grains, understanding how the sound travels through the wood, and knowing where to put a nail or a screw. I learned how to properly age wood to manage sap and oil content in order to create the right "bite." Foster continued, "If you can't get the right wood to start with, you can't make a quality call. Certain woods carry certain sounds better. I helped my first wood importer understand wood and have now used him for decades."

Solving problems is where opportunity lies. Foster recognized how hunters unknowingly encountered issues while incorrectly using some box calls. He said, "When it comes to box calls, you have to drag the paddle back and forth over the box side rail when calling." On a turkey box call, the desired sound is made as the paddle moves inward from the outer side of the rail. Foster continued, "I noticed people would repeatedly pick up the paddle after making each individual note, swing the paddle up and back out, then put it down to make the next call." Hunters will often make a series of five or more "yelps" or a rapid series of "cutts." That is hard to do, at least in the right cadence and speed, if one is lifting and repositioning the paddle at every note. Foster realized, "The paddle would squeak when dragging it backwards

Top view of #2 Boss Buster of Foster design for Pittman Game Calls

across the calling surface, which is why people were having to lift up the paddle between notes. In calls I make, I design them so there is no sound on the backstroke. That enables better cutting and up-close calling when hunting." His approach is an excellent example of how a designer can make life easier for the customer by engineering a solution.

Foster's quest to make a call by his own hands that met his sound standards was finally achieved. He received a Trademark for his White Feather brand in 1997. The White Feather name originates from his association with Carlos Hathcock, one of his instructors during his law enforcement days. Hathcock was the Marine Corps sniper with the most confirmed kills in Vietnam. The Viet Cong called the feared sniper *Lông Trắng,* translated as "White Feather," because of the white feather he kept in a band on his bush hat. The white feather is also significant to Native Americans, and Foster has such ancestry. Foster would not sell calls under his personal brand until 2002, given the growth his fledgling business was about to realize.

Given the good population of turkeys around Brookhaven, the accomplished hunter Brad Farris visited Foster in 1998 to record some hunting footage. Farris had just started working for PRIMOS® full time and the morning they hunted, Farris was armed with a PRIMOS® Double Play box call. Foster introduced him to a White Feather box; Farris was impressed with what he saw and heard and intrigued Foster had made it. He correctly suspected PRIMOS® might be interested.

Word traveled fast. Foster told me, "That afternoon, Will Primos called me. We got together, and he showed me his original Gibson box call, given to him years before. He was familiar with and liked the boxes I was making for Pittman and wanted to do something with me. What I ended up showing Will was the product of a long sit on a deer stand. I was hunting a recurve bow, which offers plenty of time when waiting to get a shot at a decent buck inside 30 yards. On that sit, I sketched out a design I thought would give a clear note with rasp. I thought that

Anthony Foster's White Feather logo

an arch on the box would help the rollover of the second note. I set out making a box, but when I first called, it was disappointing. Then I realized the outside curve was a problem." After returning to the drawing board and making another call, what would be The Heart Breaker box call made for PRIMOS® was born! He called Will and exclaimed, "I've got something good!"

This new box was based on Foster's Model #120 White Feather box, which he had named The Classic. It was a walnut box with a bloodwood lid. Will immediately loved it, even before Foster demonstrated how it sounded even better at a distance. Foster shot him a price to provide the calls. At that time, he was making calls for less than $10 a call, which is hard to imagine with today's material and labor costs. With their own expense Foster said, "PRIMOS® was going to have to sell these for $49 each, which at the time was unheard of! It had to be the highest-priced production call at the time." When we launched it, it was a Sapele (mahogany-like wood) box with a purpleheart lid. They couldn't keep 'em on shelves!" The success of this double-sided box in 1998 quickly led to a single sider, The Lil' Heart Breaker, which was released in 2000. It happens to be the author's favorite, and field-proven, production box call.

A rare Limited Edition White Feather Classic Model #120

BREAKING (TURKEY) HEARTS

Anthony Foster provided these insights on the chronology of the different variants of The Heart Breaker produced by PRIMOS®:

First variant, *1998*. Only 200 were made through the first order. The PRIMOS® logo is lasered into the thumb grip. The lids on all variants are Purple Heart.

Second variant, *1999*: 2,600 were made. For the Woods is lasered onto the thumb grip; a camo silencer band came with it. All the box bodies came from one Sapele (a Mahogany like wood) tree I imported from Nigeria. The tree was over ten feet in diameter and filled three containers when they shipped it.

Third variant, *2001*: Model 228 Patent Pending is lasered in at top of the paddle. The Heritage logo and For The Hunt Will Primos is lasered onto the bottom of the paddle, and For The Woods is lasered onto the thumb grip.

Fourth variant: US Pat No 415,054 is lasered in at top of call, with the Heritage logo and For The Hunt Will Primos lasered onto the bottom of the paddle.

By the time the wood from that first tree was gone, we had changed our slogan to Speak the Language and that appears on later calls.

I have designed and built some great calls for many in the game call business, but the Heart Breaker is still one of my favorites.

Foster aimed to prove he could make a production call that reproduced the sound of a quality hand-made call. He said, "My company took my high-performing custom call and turned it into a production call using a CNC machine." Foster believes he was among the first, if not the first, company to use a CNC machine to produce turkey calls. He told me, "The machine made the parts and pieces that needed tolerance and precision, but we never took away the hands-on part to hand-tune the call to produce the right sound. I would put my calls up against any out there!"

Foster put his money where his mouth was, entering a Heart Breaker in a National Wild Turkey Federation (NWTF) calling competition in 2001. If there was any doubt about whether a production call could sound good, contemplate the results. Foster said, "That Heart Breaker box won second place in for hunting box calls, which was the Noble Descent category, as well as Best of Show, which was the King of Kings category. Foster continued, "I had kept the White Feather line and had agreed with Will & Jimmy to never sell my calls at a lower price. Even with the success of those models, PRIMOS® had not ordered enough calls to fill my line capacity, so I started doing work for KNIGHT & HALE as well."

The KNIGHT & HALE Kentucky Longbox, made on Foster's production line, was released in 2002. Foster said, "PRIMOS® noticed, and Will also wanted a longbox. He decided to do The Heart Breaker Battleship, which is a longbox in the Heart Breaker series, in 2002." Through persistence and diligence, Foster's callmaking business attracted much attention. "I wasn't using money from the cabinetry business to fund my callmaking venture," Foster informed me. He turned out to be a good steward of his talent and resources; with that re-investment of his earnings, he built a company of fourteen employees with over $1 million of equipment on the floor.

To maximize his capacity, he began making fishing lures on the CNC and calls for many more game-call businesses. While not all the design work he did led to contracts, it created many friendships and an appreciation in the industry for his abilities. Over time, he did design work or produced calls for Preston Pittman, PRIMOS®, KNIGHT & HALE, M.A.D. Calls, QUAKER

PRIMOS® The Heart Breaker Battleship and KNIGHT & HALE Kentucky Longbox

BOY®, Penn's Woods, Lohman, Allen Sports, Heart of Dixie, Illusions Game Calls, Rich-N-Tone, Echo Calls, Dead Ringer Game Calls, Woods Wise, and several duck call companies.

While working for others was his primary focus, Foster did, at last, make and sell some calls under his White Feather brand. That ended up being for a very short time, during portions of 2002 and 2003, given that he was about to sign a game-changing contract. As a result, Foster's White Feather calls are hard to find and are expensive to purchase second-hand.

Illustrating the cult-like status of Foster's White Feather calls, In 2013, outdoor writer Mike Gaddis wrote a tribute to Foster in the Sept-Oct issue of *Sporting Classics* magazine. He told the story of wanting to identify the maker of the White Feather box call he'd been using with great success. That led him to Anthony Foster. He praised Foster's White Feather Classic Model #120 single-sided box as having "that super-keen, falsetto, narrow-band sweet spot the 120 does – that so reliably yawks in the hard cases." Foster originally sold them for $42; it is rare to see one go for less than $1000 now. Some have brought double that!

Foster believes he only made around 2,400 of that Classic Model #120. He shared, "There were 2,000 made in the main production run, and they consisted of a bloodwood lid on a walnut body. Around 100 were canary wood on mahogany, and others were made of various woods as I was experimenting." In 2002, he did a limited run for the Mississippi Wild Turkey Federation of around 200 Model #120s. They had a bubinga lid on a walnut body. Those calls would be used to raise money for the nonprofit organization. The art on the call was to commemorate the heroics of the service people and responders of the 9/11 terrorist attacks a year earlier. "With my background in law enforcement, I have always strove to honor and recognize such people," Foster said.

Foster did not limit his callmaking to box calls. He designed and made several types of turkey calls, even some duck and goose calls for himself, and later for game call companies. Within the stable of products Foster made and briefly sold under his White Feather brand, here are the calls you should know about:

> **The Classic** (a single-sided box), Model 120. This call would later be the inspiration for PRIMOS® dynamite seller, the Lil' Heart Breaker
>
> **Ol' Faithful** (a single-sided box), Model 130. This call would later inspire another PRIMOS® bestseller, the Box Cutter.
>
> **Sure-Strut Slate** (a slate-surfaced pot call), Model 150.
>
> **Sure-Strut Aluminum** (an aluminum-surfaced pot call), Model 151.
>
> **Deadly Diamond** (an aluminum slate trough), Model 140.

The Duel'n Hen (a two-reed mouth diaphragm), Model 102.

The Smokin' Hen (a four-reed mouth diaphragm), Model 104.
There were two additional mouth diaphragms. (no info on those).

White Feather Sure-Strut pot call *White Feather Deadly Diamond trough call* *White Feather mouth call*

Success comes with sacrifice. Like others who built successful companies that paralleled the wild turkey restoration, demand for new products was a constant focus. For a perfectionist like Foster, his response was to work harder. He admitted, "In those early days, it was running me ragged. I'd be up in the middle of the night changing over machine setups. I'd been offered a chance to work full time for KNIGHT & HALE in 2001, but I had concerns that if they were acquired by a larger company, production would be moved out of my home of Brookhaven."

The answer to his problems came in 2002 when Will and Jimmy Primos took him to dinner. Foster recalled, "Over a handshake, Will gave me a chance to do what I really wanted to do." Foster had grown to love running the production plant and developing products. Yet, his time was consumed by seeking contracts to fill his production capacity. Will advised him, "You can do what you want to do for us full time, run our plant. You know how to do it." It was also important to Foster to have call design responsibility, which he was granted. "I was also put in my PRIMOS® role to invent; that is my passion, and running a production plant just comes naturally," he said.

So, in 2003, Foster became a PRIMOS® employee, and to this day, he oversees production and designs new products. This deal allowed him to stay in Brookhaven, and filling capacity was no longer his problem to solve. This meant an abrupt halt to his White Feather callmaking business, although his designs would live on in the PRIMOS® brand. Foster shared one example: "Will watched me cut on a White Feather call model named Ol' Faithful, and it sparked an idea. Will thought it'd be cool if a groove could be made for the hunter's thumb, which made cutting easier." The PRIMOS® Box Cutter was the result, launching in 2004. Will and Jimmy had a commercial made to demonstrate this new call, leading to an initial sale of 20,000 calls. Now, under the PRIMOS® Select line of calls, Foster's older designs like The Heart Breaker and Lil' Heart Breaker are being resurrected for today's hunters.

Foster bringing his leisure and professional pursuits together

As with any competitive business, he saw his designs stolen or copied, which taught him lessons. Corporate buyouts were also changing business decisions and ethics. "You can only steal so much and win," was Foster's attitude. He has been involved in several patents to protect his innovations. The first one was filed for by Will Primos, the patent application for The Heart Breaker; it was awarded in 1999. Foster personally filed for several patents as well. The "bone reed" was his first. Shaped like a bone, it was a duck-call reed designed to clear water out of the call. He recalled, "When I demonstrated the call, filling it with water and then calling with no problems, eyes popped. I sold it to Knight & Hale for $75,000 with no questions asked."

Among other Foster patents were the PRIMOS® Bomb Shell and PRIMOS® Trigger Stick. He has not lost his hunger for the challenge of creating something new and different. Foster has developed as many as fifty products a year for PRIMOS®. Some never make it to market, while others have been best-sellers. His favorite call? "The PRIMOS® Hensanity is my favorite slate to use," Foster said. "Putting fingers over the holes and being able to use the middle of the surface for calling changed, to me, the way slates sound. Will and I put on a seminar at the NWTF Convention one year. After I demonstrated that call, we sold out of all we had at the show that day."

Product development is something Foster relishes, giving him a chance to exercise his creative side. The Tall Timber Gabriel box call was a neat collaborative project. Will Primos loves history and literature and has a rare copy of the book *Tall Timber Gabriels* by the late Charles Whittington. It is the first book I have identified dedicated to spring turkey hunting, published in 1971. Will had corresponded with Whittington years ago and thought the book title a good call name with historical significance. Foster recalled, "Will also loved the Lil' Heart Breaker box and had been wanting me to design another one like it but with a little higher rasp. So, I started with his favorite call and added thumb hole slots to make it easier to cutt on." The Tall Timber Gabriel was the result, released in 2018.

One of Foster's passions is the PRIMOS® Custom Mill shop. It is an interactive space where customers get to help customize a box or pot call, resulting in a one-of-a-kind item. A couple wood selections for the call are matched with limitless creative options for what can be laser engraved on the paddle of the call. They have been popular as personal hunting calls or keepsakes, gifts for wedding parties, conservation and organization fundraisers, and company events.

"We've only touched the tip of the iceberg with it," Foster told me. What some may not realize

A box call being made in the PRIMOS® Custom Mill shop

Foster and Jimmy Primos enjoy a moment after a successful hunt

when seeing the premium prices for a Custom Mill shop product is the actual work that goes into making such a call. It takes hours to do the design and then get it set up," he said. "I can take twenty, thirty, even forty hours to design something truly unique. Think about someone painting a picture; it takes time. First, I have to draw it. Then, when programming, there can be sixty to seventy shades of greyscale…" Foster quickly lost me in the details, but I gained an appreciation for what is easy to take for granted.

With Will and Jimmy Primos no longer active in day-to-day work at PRIMOS®, Foster's sense of responsibility has increased. My observation is that he is working tirelessly to ensure continued growth for the company he committed to and is doing a good job. "I want to ensure the legacy and future are secure," he told me. Foster's relationship with Will and Jimmy is a close one and another testament to the camaraderie within the game call world.

On his journey, Foster has many he admired and that inspired him. "Preston, Will and Jimmy, Harold, and David, they all did right by me. The late Rev. Wiley Reid, a Baptist preacher, and his wife, Miss Katie, who is still living, were also salt-of-the-earth folks. Rev. Wiley practically lived at PRIMOS®, and he and Miss Katie were kind and giving people. Rev. Wiley contributed to the early success of PRIMOS® by being the builder of the YAWK BOX scratch box, and Miss Katie sewed the carrying pouches for it. They would bring by food, and they embodied what is best about turkey hunting culture." In a testament to how meaningful that relationship was, Foster was a pallbearer at Rev. Wiley's funeral.

Finally, Foster shared that Mike Battey, an accomplished inventor in the game call industry, was another influencer and friend. "The first time Mike heard me cut on a box call it really caught his attention," Foster told me. "I have a lot of respect for Mike; he offered a lot of ideas in terms of business decisions and callmaking materials." Both men have left their mark by providing each of their unique talents to numerous game call companies. Through their work and that of others like Ron Eppley (a long-time manufacturer of call parts), production companies have been able to make great-sounding calls on a factory line. The story of successful game call companies couldn't be told without their ideas and involvement.

The parting words from Foster sum up who he is and what is most important to him. "I have only been able to do this because of support from my family." Foster is a hard man to reach, not just because he is busy at work but because his family is a priority. That is his recipe for success. He has not only lived his dream but helped fulfill those of others. That has been accomplished by manufacturing game calls for hundreds of thousands of people who have carried them afield to make special memories.

A higher purpose drives Foster. He told me solemnly, "I was an Eagle Scout; one of the things you're taught is to leave things better than you found them. That is also part of my family

Author's small collection of White Feather calls

tradition and Native American heritage. In general, people are not as effective at puttin' back than at takin' out. As outdoor people, we must love what we hunt more than we love killin' it. That may seem like blasphemy from a callmaker, but a little conservation in a hunter is important to ensure there will be turkeys for future generations to hunt." If more folks adopt Foster's mindset, that future will be secured.

YELP & GOBBLE, INC.

ANTHONY FOSTER TIMELINE

(* = approximate date)

1898 – Henry Gibson receives a patent for his box call. In 2018, Anthony Foster and Will Primos will later make replicas to help the National Wild Turkey Federation raise money for conservation.

Early 1900s* – Anthony Foster's grandfather hunts Mississippi's elusive wild turkeys, carving notches into an old hewn-out box call to commemorate successful hunts.

1940 – M.L. Lynch begins selling turkey calls. One of Lynch's calls will spark interest in a young Anthony Foster in learning more about how box calls are made and how they can be improved.

1970 – Anthony Foster is born on Feb 5th.

1978 – A precocious Anthony Foster is regularly exploring the woods.

1979-1985 – Anthony Foster learns to hunt small game like squirrel as well as deer; he also discovers wild turkeys and begins calling them in, first with his voice and then with calls.

1981 – Anthony Foster makes his first call, a scratch box. He makes a few hundred, striving for an ever-better-sounding call.

1984 – Box calls become a fascination for Anthony Foster, and he starts modifying them to get the sound he likes. Foster also serves as a pallbearer at the funeral service of Rev. Wiley Reid (a Baptist preacher) from the Brookhaven area; Rev. Reid made the YAWK BOX scratch box for PRIMOS® and was an inspiration for Foster.

1986 – After regularly calling in wild turkeys for sheer enjoyment, Anthony Foster takes his first turkey.

1989 – Anthony Foster and his father, Jack, establish Foster Millworks, a cabinetry business focused on hotels.

1996 – The passion for building box calls resurfaces, and Anthony Foster mills out his first one-piece box body using a CNC.

1997 – After a friend sees and hears a box call that Anthony Foster built, Foster takes his friend's recommendation to show it to renowned turkey caller and callmaker Preston Pittman. Pittman loves it; Foster re-designs Pittman's double-sided Gobble Box to have a one-piece box body. Foster receives a trademark for his White Feather brand.

1998 – Preston Pittman and Anthony Foster do their second collaboration as Foster designs a one-sided Boss Buster box call with a one-piece box body. Brad Farris visits Foster while filming a turkey hunt for PRIMOS®, is impressed with Foster's box calls, and shares that with Will Primos. This quickly leads to Foster designing and patenting a call based on his White Feather Model #120 The Classic box call for PRIMOS®: The Heart Breaker.

ANTHONY FOSTER: THE MILLWORKER

2000 – The success of The Heart Breaker leads to another Foster/ PRIMOS® box call, a single-sider called the Lil' Heart Breaker.

2001 – Anthony Foster enters a PRIMOS® Heart Breaker box Heart Breaker box call in an NWTF Callmaking Competition; the call wins second place in hunting box calls and best of show.

2002 – Knight & Hale launch the Kentucky Longbox, which Anthony Foster made on his production line.

2002-2003 – For part of 2002 and 2003, Foster makes several calls in his White Feather line; these calls will end up being rare, given Foster will shortly sell his business and cease making his own calls.

2003 – The third call in PRIMOS® Heart Breaker family is launched, a longbox called the Battleship. Foster is invited to dinner by Will and Jimmy Primos; he is offered a job to manage production for PRIMOS®, which he accepts, along with asking for call design responsibilities. Foster's callmaking business in Brookhaven, MS, becomes part of PRIMOS®.

2004 – The PRIMOS® Box Cutter premieres. This box call is based on Anthony Foster's White Feather Model #130 Ol' Faithful with a twist; Will Primos contributes the idea for a thumbhole groove to allow better reproduction of the cutting call of a wild turkey.

2013 – Mike Gaddis writes a tribute to Foster in the Sept-Oct issue of *Sporting Classics* magazine.

2018 – Anthony Foster and Will Primos make replicas of the Henry Gibson box call that Will had been gifted to help the National Wild Turkey Federation raise money for conservation. The two also work together to reproduce a Limited Edition series of Henry Gibson boxes to help the National Wild Turkey Federation raise money for conservation. The Tall Timber Gabriels box call, which Will Primos and Anthony Foster worked together on, is released.

2019 – Anthony Foster's favorite call, the PRIMOS® Hensanity is first launched.

2022 – The Heart Breaker and Lil' Heart Breaker box calls are resurrected for today's hunter under the PRIMOS®. Select call line.

SOURCES

Preface: The Survivor
1) The *Vineyard Gazette,* Friday, April 21, 1933.
2) Cokinos, Christopher, *Hope is the Thing with Feathers: A Personal Chronicle of Vanished Birds,* Jeremy P. Tarcher, 2000. Gross, Alfred O., "Banding the Last Heath Hen," Bird-Banding, 1931.
3) Eckert, Allan W., *The Last Great Auk*, Jesse Stuart Foundation, 2003.
4) Fuller, Errol, *Extinct Birds-Revised Edition*, Comstock Pub. Associates, 2001.
5) Bartram, William, *et al.*, Thomas P., *Travels & Other Writings*, Library of America, 2001.
6) Audubon, John James, *Ornithological Biography, Vol. 1*, Philadelphia, PA., 1832.
7) Schorger, A.W., *The Wild Turkey: Its History and Domestication*, Norman, OK, University of Oklahoma Press, 1966.
8) Hewitt, Oliver H. (Editor), *The Wild Turkey and Its Management*, Washington, D.C., The Wildlife Society, 1965.
9) Bailey, Wayne (Editor), *Proceedings....First National Wild Turkey Symposium,* The Wildlife Society, 1959.
10) Dickson, James G. (Compiler & Editor), *The Wild Turkey: Biology and Management*, Harrisburg, PA, Stackpole Books (for National Wild Turkey Federation), 1992.
    Lovett, Brian, *et al*, *The Turkey Hunters*, Iola, WI Krause, Publications, 2003.
11) Swisher, Brodie, (March 13, 2023), "*NWTF's State by State Spring Hunt Guide*," Bowhunting.com, https://www.bowhunting.com/article/nwtfs-state-by-state-spring-hunt-guide/
12) National Shooting Sports Foundation, "*Hunting In America: An Economic Force For Conservation*," Wildlife and Sport Fish Restoration Programs of the U.S. Fish and Wildlife Service. 2016.
13) Smith, Malcolm, *Back From The Brink*, Whittles Publishing, 2015.
14) Iowa Department of Natural Resources, "*Wild Turkeys and Crops: Identifying Crop Depredation,*" Pamphlet.
15) Hutto, Joe, *Illumination in the Flatwoods*, NY, Lyons & Burford, 1995.
16) *Nature: My Life As A Turkey* [DVD], (2011), PBS Nature.
17) Gladwell, Malcom, *Outliers: The Story of Success*, Little, Brown, and Company, 2008.
18) Denka, Jr., George with Brent Rogers, *Turkey Call and Literature Collector's Guide*, Privately Printed 2023.
19) Mickel, Earl, *Turkey Callmakers Past and Present: Mick's Picks*, Beach Lake, PA, Privately Printed, 1994.

Introduction: Answering the Call
1) Masciarella II, Raymond M, *"The Most Perfect" An Illustrated Guide to M.L. Lynch Turkey Calls*, Privately Printed, 2013.
2) Spencer, Jim, *Bad Birds*, Bolivar, MO, Lightin' Ridge Books, 2010.
3) National Shooting Sports Foundation, "*Hunting In America: An Economic Force For Conservation,*" Wildlife and Sport Fish Restoration Programs of the U.S. Fish and Wildlife Service. 2016.
4) Davin, Laurent, *et al*, "*Bone aerophones from Eynan-Mallaha (Israel) indicate imitation of raptor calls by the last hunter-gatherers in the Levant,*" *Nature Scientific Reports*, June 2023.

SOURCES

5) Williams, Jr., Lovett E., *The Voice & Vocabulary of the Wild Turkey,* Gainesville, GA, Real Turkeys, 1984.
6) Harlan, Howard, *Turkey Calls: An Enduring American Folk Art,* Nashville, TN, Harlan/Anderson Press, 1994.
7) Hale, David E, *Adventures In Hunting With Knight And Hale*, Privately Printed, 2023.
8) Wright, Albert Hazen. "Early Records of the Wild Turkey," *The Auk*, Vol 31, 1914, pages 463-71.
9) Denka, Jr., George with Brent Rogers, *Turkey Call and Literature Collector's Guide*, Privately Printed, 2023.
10) Burke, Monte, "Collections: Sounds of the South," *Garden & Gun*, Feb-Mar 2018.
11) Mickel, Earl, *Turkey Callmakers Past and Present: Mick's Picks*, Beach Lake, PA, Privately Printed, 1994.
12) Casada, Jim, *Remembering The Greats*, Rock Hill, SC, High Country Press, 2012.
13) Newark, Tim, *The Book of Camouflage: The Art of Disappearing*, Osprey Publishing, 2013.
14) Hunter, John, D, *Manners and Customs of several Indian Tribes located west of the Mississippi,* Philadelphia, 1823.
15) Schorger, A.W., *The Wild Turkey: Its History and Domestication*, Norman, OK, University of Oklahoma Press, 1966.
16) Kelly, Tom, *Tenth Legion*, Brooklyn, NY, Theo, Gaus' Sons, Inc., 1973.
17) Williams Jr., Lovett E., *Hunting The Gould's Wild Turkey In Mexico*, Cedar Key, FL, Real Turkeys, 2002.
18) Williams Jr., Lovett E., Baur, Erick H., Eichholz, Neal F., *The Ocellated Turkey In The Land Of The Maya*, Cedar Key, FL, Real Turkeys, 2010.

Chapter 1: KNIGHT & HALE

- Galiagno, Andy, host, "*007a: Turkey Hunting Public Land with Harold Knight,*" The Turkey Hunter Podcast, Wednesday Aug 6, 2014, https://www.theturkeyhunterpodcast.com/e/007a-turkey-hunting-public-land-with-harold-knight/
- Galiagno, Andy, host, "*007b: Turkey Hunting Public Land with Harold Knight,*" The Turkey Hunter Podcast, Wednesday Aug 13, 2014, https://www.theturkeyhunterpodcast.com/e/007b-turkey-hunting-public-land-with-harold-knight/
- Galiagno, Andy, host, "*007c: Turkey Hunting Public Land with Harold Knight,*" The Turkey Hunter Podcast, Wednesday Aug 25, 2014, https://www.theturkeyhunterpodcast.com/e/007c-turkey-hunting-public-land-with-harold-knight/
- Hale, David E., *Adventures In Hunting With Knight And Hale*, Privately Printed, 2023.
  Harbour, Dave, "*My Old Kentucky Gobbler*," Sports Afield, April 1972.
- Interview with David Hale.
- Interview with Harold Knight.
- Interviews with Anthony Foster, Bill Jordan, Cuz Strickland, Jim Strelec, Keith Wahlig, Korby Taylor, Mark Prudhomme, Mike Battey, Preston Pittman, Rob Keck, and Will Primos.
- KNIGHT & HALE Catalogs. 1982, 1983, 1995-2015.
- Knight, Harold, and David Hale with Wade L Bourne, *Harold Knight & David Hale's Ultimate Turkey Hunting*, Cadiz, KY, Atlantic Publishing Co., 1994.
- Mickel, Earl, *Turkey Callmakers Past and Present: Mick's Picks*, Beach Lake, PA, Privately Printed, 1994.
- Mossy Oak staff, September 2, 2016, "30 Years of Mossy Oak: David Hale," Mossyoak.com, https://www.mossyoak.com/our-obsession/blogs/prostaff/30-years-of-mossy-oak-david-hale
- Mossy Oak staff, October 28, 2016, "30 Years of Mossy Oak: Harold Knight," Mossyoak.com, https://www.mossyoak.com/our-obsession/blogs/prostaff/30-years-of-mossy-oak-harold-knight
- Strickland, Cuz, host, "*A Bucket List Hunt with Knight & Hale*," Cuz 411, May 10, 2022, https://www.youtube.com/watch?v=e1yuvKu8hYY

Chapter 2: PRIMOS® HUNTING

- Interview with Jimmy Primos.
- Interview with Will Primos.
- Interviews with Alex Lee White, Anthony Foster, Bill Jordan, Brad Farris, Chris Kirby, Cuz Strickland, Harold Knight, Jeff D'Agostino, Lorena Lipe, Mike Battey, Ron Jolly, Ronnie Smith, Toxey Haas.
- Jolly, Ron, *Memories of Spring*, Jolly's Outdoor Visions, LLC, 2020.

- PRIMOS® HUNTING Catalogs. 1986-2023.
- Mickel, Earl, *Turkey Callmakers Past and Present: Mick's Picks*, Beach Lake, PA, Privately Printed, 1994.
- Mossy Oak staff, October 14, 2016, "30 Years of Mossy Oak: Will Primos," Mossyoak.com, https://www.mossyoak.com/our-obsession/blogs/prostaff/30-years-of-mossy-oak-will-primos
- Newcomb, Clay, host, "*Episode 48: The Trouble With Lovin' Gobblin' Turkeys With Will Primos And Dr. Mike Chamberlain*," April 6, 2022, Bear Grease Podcast, https://www.themeateater.com/listen/bear-grease/ep-48-the-trouble-with-lovin-gobblin-turkeys-part-1-will-primos-and-dr-mike
- Strickland, Cuz, host, *FFOD053: Fist Full of Dirt*, "*A Fist Full of The Truth with Will Primos*," March 2, 2021, https://podcasts.apple.com/us/podcast/ffod053-a-fist-full-of-the-truth-with-will-primos/id1505260479?i=1000511264145

Chapter 3: QUAKER BOY®
- Casada, Jim, *Remembering The Greats*, Rock Hill, SC, High Country Press, 2012.
- Cost, Neil D. "Gobbler" (with Scott Branton and Ray Berryhill), *The Last Hurrah*, Brainerd, MN, Branton Berryhill Publishers, 2002.
- Interview with Bev Kirby.
- Interview with Chris Kirby.
- Interviews with Bill Jordan, Bob Wozniak, Cuz Strickland, Ernie Calandrelli, Marlin Watkins, Mike Battey, Paul Butski, Preston Pittman, and Rob Keck.
- Mickel, Earl, *Turkey Callmakers Past and Present: Mick's Picks*, Beach Lake, PA, Privately Printed, 1994.
- Mossy Oak staff, September 9, 2016, "30 Years of Mossy Oak: Dick And Chris Kirby," https://www.mossyoak.com/our-obsession/blogs/prostaff/30-years-of-mossy-oak-dick-and-chris-kirby
- QUAKER BOY® Catalogs. 1982, 1983, 1992, 2000-2023.

Chapter 4: Mike Battey
- Harlan, Howard, *Turkey Calls: An Enduring American Folk Art,* Nashville, TN, Harlan/Anderson Press, 1994.
- Hook, Roger B., "*Unknown Legend: The Work of Mike Battey*," *Turkey & Turkey Hunting*, Winter 1998.
- Interview with Mike Battey.
- Interviews with Craig "Cornbread" Corbett, Cuz Strickland, David Hale, Harold Knight, Jimmy Primos, Paul Butski, Preston Pittman, Todd Johnson, Toxey Haas, and Will Primos.
- Mickel, Earl, *Turkey Callmakers Past and Present: Mick's Picks*, Beach Lake, PA, Privately Printed, 1994.
- Williams, Jr., Lovett E., *Wild Turkey Hunting & Management*, Cedar Key, FL, Real Turkeys, 2006.

Chapter 5: Anthony Foster
- Gaddis, Mike, "*First Light,*" *Sporting Classics*, September/October 2013.
- Interview with Anthony Foster.
- Interviews with Alex Lee White, David Hale, Harold Knight, Jimmy Primos, Preston Pittman, and Will Primos.
- PRIMOS® HUNTING Catalogs. 1986-2023.
- Tate, Kevin, "*In the Grain: Wooden Turkey Calls Play the Music of Springtime*," *Mississippi Outdoors*, March April 2017.

APPENDIX – WILD TURKEY HISTORICAL TIMELINE

The restoration of the wild turkey spurred on a game call boom, as a growing number of hunters found they needed turkey calls and other gear. Data on wild turkey populations are not available for many individual years over the past decades. Some of it is only found on a state-by-state basis, and all of it is, at best, an estimate. As Rob Keck, former CEO of the National Wild Turkey Federation (NWTF), told me, "Those are the best estimated numbers. Turkey populations are very difficult to assess; states often had different methodologies to census turkeys." The following are estimates from sources listed in this book and publicly available sources assembled by the author over the past decade. Also included are vital dates influencing wild turkey populations and turkey hunting. Some dates are approximate. Thanks to Dr. James Earl Kennamer and Dr. Michael Chamberlain for their edits and adds.

300 B.C. – Mayans domesticated native Mexican wild turkeys in Central America. That subspecies, Meleagris gallopavo gallopavo, is now extinct but is the origin of today's domestic turkeys.

200 BC – Ancestral Puebloans (Anasazi) who lived on the Colorado Plateau domesticated turkeys in the Four Corners region. These birds had their roots in the Eastern and Rio Grande subspecies.

Early 1500s – Spanish conquistador Hernan Cortes is gifted 1,500 turkeys by Aztec emperor Montezuma.

1519 – The Spanish took domesticated turkeys to Europe, where its palatability helped it quickly spread.

1608 – Europeans who settled in Jamestown brought domesticated turkeys "back" to the U.S.

1620 – 10 million wild turkeys are estimated to be found in 39 continental U.S. states.

1621 – Pilgrim governor William Bradford wrote about how the colonists hunted wild turkeys during the autumn of 1621, noting they found "a great store of wild turkeys, of which they took many."

1708 – For the first time in the New World protection orders were issued for turkeys by the colony of New York. Despite that, they were extirpated there by 1844.

1748 – 18 months after Congress adopted the Great Seal, Benjamin Franklin wrote a letter to his daughter to express his disapproval of the bald eagle as the national symbol. He opined it should be the American wild turkey.

1774-1777 – Naturalist William Bartram travels the southeast U.S. and often encounters wild turkeys, writing, "The high forests ring with the noise... of these social sentinels, the watch-word being caught and repeated, from one to another, for hundreds of miles around; insomuch that the whole country, is for an hour or more, in an universal shout."

1827 – Naturalist John James Audubon published in his 1827 *The Birds of America*; the first photo plate in the book was of a wild turkey gobbler. He noted they were "less plentiful in Georgia and the Carolinas, becomes still scarcer in Virginia and Pennsylvania, and is now very rarely seen to the eastward... through Long Island, the State of New York, and the country around the Lakes, I did not meet with a single (one)...Turkeys are still to be found along the whole line of the Alleghany Mountains, where they have become so wary as to be approached only with extreme difficulty."

1830s- 1920 – Intensive logging removes tens of millions of forest acres across the U.S. His notes on the wild turkey in his 1832 *Ornithological Biography* are vaster than he records about any other bird, revealing the use of wingbone calls by hunters.

1863 – Abraham Lincoln proclaimed Thanksgiving a national holiday, and turkey became Americans' center of table choice.

1874 – New Jersey became the first state to establish a "Closed season" for wild turkeys.

1879 – Charles L. Jordan writes in *Forest & Stream*, "I expect to catch thunder from somebody on this score, but I don't care for all their thunder, so they don't stop me from shooting old gobblers in March and April." At the time of 28 states with seasons, 11 bridge into spring.

1898 – Charles L. Jordan published a series of articles in *Shooting & Fishing* that would become the book Edward A. McIlhenny published in 1914, *The Wild Turkey and Its Hunting*.

1900 – Congress passed the Lacey Act making illegal transport of game across state lines illegal but there is little funding for enforcement, game management, and conservation work.

1901 – The League of American Sportsmen lobbied for better protection for big game and wild turkey, leading to a closed season for turkeys in 2 states: Indiana and Nebraska.

1901-1909 – Theodore Roosevelt was the conservation President and helped establish the case for preserving our natural resources.

YELP & GOBBLE, INC.

1910 – Wild turkeys were protected in 26 states, given drastic declines or extirpation.
1914 – Edward A. McIlhenny published the first book on turkey hunting with material originating from Charles Jordan: *The Wild Turkey and Its Hunting*. Jordan's friend John K. Renaud provided the manuscript to McIhenny after Jordan, a game estate manager, was killed by a poacher in 1909.
1920-1930s – 30,000-200,000 wild turkeys survive in 21 states out of the 39 in their original range.
1920s-1950s – Much of the work to restore the wild turkey is rooted in a misguided effort to introduce farm raised birds into the wild.
1926 – A historical low occurred where only 13 states had a stated wild turkey season.
1929-1941 – The Great Depression sees many farms abandoned or gone fallow, which increases habitat needed for wildlife like wild turkeys to survive.
1933 – Aldo Leopold became the first professor of wildlife management in the U.S.
1934 – Congress passed the Fish & Wildlife Coordination Act so state agencies could work together.
1937 – The Federal Aid in Wildlife Restoration Act of 1937, also known as the Pittman-Robertson Act, taxed hunting guns and ammunition to pay for wildlife restoration efforts.
1939-1945 – World War II spurred technological advancements that would later aid in wild turkey restoration efforts, such as the cannon net and radio telemetry.
1943 – Henry Mosby and Charles Handley led the way in new wild turkey research and management practices detailed in their book *The Wild Turkey in Virginia*.
1948 – H.H. Dill and W.H. Thornsberry invented a cannon net that could be fired over a flock of birds.
1951 – Herman "Duff" Holbrook captures the first wild turkeys with a cannon net in the Francis Marion National Forest in Huger, South Carolina.
1958 – 20 states with wild turkeys have stated turkey seasons.
1959 – 320,000 wild turkeys estimated to be in the U.S. 31 states are now active in wild turkey restoration or well into the planning process. The first Wild Turkey Symposium is held between notable state biologists and game managers, resulting in the recognition that farm-raised turkeys do not survive or reproduce as compared to trapped and transferred turkeys.
1973 – 1.3 million turkeys are believed to be in the U.S., and 22 states have spring gobbler seasons. Tom Rodgers founded the National Wild Turkey Federation as a conservation organization.
1974 – 39 states now have turkey seasons; 16 of those states are outside its historical range.
1978 – 1.8 million wild turkeys are estimated in the U.S., and around 30 states now have seasons.
1980 – A groundbreaking for the NWTF's Wild Turkey Research Center in Edgefield, SC was held. Wild turkey researcher James Earl Kennamer, Ph.D., was hired to lead wild turkey management.
The 1980s – 47 states now have wild turkey populations, thanks to trap and transfer programs.
1990 – 3.5 million wild turkeys are estimated in the U.S.
1991 – For the first time, 49 states hold wild turkey seasons (Alaska is the exception).
1994 – 4.2 million wild turkeys are now pursued by 2.1 million hunters; An estimated 654,000 birds are taken annually.
1999 – 5.4 million wild turkeys are estimated in the U.S.
2004 – 6 million or more turkeys estimated to be in the U.S.
2008 – Despite estimates of historic wild turkey population levels, agency biologists and researchers begin discussing apparent declines in wild turkey populations and productivity based on data collected by agencies throughout the southeastern and eastern U.S.
2010 – At a meeting in Live Oak, Florida, biologists representing agencies throughout the southeastern U.S. agree that research is warranted to identify the magnitude of apparent declines in the productivity of wild turkey populations throughout the region.
2014 – 6.2 million turkeys wild turkeys are estimated in the U.S.
2015 – Researchers publish peer-reviewed work showing that wild turkey populations across the southeastern U.S. have exhibited long-term declines in production and populations.
2017 – 7 million wild turkeys are estimated in the U.S. after 200,000 wild turkeys have been transferred since the 1950s; this may prove the high water mark in post-restoration populations, as a decline biologist predicted, including the late Wayne Bailey, follows.
2019 – 6.9 million wild turkeys and 2.5 million hunters are found in the U.S.
2021 – Another conservation organization for wild turkeys, Turkeys For Tomorrow, is founded.
2023 – 6 million (perhaps slightly more) wild turkeys are now estimated to be in the U.S.

ABOUT THE AUTHOR

Brent Rogers received a bachelor's degree in biology from William Penn College and has spent his 30-year career in food research & development. Simultaneously, he has exercised his keen interest in conservation and history as a nonprofit volunteer. Foremost among them has been the National Wild Turkey Federation. He has served the organization in elected or designated positions at the local, state, and national levels. He is on the Hall of Fame committee for the Grand National Callmaking Competition and provides educational seminars.

Fusing his professional and personal pursuits led to Rogers researching the history of wild turkeys and turkey hunting culture in North America. As a freelance outdoor writer, his articles have appeared in various magazines; he co-authored his first book with George Denka in 2023: the *Turkey Call and Literature Collector's Guide.*

Growing up on a farm and keeping a small flock of domestic bronze turkeys led to Rogers' fascination with the species; that appreciation was deepened through discovering the American wild turkey upon its local restoration. Born to a hunting tradition, he also practices active stewardship of natural resources through conservation work.

He curates thousands of wild turkey items: calls, books, magazines, catalogs, audio and video material, clothing, and art. Rogers believes that the knowledge and stories of generations of hunters and biologists enhance the hunting experience and deepen our appreciation for the wild turkey.

Built upon a foundation of faith and family, Rogers has resided in rural Iowa his entire life. He has been married to his wife, Renee, for 26 years. The couple has raised two children: a son, Cyrus, and a daughter, Hannah. In his leisure time, he enjoys food preservation, family, reading, and traveling coast to coast in pursuit of the wild turkey and related collectibles.

YELP & GOBBLE, INC.

www.ingramcontent.com/pod-product-compliance
Lightning Source LLC
Chambersburg PA
CBHW061404010526
44119CB00010B/257